EVANGELICAL IDOLATRY

Evangelical Idolatry

How Pastors Like Me Have Failed the People of God

Jeff Mikels

William B. Eerdmans Publishing Company

Grand Rapids, Michigan

Wm. B. Eerdmans Publishing Co.
2006 44th Street SE, Grand Rapids, MI 49508
www.eerdmans.com

Book design by Lydia Hall

Printed in the United States of America

31 30 29 28 27 26 25   1 2 3 4 5 6 7

ISBN 978-0-8028-8466-4

Library of Congress Cataloging-in-Publication Data

A catalog record for this book is available from the Library of Congress.

Biblical quotations are from the New International Version unless otherwise noted.

Contents

Foreword

FOLLOWING THE SHOCK OF 2020, with its triple whammy of Covid, the murder of George Floyd and the racial unrest that followed, and the presidential election and its aftermath, I have heard many pastors, in various ways, say: "I thought I was discipling my church. I thought I was growing my people in the way of Jesus. I thought I was building them up to maturity in Christ. And then 2020 happened." People whom pastors believed to be mature followers of Jesus became Twitter trolls; congregants who had seemed close got into screaming matches; and congregations that seemed to be dwelling together in unity were suddenly at war.

The year 2020 was a deep shaking of the American church that was, in the very true sense of the word, *apocalyptic*. The year 2020 was a revelation of deep fissures in the church, of structural weaknesses in our ecclesiology and visions of pastoral success and reliance on vision statements. The year 2020 brought into the open what had been hidden under the surface: in various ways and for lots of reasons, much of the American church was built on sand. The political and cultural waves came crashing in, and the house could not stand unified on the foundation of Jesus Christ.

Over the past few years, a great many books have been written about the condition of American evangelicalism, offering diagnoses of what the authors believe has gone wrong and programs for how the authors believe things can be made right. These books have come from historians, sociologists, journalists, and professors, providing wide-ranging visions of the past and future of the evangelical movement.

But what has been missing in all the analysis of the past few years has been a pastoral voice of lament and repentance, a considered analysis of what pastors have done, or not done, that has contributed to the weakening of the church. In this book, Jeff Mikels offers us this pastoral lament and calls us to repent. Taking us along on his journey, Jeff reflects deeply on important questions: What things did pastors give our hearts to that weren't, in fact, building up the church? What did we buy into that left the church vulnerable to the winds and waves? What are the idols that evangelicalism, and her pastors, have worshipped?

An idol is anything that takes the place of devotion in our hearts that belongs to God alone. Jeff's call to lament and to repent is vital to the work of pastoring today. The church, and her pastors, continue to be caught in idolatry, which is clearly seen in the anger, division, and anxiety that mar the church. We continue to be seized by idols that draw us away from the formative work of the Holy Spirit. We continue to be conformed to the pattern of the age, rather than having our minds renewed by the Lord Jesus Christ.

Pastoral leadership today must be courageously filled with invitations for the Lord of the church to confront our idols. Inevitably, different readers will need to reflect on their own idols. Perhaps others will find different idols in their hearts than Jeff found in his. But Jeff's analysis points to a way forward that calls all the shepherds of the church to walk, perhaps as never before, in the way of God's grace, a way that drives us to our knees as we surrender our idols. Only then, in true dependence on the Lord, will we be free to worship Christ and lead the church to be renewed in our true worship of the triune God who sets us free.

Joel Lawrence
President, Center for Pastor Theologians

Introduction

IN 2006, WHEN JENNIFER and I moved to Lafayette, Indiana, to start a church, we were just like most church planters. We were convinced God was leading us. He had affirmed it through our own times of prayer, through affirmation from trusted leaders, and through the financial and prayerful support of many in our lives who made sacrifices toward the effort. Like most church planters, we were eager to do a different kind of church that was not beholden to any sort of *that's-how-we-always-do-it thinking*. We wanted to leverage modern technologies and marketing techniques to connect with people that other churches weren't reaching and to inspire people with hope that maybe this church could be their spiritual home.

Most of all, we were prepared to fall in love with the city and the people of Lafayette and the greater county. Both of us had an affinity for this area, and Jen was a graduate of Purdue, so we believed Lafayette would be as much of a blessing to us as we believed we could be for the people of Lafayette. Also, our hearts were burdened by the statistic that only 20 percent of people in the surrounding county could be claimed by any church. For an area as Christian as the middle of Indiana, Lafayette had a terribly low level of commitment to church participation. We believed the time was right for a new expression of the church in our city, a new style of teaching, a new style of worship, a new kind of authenticity, and a new openness to cultural and economic diversity within a church body.

In other words, we were just like most church planters in the early 2000s.

Unlike many church planters, though, we never saw ourselves in competition with the existing churches of Lafayette. Back in high school, I developed a deep passion for Christian unity. I loved the capital "C" Church. I loved the vision of the body of Christ. I was sold out to evangelical cooperation, and my wife shared that vision with me. We wanted our young church to be a catalyst for Christian unity throughout the county. We wanted to win people to Christ, and we wanted to win Christians to each other. We wanted to love our neighbors well and help them take next steps on their spiritual journey, and we wanted to do it together with other churches.

It was a difficult road but a good one too. We saw people come to faith, and we saw people walk away. We saw churches come together and split apart, and through it all, our two original passions morphed into my two personal struggles. We wanted to see people grow in faith and see churches cooperate, but our church never hit the stride of rapid growth promised by church-planting anecdotes, and my efforts at multichurch cooperation never materialized into anything of real impact in our community.

We baptized a lot of people, but very few of them ever matured into spiritual leaders in our church, and nearly all of them eventually went on to other churches or dropped out of church attendance altogether. We reached average attendance levels near three hundred for a few months after buying and remodeling our first building, and we had single Sundays near four hundred, but even at our peak, our volunteerism and giving were so low that we struggled to maintain core ministries and pay staff. As a result, our capacity for ministry *beyond* our walls was low. We deployed many leaders who by failing to flourish or even endure in their positions ended up causing great pain to the church. We had incredible opportunities but were never able to fully take advantage of them or sustain the ministry arising from them.

I share these things because I want you to know that I was a "normal pastor." Ours wasn't a church with remarkable success. We never obtained significant social media recognition, the people in our community didn't universally know our name, and just like any other church, our leaders struggled to stay optimistic in the face of our hardships.

In the summer of 2019, after a year of declining finances, and with a weekly Sunday attendance hovering around two hundred, I invited the elders of the church to join me on a journey of redevelopment, rediscovery, and reimagining for the church. We started working through a book to help us understand church dynamics better. We made plans to divide up leadership more efficiently. We brainstormed new formulations of our mission statement.

However, there was a growing tension among us. Some elders were optimistic about our future. They thought a refocus on core values and mission would spark a new momentum. Other elders thought we needed to blow things up and start over. One voice in those conversations suggested it was time to declare the experiment over, close the church, and go our separate ways.

For the first time in our history, we had a leadership team that was divided over whether we should even be a church. The tension among the elders was tangible, but I was convinced that God had called me to this work, and I didn't have any reason to give up on it yet. I was doing my best to maintain my enthusiasm, and I was trying to build these other men into mature, enthusiastic leaders themselves, even though we were all more burned out than we cared to admit.

I knew I was tired, but I was also highly optimistic. I believed the solutions to be simple. All I needed to do was to get the leaders leading and the people serving. If the leaders were unified and cooperating, and if the people could see themselves united as members of a shared family on a shared mission, and if we could all stay faithful to serve people outside our church, we would regain our original momentum. I was eagerly looking forward to the year ahead, and we launched into 2020 with that mindset. We changed our mission statement to be *empowering people to live the life God made them for*, we dropped back to only one worship gathering so Sundays could feel more energetic and people could feel more connected, and we committed to significant changes in our leadership structure.

But 2020 in so many ways undermined everything I was hoping for.

GROWING DISILLUSIONMENT

It started with Facebook. One of our church fundamental strategies had always been to have strong online community engagement throughout the week. We encouraged people each Sunday to join our Facebook group so we could build relationships online with each other, but even as we encouraged greater participation there, I saw more and more people falling into the hole of inflammatory statements, political fervor, misinformation, and ridicule. It was the modus operandi of Facebook in those days, and it infected us too. Misunderstandings and animosity began to build. People on Facebook started acting like enemies even when they were claiming to be followers of Jesus. That's when I first began to sense there was something wrong, deeply wrong, not just with my church but with American Christianity more broadly.

It started as disappointment. I was disappointed that our church family wasn't immune to vitriol as I saw it show up in more and more of our online interactions. I saw people develop resentment toward each other, and I began to feel especially bothered by the visible and aggressive loyalties people had adopted toward political figures, conspiracy theories, and racist attitudes. Still, I thought it was a phase we could work through if I continued to engage our church people with open conversation, prodding them toward Christlike speech. I attempted to initiate discussions where people on either side of the growing political divide would openly discuss important and divisive issues and do so with Christlikeness, but those discussions repeatedly devolved into name-calling and nastiness. I deleted comment after comment in an attempt to coach people toward kindness, but it only served to bring more accusations against me. I naively tried to use Facebook as a discipleship tool. I tried to move people toward graciously understanding differing perspectives, but the Christians in my circle kept moving toward anger and fear.

Still, when the COVID lockdowns happened in March of 2020, I wasn't initially worried. Another of our church fundamental strategies had always been to leverage technology and creativity for our Sunday experience, so when other churches were scrambling to figure out how to do live streaming and online ministry, we were already comfortable with it. With one of the best live-stream productions in town, we decided to lean into it. While people were in home lockdown, we turned Sunday morning into a creative TV show experience complete with comedic moments, guest interviews, and professional quality music videos we produced ourselves. It was fun and funny and inspirational. One commenter said that Easter 2020 was the best church experience they ever had; however, not everyone was pleased. Some families actually left the church after our second week, claiming it didn't feel like church anymore. At the time, I didn't know how many other churches in town were just continuing to meet in person despite the recommendations against it.

I was disheartened that those families couldn't see the outreach potential of those few weeks or that they would be so willing to leave knowing we had made only a temporary change for the specifically strange circumstances we were all in, but I pressed on nonetheless.

When it became clear that the COVID pandemic was fully present in the United States, I still wasn't worried. From my perspective, it was obvious that the pandemic was a challenge that could be addressed with solid science and mutual cooperation. I thought the church was the perfect place to find a clearheaded response to the pandemic because we claim to value truth, cooperation, and making sacrifices for the sake of others. Additionally, one of my perspectives in ministry has always been to respect the work of the scientific community, and so, following recommendations from the smartest people in epidemiology, I made the call to stay primarily virtual, close our in-person children's programs, and encourage mask-wearing for all who wanted to come to worship gatherings in person. However, many people left us altogether, searching for churches without similar restrictions, and as time wore on, more and more families did the same. After all, in our town, plenty of those churches could be found.

All those departures weighed heavily on me, but again, I continued to press on with optimism. During the first few months of the pandemic, I still had the verbal support of the other elders in our church, and we all hoped that things would get back to normal soon.

However, something was changing in me. All those disappointments were coalescing into a new kind of burden. More and more, I saw the way Christians and Christian churches were responding to the events in the world around them, and more and more, I saw them adopting the same language and perspectives as secular conservatism. Specifically, the Christians in my life were aligning themselves with the claims of then president Donald Trump and the perspective of Fox News rather than the life or teaching of Jesus. Three events of the time solidified the changes in me.

First, at the beginning of 2020, Donald Trump was undergoing an impeachment trial. Having experienced the impeachment trial of Bill Clinton during my formative years and having experienced the ground-swell of Christian outrage at his behavior and evangelical support for removing him from office, I was dumbfounded to see the evangelical Christians in my community adopt exactly opposite values as they rallied behind President Trump. Clinton had been impeached for abusing his power and attempting to cover it up, and now Trump was being impeached for the same reasons, but this time, Christians were taking the opposite approach. How had my Christian brothers and sisters flipped on their value system so easily? When it came to Bill Clinton, they said "character matters," but in the case of Donald Trump, they said, "I elected Trump to be my president, not my pastor." I still don't understand that logic.

Second, at the beginning of the pandemic, even though scientific consensus said the COVID virus was highly transmissible through the air, that it was much more deadly than influenza, that it had the potential to flood our hospitals with patients, and that we could avoid the worst by making a few lifestyle changes like limiting exposure to large indoor gatherings and wearing face coverings, I was confused when my Christian brothers and sisters decided to ignore the available data, reject public health guidelines, and instead dive into misinformation, conspiracy theories, and outright lies. Not only were they listening to these false claims, but they were also embracing and perpetuating them as if doing so were the proper Christian response! Christian friends wore T-shirts saying "Faith not Fear" as a protest against wearing masks.

I was confused. Had my Christian community suddenly become irrationally gullible, or had they always been so, and I had never let myself see it? Though I was raised to believe that Christianity was a faith built on absolute truth, and though I had learned that the Christian search for truth was the historical foundation for science itself, I now found myself in a Christian culture that had no interest in science unless that science agreed with their own biases or desires. If you want to worship in large groups without masks, find the post on Facebook claiming COVID is a fraud or that masks are dangerous and run with it! I'm not saying the CDC holds absolute truth, but the outright rejection of scientific data in favor of anecdotes and conspiracies baffles me even to this day. (I know *pastors* who adamantly assert COVID is a hoax, manufactured by liberals under the influence of Satan.)

But third, and most importantly for my journey, the events surrounding the murder of George Floyd hit me hard. In the years leading up to 2020, I had built some strong relationships with Black pastors and other members of the African American Christian community in Lafayette, and those friendships allowed me to start seeing racial disparities through their eyes. As the pandemic lingered, my heart broke to learn that COVID-19 was disproportionately worse among people of color whether in terms of economic impact, hospitalizations, or deaths. With the benefit of hindsight, we now know those disparities were real.[1] I saw those disparities second-hand. In 2020, when I spoke with my African American friends, I heard regular stories of them going to one more funeral for one more family member or of them needing to spend another few nights in the hospital themselves. By the fall of 2020, none of my white friends had to bury a relative from COVID, but *all* of my Black friends had at *least* one family death, and most had more. The disparity of COVID outcomes for different groups of people produced a strong sense of empathy in me for them, and then, when George Floyd was killed (following the deaths of Breonna Taylor and Ahmaud Arbery), and when the protests came and the police and politicians responded as they did, my empathy for my Black brothers and sisters reached a new level.

I had been raised to think of Jesus as the one who came to seek and save the lost, the one who offered hope to the hurting and the broken, the one who would touch a leper, and the one who taught us to love one another in sacrificial ways. I was taught to bear one another's burdens and so fulfill the law of Christ. So too, in my soul, I began to feel the burdens of my brothers and sisters of color whether that burden was racial inequities in the criminal justice system, the economic system, or the medical system. Then my burden became twice as heavy when I noticed that very few of my white brothers and sisters were even willing to *acknowledge* the disparities, let alone *address* them. I began to see even *mask-wearing* through the eyes of social justice. If I wore a mask (or later, got a vaccine), I could be one more brick in the protective wall surrounding my Black brothers and sisters, but as I looked around, I saw more and more of my white brothers and sisters behaving carelessly in that regard. On issue after issue, the teaching of Jesus to sacrifice ourselves to love others, so dear to my heart, was disregarded by evangelical Christian culture, and *I no longer found any alignment between the Jesus I followed and the practices of the Christians in my evangelical subculture.*

I was on the border of a full deconstruction meltdown. You could accurately say that I had become disillusioned with the Christian church I had loved my whole life.

What changed?

I did.

The great disparity between the life and words of Jesus and the life and words of my Christian culture shook me. It opened my eyes. It woke me up.

Not everything changed. My heart for God, my motivation to serve others, my fervor to see the people of my church thrive in their walk with Christ and in their testimony before the world, and my passion to accurately teach the Bible didn't change. But my perspective regarding how to *apply* the teaching of Jesus in our current world changed a lot. My strengthening relationships with African American pastors in town led me to see George Floyd's death, the political rhetoric of the president, and the economic and medical inequities brought on by COVID-19 in a completely new light—a light that demanded my engagement. I began to see that following Jesus required me to sometimes say things out loud, to verbalize blessing for the outcast and to address the idolatry of the religious establishment.

In my mind, I hadn't changed much, but it was still too much for many. I was getting a new perspective on my calling, and there were people in my life who were uncomfortable with my journey. People who previously asserted their love for me decided that they couldn't continue in relationship with me. They and others in my white religious circles had become dependent on media and messaging that aggressively opposed things I was starting to say. Whereas previously I would intentionally avoid political talk, in 2020 I found myself in a world where *accurate* talk, *moral* talk, and even *nuanced* talk were all perceived as *political* or even *liberal*! However, I was a pastor, charged with bringing the truth of God's word and the calling of Jesus to my people each week. I was feeling an ever-increasing burden to speak truths I hadn't spoken before, to oppose evils I hadn't opposed before, and most of all to call Christians to rekindle their commitment to the imitation of Christ against all other political loyalties.

So I spoke up, but when I did, I sounded like one of the voices that many in my own church had already decided to reject. So, they left. A full 80 percent of our church left, including every elder except one, who lasted one more year before also leaving. Some went to other churches. Some quit church altogether. I felt rejected, and that sealed my disillusionment.

I cannot accurately describe how deeply disconnected I felt and continue to feel from the rest of my Christian subculture since then. I have wrestled and struggled to figure out what is really going on.

- Why were/are the Christians in my subculture so rigidly loyal to Donald Trump regardless of his character or the way his policies were making life harder for already marginalized people?
- Why were/are the Christians in my subculture so opposed to the science of COVID-19 and the related public health measures? And why were they so drawn toward conspiracy theories and false information? (Remember that this was before the "Big Lie," before the January 6 insurrection, and before the rejection of COVID vaccines!)
- Why were/are the Christians in my subculture so in favor of personal freedom as opposed to the sacrificial values of Christ that they would refuse to even wear a minimal face covering out in public?
- And why were/are the Christians in my subculture so apparently insensitive to the conditions caused by systemic racism and implicit bias that they would label antiracism as "wokeism," turn it into a cultural bogeyman, and deny the existence of modern-day racism?

I was disillusioned, discouraged, and confused. I felt isolated, ostracized, and abandoned by people I had considered family. Furthermore, my attempt to use the words of Jesus to address the moral issues of our day was met with such opposition from people I loved that all the other emotions coalesced into anger. I even tried to embrace it. I thought that I could leverage the intensity of my feelings to open someone's eyes.

I thought expressing my anger might do some good. I thought sharing my emotions honestly would reveal my vulnerability to people who loved me and that their sympathy for me personally might help them understand the seriousness of the issues I was confronting.

That strategy backfired, accomplishing exactly the opposite of my intent. Instead of inviting people who loved me to take me seriously and enter into conversation with me, my expressions of negative emotions like anger and disgust gave people the sense that I had become impulsive, arrogant, or at least improperly aggressive and, therefore, untrustworthy. Some questioned my mental health. Some concluded I shouldn't be a pastor at all, and they told me so. I was tempted to agree with them and thought often about quitting and walking away. When my wife applied for a job in a different city, one of her motivations was to give me an excuse to leave the church, and when she got the job offer, we prayerfully decided to take it and leave Lafayette. The church we planted, Lafayette Community Church, recently decided to close, and I'm currently not serving as a pastor in any church.

Still, I cannot shake the assurance of God's calling on my life and this new clarity that he brought to me through the events of 2020. It's years later, and I am still acutely distressed by the infiltration of political ideologies and earthly allegiances into the body of Christ, I'm convinced that something needs to be done about it, and I'm trying to be part of the solution.

GRAPPLING WITH FAILURE

I have thought a lot about my ministry in Lafayette, and the word "failure" comes to mind often not because the church failed to reach megachurch status or because the church lasted only a year after I left or because we didn't have huge numbers of salvations. I sometimes feel like a failure for this one reason:

> I didn't adequately prepare people for the turmoil of 2020. Specifically, I didn't adequately cultivate an allegiance to Jesus, his life, and his words that surpassed other traditional and cultural allegiances.

When push came to shove in 2020, people were more ready to trust the words of Fox News than the words of Jesus, who called us to deny ourselves, love our neighbors sacrificially, be a blessing to others, and oppose performative religious idolatry. Of course, that reality wounded me deeply, but it also forced me to do some hard reevaluation of my ministry.

At the heart of it all was a simple but obvious logical conclusion: If, after seventeen years of being under my ministry, their hearts resonated more with Fox News than with Jesus, I had failed to accurately portray Jesus as our example, authority, and only King.

But how?

How did my teaching fail to counteract the influence of conservative media?

More than that, I began to wonder whether my teaching somehow *reinforced* the perspective of conservative media? What part did I play in training my people to think like Tucker Carlson of Fox News instead of like Jesus of Nazareth? How did I fail to prepare my people to handle a global pandemic? How did I fail to prepare my people to see through the lies of QAnon? How did I miss the slide toward Christian nationalism that so many have embraced?

After much consideration, I'm convinced that I am complicit.

My approach to preaching, teaching, and discipleship not only kept the door open to conspiratorial conservatism, but it also helped people usher it right into their hearts. And it's not just my approach that was at fault. I have since come to realize that some bedrock principles of Evangelicalism are fundamentally tied to conservative cultural idols, but I never saw them or exposed them.

WOOD, HAY, AND STRAW

Throughout this book, I'll be returning to a metaphor from the apostle Paul:

> By the grace God has given me, I laid a foundation as a wise builder, and *someone else is building on it*. But each one should build with care. For no one can lay any foundation other than the one already laid,

which is Jesus Christ. If anyone builds on this foundation using gold, silver, costly stones, wood, hay or straw, their work will be shown for what it is, because the Day will bring it to light. It will be revealed with fire, and the fire will test the quality of each person's work. If what has been built survives, the builder will receive a reward. If it is burned up, the builder will suffer loss but yet will be saved—even though only as one escaping through the flames.

1 CORINTHIANS 3:10–15

When Paul wrote those words to the people of Corinth, he was afraid for them. Even though he gave them the permanent spiritual foundation of Jesus Christ, he was afraid that others would build on that foundation with something less enduring. The spiritual life can be built from a variety of materials—gold, silver, precious stones, wood, hay, or straw—but only some of those materials will endure the fire of testing. Whether that testing is the fire of future judgment or a reference to the trials we face here and now, the point remains. Flammable items will not survive. If a person's life is built with wood, hay, or straw, their works will burn, which will leave them nothing to show for what they've done.

Paul was afraid that others after him would give people shoddy and flammable materials with which to build their lives, but who would do such a thing? Who would lead people to build their lives with things that won't endure?

Me, that's who.

As a pastor, I fall into the category of "someone else." Paul gave people the foundation of Jesus, but his foundation-laying ended a long time ago. Now, every single week, pastors like me are responsible to build on that foundation and to help other people build on that foundation with a variety of building materials. I want to help people build their lives on the foundation of Jesus, and I want to help them build with bricks of gold or maybe silver. I want to help people establish their lives with the glorious truths of God, but the more I reflect on the past years of my ministry, the more I think I've been giving people wood, hay, and straw.

Now, I don't think that my entire ministry has always been a failure, and I don't think all of Evangelicalism is exclusively flammable, but still, I have come to realize that much of my ministry and much of American

Evangelicalism has been devoted to giving people wood, hay, and straw and to protecting the wood, hay, and straw already in circulation!

THIS BOOK IS FOR BOTH OF US

This book is my attempt to identify my own false teaching, to expose the idols of Evangelicalism, and to call out the faulty perspectives that undergird and empower them. The issues I faced in 2020 are continuing today, and I believe, endemic to American evangelical Christianity itself. As I see it, they must be addressed directly, for the sake of the gospel.

For the pastors who ignore these issues, their churches might remain viable and perhaps even successful organizations when evaluated by earthly measures, but the people in those churches will be unknowingly conformed to the image of modern conservative politics and not to the image of Christ. Other people in those churches might sense their own disillusionment and conclude that the problem is with Christianity itself rather than with the idolatries of Evangelicalism. In either case, the souls of these people will be deeply harmed, and eventually all that work might be revealed to be nothing more than sticks and straw.

Still, for the pastors who address these issues, and who do it better than I have, they might be able to rekindle an allegiance to Christ and his kingdom that overshadows all competing allegiances and results in the transformation of many lives and the transformation of our very culture. That's the kind of pastor I want to be, and that's the kind of pastor I want to help.

Perhaps you are that pastor.

Perhaps you are the church leader who is called to help that pastor.

Perhaps you are the church member who needs language to describe your own disillusionment.

My calling is to help you.

I want you to see our current situation for what it is, and I'll be blunt. It's idolatry. American white evangelical Christianity has adopted allegiances to a number of evil idolatries that if not addressed will wound our souls and undermine our entire witness for the gospel of Christ in our modern world. These idols don't stand on their own. They are propped up by a scaffolding of sticks, structures we have built on the foundation of Christ as if they are Christian when in fact they violate much of what he actually taught. While the idols are worshiped in the heart, the structures are weekly reestablished in sermons, podcasts, blogs, and books throughout the evangelical subculture.

If this is true, those of us who feel the need to point it out are in for a difficult journey. As a pastor friend of mine warned me recently, "The problem with idols is that people will fight to defend them." I feel that burden. My calling is to plead for people to return to an authentic Christlikeness despite the opposition. Therefore, I am assembling these thoughts for you who choose to read.

Perhaps you are a pastor facing my same dilemma, and you need to know that you aren't alone. You need courage and boldness to speak up for truth.

Perhaps you are a disillusioned Christian wondering how the church of Jesus got off the rails of Christlikeness, and you need a rekindled hope.

Perhaps you are confused, wondering why I've turned from the evangelical camp, but you're curious and willing to give this some of your time.

Perhaps you have a completely different perspective and are preparing to do battle with me over these ideas. Whoever you are, I welcome you.

These reflections are my own. They are at times critical and at times constructive. But I offer them to you humbly. If I speak incorrectly, may God lead you to forget my words. If I speak the truth, may the Spirit confirm it to your heart. But no matter what, I pray for you now that God will lead you, perhaps through these words, to rekindle your love for him and to embrace anew the purity of the gospel of a God who loves enemies and sacrifices extensively for people who don't deserve it. I offer the following reflections in the hopes that God will use them to further cleanse, refine, and beautify the bride of Christ.

CHAPTER 1

Our Hezekiah Moment

EVANGELICALISM HAS IDOLS. We shouldn't be surprised by that. Every religious tradition has its idols. However, for most of my ministry, I've been blind to my own. Without the challenges of the past few years, I might never have seen them for what they are. Idols are sneaky. They accumulate over time, gradually, and always from the good intentions of well-meaning people. Rarely does someone invent a new idol, set it up as an idol, and convince others to worship it. No. Idols develop organically starting from just a good idea or a curious concept. Then, over time, they are woven into the fabric of the faith and feel indistinguishable from it. There's a fascinating example of this in the Old Testament. It's the story of Hezekiah and Nehushtan.

HOW IDOLS HAPPEN

Modern evangelical Christians are familiar with many of the Old Testament accounts of idolatry. Sermons and studies regularly cover the story of the golden calf, the story of Dagon falling down in front of the ark, or the story of three faithful boys choosing a fiery furnace rather than bowing before the statue of Nebuchadnezzar, but few sermons cover this one.

> In the third year of Hoshea son of Elah king of Israel, Hezekiah son of Ahaz king of Judah began to reign. He was twenty-five years old when he became king, and he reigned in Jerusalem twenty-nine years. His

mother's name was Abijah daughter of Zechariah. He did what was right in the eyes of the LORD, just as his father David had done. He removed the high places, smashed the sacred stones and cut down the Asherah poles. He broke into pieces the bronze snake Moses had made, for up to that time the Israelites had been burning incense to it. (It was called Nehushtan.)

2 KINGS 18:1–4

The story of this idol begins during the wilderness wanderings of the people of Israel. God had sentenced them to forty years in the wilderness, and once again, the people were complaining about their situation.

Then the LORD sent venomous snakes among them; they bit the people and many Israelites died. The people came to Moses and said, "We sinned when we spoke against the LORD and against you. Pray that the LORD will take the snakes away from us." So Moses prayed for the people.

The LORD said to Moses, "Make a snake and put it up on a pole; anyone who is bitten can look at it and live." So Moses made a bronze snake and put it up on a pole. Then when anyone was bitten by a snake and looked at the bronze snake, they lived.

NUMBERS 21:6–9

It's an amazing picture of God's grace in conjunction with his wrath. It's also a foreshadowing of Christ on the cross. Jesus, talking to Nicodemus, cited this story as a prophecy of himself (John 3:14-15). However, no matter how important the bronze serpent was in the story, it was designed to be for that one moment alone.

God never told the people to keep it around, but that's exactly what they did. Someone decided that this relic was an important reminder of an important time in the history of the people, and so it was preserved. Later, someone decided it should be on display. Later, someone decided it was worthy of a name and chose *Nehushtan* probably because it sounded like the words for "bronze serpent." Later, someone decided that since it represented a move of God, it represented something about

God himself. Later, someone decided that as a representation of God, it was a relic similar to the tabernacle. Later, someone decided that just as incense was burned at the tabernacle to represent the presence of God, burning incense in front of Nehushtan made sense too.

It's logical, right? One concept leads to another. Each concept makes perfect sense. Each step, each move seems to be the right step, the right move. God moves in history, the people remember what he did, and the memories and relics of those moves take on a life of their own.

That's the problem with idols. Not all of them are as simple and straightforward as the golden calf, the image of Dagon in the Philistine temple, or the idol King Nebuchadnezzar set up in his own image. In fact, only a few follow that paradigm. Most idols are far more insidious. Their idolatry grows gradually over time, and it usually stems from the good intentions of good people making incremental, logical decisions based on some experience they had with God at some point. Still, good intentions and good reasons never absolved Israel from her idolatry, and neither will they absolve us of ours. Hundreds of years after that one moment in the desert, Nehushtan qualified as an idol, and we can take courage that Hezekiah somehow mustered the determination to destroy it.

Praise God that even though Hezekiah moments are rare, they happen, and we are in the midst of one right now. Many voices are rising up to highlight the idolatry within modern American Evangelicalism. Beth Moore, Russell Moore (unrelated), Jemar Tisby, and Kristin Kobes Du Mez are just some of the voices that have inspired me, and if my voice can be added to theirs, I will consider it an honor. But my goal isn't to sound like them. My goal is to sound like Jesus. My goal is to point you and me back to Jesus. He's the real deal among a world of idols. The people of God have always needed men and women of clarity and courage, prophetic voices that will call an idol what it is and do the work to dismantle it. For too long, I kept silent even when others spoke up, but it's time to undo that mistake.

THE TASK AHEAD

I don't think it makes much sense for me to just list all the idols I see in present-day Evangelicalism, propose some deconstructions, and hope the message sticks with you. I wouldn't have been able to receive that a few years ago. It would have felt like an attack on my fundamental beliefs then, and I don't want to do that to you now. We need to take this journey slowly if we are to take it together. Idols are accompanied by too much tradition, engender too much commitment, are wired too deeply into our faith, and are supported by too much doctrinal scaffolding. But I believe in this dialogue between you and me. I trust that God can open both of our hearts to the idols therein so we can identify them and tear them down. Therefore, my approach in the rest of this book will follow four distinct but related paths.

First, I'm going to take you back to the roots of Evangelicalism, not historically but doctrinally. We are going to start with the most difficult question God's people have ever had to ask themselves. It's the question that has plagued the people of God from the moment Jesus showed up on the scene. It's the question of how God wants us to relate to him and to the world around us. *Are we called to believe something, be something, do something, or a combination of all three?* How you answer that question arises from and then controls what you think of the central doctrine defining Evangelicalism: the gospel. The question and the doctrine are intertwined, and many idols are built on faulty definitions of the gospel. I'll start by addressing this issue directly. Specifically, I'm going to claim that Evangelicalism in America has embraced an overly narrow definition of the gospel, a definition that leaves out important biblical truth, and therefore finds it too easy to focus on Christian terminology and proper doctrinal formulations while ignoring issues of character and behavior. This will be challenging, because evangelicals aggressively protect their gospel. Stick with me through that section, because it makes all the difference in the world.

Second, after doing the hard doctrinal work of reexamining the gospel and its implications from the teaching of the New Testament, I'm going to take a detour from that line of reasoning to offer a personal confession of sorts. I'll expose by way of that confession how cultural and doctrinal aspects of Evangelicalism led me to certain conclusions and convictions that went beyond and stood in contrast to the true gospel. I'll share how I came to see the idolatry embedded in many of my earlier convictions and the scaffolding I once used to erect and protect those idols. Then, I'll expose how a few specific evangelical doctrines led me to false beliefs, improper behaviors, and many additional idols. I'll warn you: those chapters will be rough. Working through those issues has been rough for me, and I've had the benefit of years to process them. That's why I'll try my best to keep those chapters about me and how my thinking has changed. I'll cover some of my own evolving thoughts on some truly difficult topics. I didn't come to this way of thinking easily, so I don't expect it to immediately resonate with you either.

Third, I'll then return to the relatively safe ground of Bible study to address the responsibility of Christians in the world today. We'll consider what the Bible really says about Christian morals and values. What does the moral life of a Christian look like? What values should Christians have in response to the teaching of the Bible? We won't stop there, though. I'll press further to ask the question of moral relevance between the people of God and the people of the world: *Which Christian moral values are translatable to the world around us, and how should we do the translation?* This is the question modern Evangelicalism has failed to address because it assumes something contrary to our preferences. Specifically, this question assumes that something we like, our Christian values, are perhaps for us alone and not for the surrounding society. Evangelicals don't like that thought, and that's why the question is so important. We must ask it because our temptation is to mix evangelism for Jesus with evangelism for our preferences, and this temptation is behind many idols.

Finally, after identifying the true gospel, confessing my own biases and failures, and addressing what Christian morality should look like and does look like in the modern world, we will finally be ready to address the most difficult items and the main thrust of this book. I'll call out by name idols built of worthless wood pervasive in the evangelical world. I'll identify the temples that house them, and I'll recommend ways for their dismantling. In some cases, I might overstate the case for a particular idol, or I might go too far in recommending the destruction of that idol, while in other cases, I might miss an idol entirely. I will not be able to exhaustively list all the idols existing in the church, the idols of particular interest to you, or even all the idols still residing in my own heart. But I promise not to leave you with a list of my own grievances against modern American Christianity. These chapters are intended to shift perspectives, yes, but more than that I want them to motivate. I want them to be aspirational. I want us together to embrace a new optimism for the work of God in our day. It is my prayer that God will use my words to open wide a new dialogue desperately needed by today's evangelicals.

I'll end the book with hopeful optimism, and I'll recommend a path for you. Actually, I'll recommend three paths for you. There's room for us to disagree on the practical outgrowth of the principles I will share, but there's a call on all of us just the same. We who claim to be followers of Jesus have to actually walk out the life of faith. We will have to live out the way of the cross, and there's no more fitting way to end a book than to call us back to the image of Jesus himself.

Let's begin. We start with the foundation Paul said he put down as an expert builder, the root of modern Evangelicalism's self-identity: the understanding of Jesus and his gospel.

CHAPTER 2

A Jesus-Centered Gospel

NOT LONG AGO, I was in a meeting with a variety of pastors from a variety of traditions, and we were talking about something scholars call liberation theology. I was feeling uncomfortable about the whole affair, because my seminary had trained me to think of liberation theology as a heresy against the true gospel. I spoke up a few times and found that a couple pastors in the room shared my perspective too. Before long, it was us against the others in a heated debate over the true meaning of the gospel.

For the unfamiliar, "gospel" is the English word we use to translate the Greek word *euangelion* (the word behind both "evangelism" and "evangelical"). Literally, the Greek word means "good message," but in the church world, "gospel" is a technical term, and it can have very different meanings depending on which part of the Bible you are emphasizing at the time. It's even reflected in our translations. For example, many English versions translate it "good news" when Jesus says it and "gospel" when Paul says it.

The same Greek word is behind both translations, and whatever Paul thought of the word, he got his concept originally from Jesus, but we, along with translators and hundreds of years of church tradition tend to focus on the differences. We translate the words differently, we prioritize them differently, and the lines we draw between Paul and Jesus become lines we draw between ourselves and other Christians. They are at the core of the Protestant-Catholic divide, and at the core of what we could call the conservative-progressive divide as well.

I was taught the conservative Protestant perspective so passionately that I felt animosity toward anyone who had a different perspective. But I've softened. Meetings and dialogues and debates like the one I had with those other pastors have helped. They prompted me to spend more time studying our differences, and I've started to realize the dividing line is blurry. I want to help you blur this dividing line too, but to do that, I first need to help you understand the division. As we look at some different passages about the "good news," you'll be able to see the differences between how Jesus uses the word and how Paul uses the word, but I won't stop there. I'll also show you how they really are the same, how Paul's usage flows from Jesus's.

THE GOOD NEWS ACCORDING TO JESUS

In Jesus's first public affirmation of his ministry, he quoted Isaiah 61, saying he had come to "proclaim good news." Matthew, Mark, and Luke all tell us that Jesus went about "preaching the good news of the kingdom" (Matt. 4:23; 9:35; 11:5; Mark 1:14; Luke 4:43; etc.). However, if you look closely at the ministry of Jesus, you don't find many times when he ties a doctrinal affirmation to that good news. He never says forgiveness is the good news or that heaven is the good news. In fact, reading his words and deeds, you realize the good news can't be limited to a message of doctrinal facts. Jesus didn't just say good things and then move on from town to town; he accompanied his message of good news with good actions—actions so good, people reported them to others as good news.

> People were overwhelmed with amazement. "He has done everything well," they said. "He even makes the deaf hear and the mute speak."
>
> MARK 7:37

More than a message, Jesus himself and the entirety of his ministry on Earth—showing love to sinners, healing the sick, and casting out demons—was a literal expression of his good news to the world, and if you had been there in person, you most certainly would have mixed the message of the words and the message of the actions together. If I tell you I have a million dollars for you but never give you a check, that's a burden, not good news. If I tell you I've found the cure for cancer but don't help your mom, that's not good news. If someone says, "the kingdom of God is coming," and then walks away, that's also not particularly good news. But when Jesus said, "The kingdom of heaven is here!" and followed it by raising a child from the dead, people got the idea the two were linked, and they went home talking about the good news.

The gospel as recorded in the books we call the Gospels is *both* message and ministry:

> After John was put in prison, Jesus went into Galilee, *proclaiming the good news* of God. "The time has come," he said. "*The kingdom of God has come near*. Repent and *believe* the good news!"
>
> MARK 1:14–15

> But he said, "I must *proclaim the good news* of the kingdom of God to the other towns also, because that is why I was sent." And he *kept on preaching* in the synagogues of Judea.
>
> LUKE 4:43–44

> When Jesus had called the Twelve together, he gave them power and authority to drive out all demons and to cure diseases, and he sent them out to *proclaim the kingdom of God and to heal the sick*. . . . So they set out and went from village to village, *proclaiming the good news and healing people* everywhere.
>
> LUKE 9:1–2, 6

As Jesus used it, the gospel is a message that the kingdom of God has come near, a message that should be believed or received, but also a message deeply connected to works that prove its truth, works of miraculous liberation from the brokenness of sin. Those who receive the good news receive an experience, a moment of freedom. Those who talk about the good news talk about the present reality of a new reality better than the old reality. Those who are deputized for the gospel carry the message *and* the works wherever they go.

Also important, consider that when Jesus sent out his disciples, whatever the "good news" meant to them, it definitely involved nothing about Jesus dying for the sins of the world. Throughout the Gospels, every time Jesus said anything about his coming death, the disciples ignored or rejected it. Peter once even opposed Jesus to his face about it. In their preaching, they would *never* have said, "Jesus died for your sins." Jesus hadn't died yet, sure, but also, the disciples didn't believe he would! If the Gospels are correct that the disciples were preaching good news, then the "good news" must be different from or at least more than "Jesus died for your sins." We'll come back to that. For now, let's consider how the good news transformed from something tangible and experiential into a doctrine to be merely understood and believed.

THE MOVE TOWARD A DOCTRINE

In the decades after Jesus's resurrection, beginning in the book of Acts and continuing through the epistles of the early church, the gospel gradually took on a more doctrinal tone. Increasingly, the emphasis was placed on the specifics of the message that must be believed, and the accompanying works of liberation received less attention.

> Day after day, in the temple courts and from house to house, they never stopped teaching and proclaiming *the good news that Jesus is the Messiah.*
>
> ACTS 5:42

It makes sense. During the ministry of Jesus, the message of the gospel was about a future that was invading the present, and the miracles were the evidence, but during the first days of the church, the message of the gospel centered around a specific miracle that happened in the *past*. When the first Christians were spreading the good news, they couldn't do so without mentioning the most remarkable, best news of all: a dead man came back to life and promises resurrection for us too. It still had future impact, but it was based on something in the past. That's why in the book of Acts, the good news repeatedly arrives as a claim that something happened, a claim that the Messiah (Anointed, Promised King) *has come*, that Jesus is he, and that we must join him.

For Jewish people, the message of an arrived Messiah was good news because they had waited for him for centuries, but outside the Jewish context, the message of a Jewish Messiah wasn't self-evidently good. The gentiles weren't hoping for a Jewish king, and that's why Paul's ministry was so significant. As a citizen of Rome, trained by Pharisees, he was perfectly positioned to understand the universal significance of a resurrected Messiah and to contextualize the message of Jesus to non-Jewish people. When he took the gospel of Jesus into contexts that didn't care about a Jewish King or Jewish prophecies, he could highlight how the gospel was even more than a mere historical claim; it was a universal life-changing truth for all people of all time.

> While Paul was waiting for them in Athens, he was greatly distressed to see that the city was full of idols. So he reasoned in the synagogue with both Jews and God-fearing Greeks, as well as in the marketplace day by day with those who happened to be there. A group of Epicurean and Stoic philosophers began to debate with him. Some of them asked, "What is this babbler trying to say?" Others remarked, "He seems to be advocating foreign gods." They said this because Paul was preaching *the good news about Jesus and the resurrection*.
>
> ACTS 17:16–18

In Athens, Paul's point was that someone had beaten death! Resurrection was a reality, and Jesus proved it! It's still a statement of history, but it's also a statement of universal truth and a promise for the future. If you put your trust in Jesus, you can also share in his resurrection life. That's good news even to gentiles.

Finally, near the end of Paul's life, as he was anticipating his trip to Rome, he assembled everything he thought about the good news and wrote his most complete thesis on the gospel. In his letter to the Romans, he says things like this:

> That is why I am so eager to preach *the gospel* also to you who are in Rome.
> For I am not ashamed of *the gospel*, because *it is the power of God that brings salvation* to everyone who believes: first to the Jew, then to the Gentile. For *in the gospel the righteousness of God is revealed*—a

righteousness that is by faith from first to last, just as it is written: "The righteous will live by faith."

ROMANS 1:15–17

In Romans, the translators exclusively use "gospel." That's a good translation. By this point, Paul is using the word to describe a doctrine of historical claims with promises for the future. It's a doctrine that contains power all by itself. It's a truth that God will leverage to bring *salvation* to people by connecting *his righteousness* to people of *faith*. It's a doctrine of spiritual cleansing, restoration, and empowerment. It's still deeply connected to how one *lives*—life is to be characterized by *righteousness* and *faith*—but one can easily come away from Paul's words with the idea that accurate belief somehow matters more than behavior. In fact, this understanding became the foundation of the movement we call the Protestant Reformation.

DOCTRINAL LOCK-IN

The biggest transformation regarding the gospel came through the work of a doctrinal activist named Martin Luther, born in 1483 in Germany. The first chapter of Romans transformed his life, and it fundamentally changed the way Christians viewed the gospel. He, more than anyone else before him, is responsible for establishing the gospel as a doctrine to understand and believe, and his definition of the gospel created a major rift between Christians that endures today. Here's how it happened.

During his younger years, Luther wrestled with the meaning of Romans 1. His great difficulty was in understanding the phrase "righteousness of God." He had been brought up to think of God as *holy*, *righteous*, and *wrathful*. Righteousness wasn't something God had or did. Righteousness was something God *was*, and because God was righteous, he couldn't be anything other than wrathful against unrighteousness. Because God was righteous, he must oppose the sinner. The way Luther saw it, the message of God's righteousness was a message of judgment against the sinner.

However, in Romans 1, in the passage I just quoted, Paul said the righteousness of God was *good news* for the sinner! Luther thought, *How could God's righteousness ever be good news for a sinner?*

He was deeply troubled by this passage for years until one day, he saw the passage in a totally new light. He wrote,

> Then finally God had mercy on me, and I began to understand that the righteousness of God is a gift of God by which a righteous man lives, namely faith, and that sentence: The righteousness of God is revealed in the Gospel, is passive, indicating that the merciful God justifies us by faith.[2]

Luther had the sudden insight that "righteousness of God" could also be translated "righteousness from God," and that meant God was *giving righteousness to people by faith*. In other words, people who *believed* the *gospel* would be *given* righteousness. This moment changed everything. This moment locked in the idea that the gospel was a doctrine to believe and that righteousness wasn't a statement about how you lived your life but rather a statement about how you stood in relation to God. This new perspective launched the Protestant Reformation and became its most fundamental concept. It is still the main doctrine dividing Catholics from Protestants and progressives from conservatives. In general terms,

> *Catholics and progressives tend to define the gospel from the words and life of Jesus. They see it as a message of the way God is at work in the world and an invitation to join him in it.*

> *Protestants and conservatives tend to define the gospel from Paul's didactic writings. They see the gospel as a doctrine that when believed gives the believer an immediate righteous standing before God and carries the promise of future salvation.*

THE DIVISION MATTERS

For the average Christian, this probably seems like a pointless debate, a disagreement that doesn't really affect our daily life and shouldn't have any impact on us, but in fact, this division is of central importance. Our disagreement over the nature of the gospel separates Christians from each other, dividing the body of Christ, and this doctrinal division also changes the way we understand our relationship to the world. For those who embrace the Reformers' understanding of the gospel, our primary responsibility is to help people understand the gospel, embrace it as truth, and commit themselves to promote it. From this perspective, our job is to *teach* the gospel doctrine and let God's righteousness take hold in a person's life according to his own methods and timing. In other words, for most Christians in the tradition of the Reformers, Christianity is focused on getting people to understand and accept a specific set of truths about Jesus, follow it up with more doctrinal training in proper understanding, and to leave all the righteousness-building work to God. Church ministries are focused on education and doctrinal accuracy more than on character, behavior, or activism, and when character or behavior flaws arise, the solution is usually assumed to be better *discipleship* (mostly in the form of additional education).

However, for Christians in the Catholic tradition (and in many progressive Protestant traditions), the gospel has always been a message that combines the promise of God with the cooperation of human beings. From this perspective, cooperation is much more important than individual understanding. Yes, this view believes God's grace is available to humans because of Jesus, but it also holds that a person doesn't need to be doctrinally accurate to be a recipient of that grace. From that perspective, my *participation* matters more than my knowledge.

These perspectives, in their extreme versions, are incompatible with each other, and they result in vastly different attitudes toward the work of Christians in the world today. At one extreme, there are Christians who say all we should focus on is *preaching* a specific doctrine called the gospel. At the other extreme, there are Christians who say all we should focus on is *living* out a specific lifestyle that *represents* the gospel. Of course, as is usually the case, both extremes are inadequate. Why, even Paul in his introduction to the book of Romans referred to the gospel in a way that rejects both extremes!

Paul, a servant of Christ Jesus, called to be an apostle and *set apart for the gospel* of God— the gospel he promised beforehand through his prophets in the Holy Scriptures regarding his Son, who as to his earthly life was a descendant of David, and who through the Spirit of holiness was appointed the Son of God in power by his resurrection from the dead: Jesus Christ our Lord. Through him *we received grace and apostleship to call all the Gentiles to the obedience that comes from faith* for his name's sake.

ROMANS 1:1–5

For Paul, the gospel was definitely a doctrine to believe, but it was also a calling to obedience flowing from that belief. It's a thing that transforms us, a thing that sets us apart, moves us toward personal righteousness and changes the way we relate to the world. Believers are called to an *obedience* that comes from *faith*. Paul wasn't giving a new gospel different from Jesus. Paul's gospel was a *Jesus-centered* gospel. He said it himself as we have already seen.

By the grace God has given me, I laid a foundation as a wise builder, and someone else is building on it. But each one should build with care. For no one can lay any foundation other than the one already laid, which is Jesus Christ.

1 CORINTHIANS 3:10–11

The foundation is Jesus. Not some doctrine about Jesus. Jesus himself. He is the way.

Our task is to come back to that gospel—to see Paul as an application and contextualization of Jesus, not an addition or counterpoint.

REDISCOVERING A JESUS-CENTERED GOSPEL

I will not attempt to reconcile all the doctrinal differences between various Christian perspectives on the gospel. This chapter is just a call for us to put Jesus, his life and teaching, back in the center of it. It's a call for my fellow evangelicals to embrace a gospel that is more than doctrine alone, a gospel that combines right thinking, personal holiness, and even social action; a gospel that changes us inside and out; a gospel that brings the good news of the kingdom into present-day living. We always express some form of social engagement, but for too long, evangelicals have missed the literal example of Jesus in his social engagement. We've lived as if doctrinal accuracy, doctrinal communication, getting people saved, and keeping specific morality codes are what matter, but the first Christians knew better:

> Religion that God our Father accepts as pure and faultless is this: to *look after orphans and widows in their distress* and to keep oneself from being polluted by the world. . . . What good is it, my brothers and sisters, if someone claims to have faith but has no deeds? Can such faith save them? Suppose a brother or a sister is without clothes and daily food. If one of you says to them, "Go in peace; keep warm and well fed," but does nothing about their physical needs, what good is it? In the same way, *faith by itself, if it is not accompanied by action, is dead.*
>
> JAMES 1:27; 2:14–17

It's almost as if James were saying we needed to love God *and* love people.

He was. He learned it from watching his half-brother and Lord, Jesus.

It's time for us to understand a bigger view of the good news, to live from and for that good news, and to promote its goodness to the wider world. This isn't new. It's the gospel of Jesus, and it has always been the gospel of Paul too.

Let's revisit Jesus's words again. Let's see the way he uses "good news," and then let me show you some things Paul wrote that we evangelicals too often skip, take out of context, or misread according to our presuppositions. Our problem is that we read the text to confirm what we already think, but we can do better. Here's my suggestion. For each of these sections, read the verses, then my exposition and summary statement, but then go back to the verses. Sit with the text of Scripture for a while. Read the verses from your Bible so you see them in their context. Read them from different translations. Let the Scripture challenge you more than what I say about it.

THE GOOD NEWS ACCORDING TO JESUS (REVISITED)

After John was put in prison, Jesus went into Galilee, proclaiming the good news of God. "The time has come," he said. "The kingdom of God has come near. Repent and believe the good news!"

MARK 1:14–15

Jesus went throughout Galilee, teaching in their synagogues, proclaiming the good news of the kingdom, and healing every disease and sickness among the people.

MATTHEW 4:23

So he replied to the messengers, "Go back and report to John what you have seen and heard: The blind receive sight, the lame walk, those who have leprosy are cleansed, the deaf hear, the dead are raised, and the good news is proclaimed to the poor."

LUKE 7:22

You can't deny that belief is a key component of the good news. From the earliest days of Jesus's ministry, he was proclaiming the gospel, saying, "Repent and believe!" But consider what the person in the audience was supposed to believe. Jesus gave a fact: The time has come; the kingdom of God has come near. Then, he told people to believe the good news. In that context, belief must mean to accept the truth of the previous claim. The time *really has come*. The kingdom of God *really is near*. I believe it. This isn't a doctrinal belief. This isn't a religious belief. It's a *reality* belief. It's a belief that God *has changed* things and *is changing* things. It's a belief that a shift is going on right now, away from the kingdoms of the world toward the kingdom of God. So here's the question: if you really believe a new kingdom is on the move, what behaviors would result?

There's a silly phrase that's been around in Internet culture for a while now, and it goes like this:

"I, for one, welcome our new _____ overlords."

Fill in the blank with whatever scary thing is going on in the world, and you get the phrase as it shows up: "I . . . welcome our new robot overlords,"

"I ... welcome our new AI overlords," and so on. The phrase arises from the fact that the Internet is permanently public. What goes on the Internet will always be saved on some computer somewhere, and there is always a trail back to the source. So, *if* robots take over the world, you want there to be a record that you aren't opposed to their authority. You want the robots to know they can trust you to be loyal. They might kill other people, but they might keep you around because you are on their side.

It's generally said as a joke.

However, Jesus instructed us to take that exact approach regarding God's kingdom. He said, the kingdom of God is coming, and it's time for you to declare your allegiance to it. That's the meaning of the word "repent." It means, "I, for one, reject my previous authority and welcome the ultimate authority of God." Before, you were following your own way in the flow of the kingdoms of the world, but now you are turning around to follow the way of God in the flow of his kingdom. Sure, there's something to believe, but you can't *really think* God is the Ultimate King without it changing you. This claim requires a response of allegiance and surrender and transformation. This is repentance: "I used to be subject to other authorities, but now I welcome the authority of God, I affirm his present and coming kingdom, and I will live as a citizen of its future reality in my present-day life."

> *The good news for Jesus is tied to the now-and-future kingdom of God. It offers many benefits but also demands surrender and transformation.*

Belief means something else too. Consider what Jesus said to Nicodemus:

> "For God so loved the world that he gave his one and only Son, that whoever believes in him shall not perish but have eternal life. For God did not send his Son into the world to condemn the world, but to save the world through him. *Whoever believes in him is not condemned, but whoever does not believe stands condemned* already because they have not believed in the name of God's one and only Son."
>
> JOHN 3:16–18

Or, later to the crowd:

Jesus answered, "The work of God is this: to *believe in* the one he has sent."

JOHN 6:29

Notice this belief is categorically different from the belief mentioned before. The previous formulation was "Here's a fact . . . believe it and let it change you." This formulation is more aggressive and more personal. "Something is desperately wrong with you and the whole world, but I myself am the solution, put your trust in me." This isn't belief *about*. This is belief *in*. This belief is the belief of *trust*, and trust is always *personal*. Yes, there are some facts to understand. The whole world is in a bad place in relation to God, but God, in his love, is doing something to redeem the world, and it centers on Jesus. However, if you accept the reality of these facts, your response must also be personal. Jesus *himself* is the answer. In order for me to enter God's work of redemption and salvation, I need to trust *him*.

> *The good news includes the message of universal condemnation for sin, the sacrificial love of God, and eternal salvation available exclusively through Jesus.*

Even when Jesus is talking about belief, it's almost never a belief about facts. He never gives a list of required belief-facts. He doesn't say *how* his death and resurrection provide salvation. He doesn't warn Thomas that his doubt puts him in danger of hell. Throughout his ministry, Jesus emphasized only the two facts we've just considered: He tells us to believe his description of the now-and-future kingdom of God, and he tells us to believe in him as the one and only Son, our Sacrifice, Savior, and Lord.

So, what does it mean to believe in the kingdom? It means to live like a subject of that King abiding by the ways of that kingdom. What does it mean to believe in the one and only Son? It means trusting him as the ultimate Agent of the Almighty God. Together, these beliefs require behavior. If he's the King describing his kingdom, if he's the Agent living out the will of God, then our response must be to *trust* and *follow* him.

> "Therefore everyone who hears these words of mine and puts them into practice is like a wise man who built his house on the rock."
>
> MATTHEW 7:24

> Jesus replied, "Anyone who loves me will obey my teaching. My Father will love them, and we will come to them and make our home with them. Anyone who does not love me will not obey my teaching. These words you hear are not my own; they belong to the Father who sent me."
>
> JOHN 14:23–24

Jesus describes himself as the Agent of the Father in a loving relationship with him and with the world, and those who love him will therefore follow his words even as he follows the words of the Father. Whatever label you use for Jesus—Lord, Teacher, Mediator—you aren't a believer in Jesus unless you are a *follower* of Jesus. A believer is a doer. They who believe in Jesus are they who do the work of Jesus. Belief and behavior do not exist separately from each other.

Additionally, following Jesus is more than just doing what he said. It also means doing what he did.

> "You call me 'Teacher' and 'Lord,' and rightly so, for that is what I am. Now that I, your Lord and Teacher, have washed your feet, you also should wash one another's feet. I have set you an example that you should do as I have done for you. Very truly I tell you, no servant is greater than his master, nor is a messenger greater than the one who sent him. Now that you know these things, you will be blessed if you do them."
>
> JOHN 13:13–17

"The student is not above the teacher, but everyone who is fully trained will be like their teacher."

LUKE 6:40

"The Son of Man did not come to be served, but to serve, and to give his life as a ransom for many."

MATTHEW 20:28

"Greater love has no one than this: to lay down one's life for one's friends."

JOHN 15:13

Jesus replied: "'Love the Lord your God with all your heart and with all your soul and with all your mind.' This is the first and greatest commandment. And the second is like it: 'Love your neighbor as yourself.' All the Law and the Prophets hang on these two commandments."

MATTHEW 22:37–40

"Therefore go and make disciples of all nations, baptizing them in the name of the Father and of the Son and of the Holy Spirit, and teaching them to obey everything I have commanded you. And surely I am with you always, to the very end of the age."

MATTHEW 28:19–20

John 13 shows us the immense sacrificial love of Jesus for twelve men who would soon totally abandon him or even betray him. Jesus demonstrated real love, and his followers must be people of sacrificial love like him. Listen, the love of Jesus doesn't end when you feel better about yourself. The love of Jesus moves into you to flow through you. It's a transformative love with an embedded calling. Because he loved us so richly, we are to love others. Because he came to us, we go to others. Because he showed us the way to the Father, we display that to others. The *work* of the gospel involves living lives of selfless love and helping others to do the same.

The calling of the gospel is to follow Jesus, doing the work of Jesus, heeding the words of Jesus, expressing sacrificial love like Jesus, and reproducing others who also identify with Christ and obey his words.

This is how Jesus presented the good news. Although he never gave us a rigid formulation of a doctrine he called the gospel, his teaching included a recognition of *something spiritual* (we can be right with God through faith in the Son) and *something social* (we need to imitate Jesus, love others, and train others to do the same). His gospel promises something to us, but it also demands something of us. His gospel is freely offered but costly to receive. His gospel is meaningful and also transformative. It changes me, and it calls me to change the world. Through me, it blesses the world so much, people call it good news.

Still, Jesus never gave us a doctrine of the gospel. That work was done for us mostly by the apostle Paul who contextualized it to the Greco-Roman way of thinking. However, as we consider Paul's words, we will be tempted to misread them. Our tendency with Paul will be to think of the gospel in cold, clinical terms about the cross and its promise for *our salvation* because that's how he often presents it to his gentile audience, and it's the view that benefits us most. We'll be tempted to see the gospel as a list of facts about the death and resurrection of Jesus along with some personal implications of those facts, but we must not forget that according to Jesus, good news was already here even before he went to the cross.

THE GOOD NEWS ACCORDING TO PAUL

Here's a passage that perfectly illustrates our tendency to misread Paul.

And so it was with me, brothers and sisters. When I came to you, I did not come with eloquence or human wisdom as I proclaimed to you the testimony about God. *For I resolved to know nothing while I was with you except Jesus Christ and him crucified.* I came to you in weakness with great fear and trembling. My message and my preaching were not with wise and persuasive words, but with a demonstration of the

Spirit's power, so that your faith might not rest on human wisdom, but on God's power.

1 CORINTHIANS 2:1–5

This passage is where we go off the rails with Paul, so I needed to start with it. The part I highlighted, quoted out of context as it usually is, communicates a *simple* gospel. It's a major verse we evangelicals use to convince ourselves that the gospel is really about one thing only: Jesus died for you. As a result, evangelicals view the cross as a symbol of Jesus's vicarious atoning sacrifice for me. The cross means he died so I don't have to. In a lot of ways, that's a true statement, but that interpretation misses the point of this passage.

Read it again and pay attention to the context. While other preachers were using eloquence and "wisdom," Paul was determined to let Christ shine. In the cosmopolitan city of Corinth, Paul could have quoted Greek philosophers like he did in Athens, or he could have quoted Hebrew Scriptures like he does in his letters, but he didn't. He says he limited himself so much that people might accuse him of knowing nothing other than stories about Jesus. Of course, we know he's under-selling his ministry a bit. We know he spent a great deal of time with the Corinthians. We know he spoke of many things other than the crucifixion. Therefore, we have to conclude, Paul wasn't making a point about the gospel and its contents; he was making a point about how the gospel made him live.

Paul's example in this passage does something evangelicals ignore too often. Paul, the very smart man that he was, describes his behavior here as self-limiting. One might call it self-denial, a willingness to lose his life for the sake of Christ. You might even call it taking up your cross. Here's the fascinating irony: Christians who use this verse to prove that the gospel is a doctrine about what Jesus did for us on the cross miss the fact that Paul wrote it to show his desire to *mimic* the cross. We misread the verse as if it is telling us to focus on a simple doctrine to believe, but Paul wrote the verse because for him, the cross was *also* a pattern to follow.

Something to believe? A pattern to follow? Yes to both. Don't over-simplify it.

WITH THAT, WE ARE NOW ready to see Paul's doctrine the way he intended it.

> Paul, a servant of Christ Jesus, called to be an apostle and set apart for the gospel of God—*the gospel he promised beforehand through his prophets in the Holy Scriptures regarding his Son,* who as to his earthly life was a descendant of David, and who through the Spirit of holiness was appointed the Son of God in power by his resurrection from the dead: *Jesus Christ our Lord.* Through him we received grace and apostleship to call all the Gentiles to the *obedience that comes from faith* for his name's sake. And you also are among those Gentiles who are called to belong to Jesus Christ.... For I am not ashamed of the gospel, because it is the power of God that brings salvation to everyone who believes: first to the Jew, then to the Gentile. For in the gospel the righteousness of God is revealed—a righteousness that is by faith from first to last, just as it is written: "*The righteous will live by faith.*"
>
> ROMANS 1:1–6, 16–17

I've quoted parts of this before, but now, with much more context, you can see what Paul intended to do with Romans. Paul wasn't personally known to the believers in Rome, so he needed to explain his ministry and his convictions in clear, concise terms. More than that, Rome was a city steeped in the analytical and logical thinking of the Greeks, so this letter will be his presentation of the gospel in logical, factual, and doctrinal ways. Still, don't be distracted by his emphasis on doctrine. His gospel was more than "Jesus died for you." His gospel was more than a description of how to be right with God. The revelation of righteousness is *in* the gospel but it isn't *the* gospel. In fact, the passage I just quoted actually contains the briefest possible formulation of Paul's gospel. It's hard to recognize because his sentences can get really long, but here it is: "Paul ... set apart for the gospel of God ... regarding his Son ... Jesus Christ our Lord." For Paul, the gospel was ultimately the message about Jesus. It's the message that Jesus is Lord. That's why his focus wasn't merely to bring *salvation* to the gentiles. In his own words, his focus was to "call all the Gentiles to the *obedience* that comes from faith." For Paul, Jesus was the *Lord* by whom we are *saved* and for whom we *live*.

The gospel is the message that Jesus is Lord, through whom God graciously gives righteousness and salvation to any person who receives it with life-changing faith.

Paul's explanations are certainly more complicated and detailed than anything we saw in the words of Jesus, but his point is clear. The gospel is a *doctrine* about how Jesus's death and resurrection prove his lordship, a *promise* that those who belong to him are given the righteousness of God, and a *calling* to respond in faithful obedience.

Here's one more from Paul:

For Christ's love compels us, because we are convinced that one died for all, and therefore all died. And he died for all, that those who live should no longer live for themselves but for him who died for them and was raised again.

So from now on we regard no one from a worldly point of view. Though we once regarded Christ in this way, we do so no longer. Therefore, if anyone is in Christ, the new creation has come: The old has gone, the new is here! All this is from God, who reconciled us to himself through Christ and gave us the ministry of reconciliation: that God was reconciling the world to himself in Christ, not counting people's sins against them. And he has committed to us the message of reconciliation. We are therefore Christ's ambassadors, as though God were making his appeal through us. We implore you on Christ's behalf: Be reconciled to God. God made him who had no sin to be sin for us, so that in him we might become the righteousness of God.

2 CORINTHIANS 5:14–21

This passage leans heavily into doctrine. Christ became sin for us, dying the death of sin for us on the cross so that we could become God's righteousness. That's vicarious atonement, a central component of evangelical doctrine. Evangelicals also focus on Paul's idea here of internal, spiritual transformation. Faith in Christ means being brought into Christ which makes us a "new creation" and "reconciled" with God. However, something amazing appears here that isn't often mentioned.

All of this is tied to behavior. *Christ's love compels us. Those who live should no longer live for themselves but for him. We are therefore Christ's ambassadors.* Sometimes Paul emphasizes faith, but here, in a passage deep with doctrine, he doesn't mention faith even once. More than that, in this passage, there is no belief-based lesson about *how* a person is reconciled to God. There's no description of a prayer to pray, or words to recite, or a ritual to do, or even a requirement to believe what he just said. It's just an assertion that we can be reconciled to God through Christ and that those who are reconciled are called to join the work of reconciliation as well. Why would Paul "implore" people to be reconciled to God without giving them a list of beliefs or a recipe to follow? How is it in any way an appeal if he doesn't ask them to believe a set of doctrines, pray the sinner's prayer, or get baptized?

When Paul says, "Be reconciled to God," that's the extent of his invitation. God has opened the door to reconciliation. That's it. What remains is for you, like the prodigal son, to simply come home. It sounds like a religious doctrine, but the only way to believe it is to do it. It seems religious, but it doesn't prop up any religious ritual or discipline. It's just a description of the simple fact that God opened the door, he let Paul come in, and now Paul is asking others to come in too. Yes, this is some really interesting doctrine, but that's secondary to Paul's main point. His main point is relational. His point is to claim that *reconciliation* is at the core of the gospel's work. The gospel reconciles *me* to God because the gospel is about God reconciling the *world* to himself. My reconciliation with God brings me into that work, and because of Christ, I am an agent of reconciliation with all of the interpersonal and societal implications of that calling.

> The gospel involves the message that God, in love, is making people new in Christ, removing their sin, giving them his righteousness, reconciling them to himself, and deploying them as his agents of reconciliation in the world.

Any honest reading of the New Testament should lead to the conclusion that Jesus, the Son of God, came into the world to demonstrate the kingdom in power, to sacrifice himself for our salvation, and to call people to follow him in repentance, faithfulness, obedience, imitation, and the work of reconciliation. There are always spiritual and social components to the claim that Jesus is Lord.

This is what the New Testament writers mean by "gospel." It is the *entirety* of the story of Jesus—who he is, what he has taught, what he has done for us, what it means to join him, and what's ahead for the faithful. The gospel brings about an eternal, future salvation, but it also brings about a right-now transformation, the righteousness of God applied to us, wrapped around us, infused within us in this present moment. The gospel compels us to move away from our own sinfulness toward an obedience that flows from reconciliation with God and drives us to participate in the work of reconciliation started by Jesus.

The gospel is a transforming message. It is a message that transforms us spiritually, and it also transforms us socially, making us collective agents of transformation in the midst of broken people God deeply loves.

A JESUS-CENTERED FORMULATION OF THE GOSPEL

Therefore, although evangelicals have largely followed the Protestant tradition of narrowing the gospel focus to doctrinal affirmations and religious responses, it's time for us to rediscover the broader understanding of the gospel as taught by Jesus and the New Testament writers. It's time that we embrace an understanding of the gospel that isn't satisfied with the extremes of doctrinal accuracy or social progressivism but that embraces the same integration of faith and life that Jesus did. A gospel that has doctrinal truth, spiritual transformation, and proper social engagement all at its core:

The Gospel

Jesus, Son of God, Lord and King, came into the world to demonstrate the kingdom life, to sacrifice himself that we might be eternally reconciled to the Father, and to invite us to follow him. We receive that reconciliation and live that kingdom life through repentance, faithfulness, obedience, and joining Jesus in his work of reconciliation.

For most of my life, if you had used that definition, I would have accused you of teaching a false gospel. I bought the idea that the gospel was narrow. *Jesus died for your sins; believe it, and you can go to heaven.* Years of church attendance and Christian education reinforced that definition. If you added anything else, I thought you were adulterating the gospel.

I've changed my perspective. The transformation started with the realization that Paul's gospel came from Jesus. I'm ashamed to admit I had to realize that, but once I realized that Paul and Jesus were talking about the same thing, that Paul was merely contextualizing the good news of Jesus for new audiences, I gave myself permission to let the words of Jesus shape and define my understanding of the good news. Along the way, I began to realize that what I had believed about the gospel needed to take second or third place behind the actual words of the New Testament. I appreciate the contextualizations, applications, and simplifications of people like Martin Luther, but my true foundation is Jesus himself and, because of him, the words of his first followers. Therefore, I have decided to live and breathe a gospel that fully embraces the teaching of Jesus, the example of Jesus, *and* the didactic instructions from Paul and the other New Testament writers.

I'm inviting you to join me in embracing a new, unified approach to the gospel that embraces both a doctrine to believe and a life to live. Christians should be people who fully receive the whole gospel from the whole New Testament, people who let it do its work of transformation in our lives, people who understand that truth transforms and belief behaves, people who are changed by the good news, who *are* good news, and who embrace our role as agents of reconciliation and transformation in the world around us. This is the journey of all who follow Jesus, and it's the journey we should wholeheartedly join.

To that end, let's consider what it means to integrate a gospel like this deeply and fully into our lives, our churches, and our world.

CHAPTER 3

Gospel Integration

NOT TOO LONG AGO, I was at a conference designed to train Christians in the practice of biblical counseling. Before the conference, I didn't know that "biblical counseling" was actually a technical term for a specific kind of counseling done by some churches. I just wanted to do a better job of helping people through their struggles, and I wanted to do that job according to the teaching of the Bible, but at the conference, I discovered a kind of counseling much different from what I was hoping to learn. Specifically, they came at counseling with a framework made up of four convictions (forgive the oversimplification):

· All mental, spiritual, relational, and emotional problems arise from sin.
· The goal of the Christian life is the reduction of sin (called progressive sanctification).
· The pathway to progressive sanctification is learning and doing what the Bible says.
· Therefore, learning and obeying the Bible will solve your problems.

I was unsettled by this at the time. Of course, I had been taught that Christians needed to become *more like Jesus* over time, and that being more like Jesus really meant being less sinful, and being less sinful really meant thinking fewer sinful thoughts and doing fewer sinful actions. I had also been taught that the process of becoming less sinful was largely a *mental and emotional* process: memorizing and studying Scripture, praying, listening to sermons, singing songs, having fellowship, doing devotions, and more. The counseling conference promoted roughly those same solutions, so why did I feel so bothered by it?

I felt bothered because they prescribed this same solution to every single nonphysical problem. No matter what the problem was, the solution was the same: think more Christian thoughts, do fewer non-Christian things. I was bothered by it at the time because neither Jesus nor any other New Testament writer gives an answer this trite to the real problems people face. Now, however, I'm bothered by it for a different reason. I've come to realize their framework depends on a gospel that's too narrow and a goal that's too small.

The gospel of the New Testament is too big to be satisfied by our individual, internal moral improvements. Sure, it affects me as an individual, but it was designed to change the world. Christ's death applies to me, yes, but his purpose was to bring about the reconciliation of "all things." The gospel is supposed to be transformative in ways both deep and wide, both personal and interpersonal. *That's* what I long for. I want the goodness of Jesus, his teaching, and his example to permeate deeply into my soul and then to flow out of me, bringing good news to others through me. Toward that end, I don't want to promote what most evangelicals call progressive sanctification, I want to promote something I'm calling "gospel integration."

When it comes to being a follower of Jesus, the real issue is not how long you've been a Christian or how much of the Bible you have memorized or even how closely you toe the line of some morality code. The real issue is how *deeply* and how *thoroughly* the message and life of Jesus have affected your life, and then, how deeply and how thoroughly that gospel affects the people and society around you. The work of us humans is not necessarily to strive for the incremental transformations we define for ourselves but to let the good news of the lordship of Jesus have deeper sway in and through our lives. The calling Paul had was far more than getting people to believe a doctrine or obey some code. He was called to advance a message so powerful that its very nature was to transform individuals and communities spiritually and socially.

Therefore, in the spirit of the apostle Paul, the job of any individual Christian and the job of any church is to work toward deeper gospel integration, integrating the truth *and* the implications of the gospel more deeply and more fully into ourselves, into each other, and even into our society at large where appropriate. Let's start by considering what it means for the gospel to move deeply into an individual person.

THE GOSPEL IN US

Recall the definition of the gospel I gave at the end of the last chapter:

The Gospel

Jesus, Son of God, Lord and King, came into the world to demonstrate the kingdom life, to sacrifice himself that we might be eternally reconciled to the Father, and to invite us to follow him. We receive that reconciliation and live that kingdom life through repentance, faithfulness, obedience, and joining Jesus in his work of reconciliation.

What does it look like as this truth settles more deeply into a person's heart and life?

First, it should be obvious that any true recipient of this gospel will be an individual who is overwhelmed by the authority of Jesus as the Son of God, the immensity of his power and his sacrifice, the promise of the kingdom, and the tragic reality of human sinfulness. As this awareness sinks more deeply into a person's life, the first result we should see is a deep *humility* regarding ourselves coupled with unquenchable *awe* regarding our Savior. This is what we mean with the words "repentance" and "worship." Repentance is the decision to relinquish control of your life to God followed by the daily, lived-out reaffirmation of that decision. Worship is the repeated recognition that there is one whose power, wisdom, and glory so overshadow your own that any concept of self-determination becomes unthinkable.

Every recipient of the gospel begins the journey with repentance and continues in that repentance by living a life of humility and worship.

Second, the work of the gospel in a person's life always leads into a life of *faithfulness*, not mere belief. Belief is fulfilled so long as your idea matches reality, but faithfulness is never finished. True faithfulness, as understood in the way of Paul, James, and Jesus, is not about assenting to specific statements of doctrine. Faithfulness is not about reducing your doubts or developing greater confidence in certain theological statements. Rather, as the gospel becomes more integrated in your life, you become more consistent in the expressions of that gospel life. Faith may start like a mustard seed, but good seeds in good soil grow, they endure, they bear fruit. This is not about church attendance, scheduled financial donations, or even an ongoing affirmation that you still believe. Faithfulness might express those things, but the true fruit of the faithful is to look more like Jesus.

> *The gospel, when lived out, produces the fruit of a life resembling Jesus: alignment with his teaching, imitation of his behavior, and participation in his work of reconciliation.*

Third, the work of the gospel in a person's life will always produce these various things *together*. An integrated gospel, deeply integrated into a person's life will not produce one fruit to the neglect of the others. A person cannot imitate Jesus while failing to obey the words of Jesus. A person can't truly recognize Jesus as the Son of God, Lord, and King without joining him in his work of reconciliation.

We fail here often. Our propensity is to display an out-of-balance gospel that aligns with our own comforts, but we must diligently oppose such misalignment. Our human sinfulness is inclined to make us prioritize one fruit over the others. We might emphasize obedience to Jesus's teaching to the neglect of any imitation of his character. We might work toward some form of reconciliation without any emphasis on his actual teaching. More than that, we will be tempted to attack each other when we think someone else is doing it wrong. There will be those voices in the church telling us to forget about all the behaviors and just focus on the belief itself. That voice will accuse us of living by law instead of grace. Other voices might accuse us of ignoring the truth and living with too much grace. In the struggle, we'll be deceived into prioritizing one of the two prongs of the gospel, and we will fall for it because it's more comfortable to live without the tension. It's more comfortable to retreat into silos of doctrinal accuracy or behavioral uniformity. But that comfort is a lie.

The gospel is not comfortable. It's a thing of tension: belief and behavior, individual and communal, now and not yet. These conflicting voices must be heeded together. Without the different voices pushing on each other, we might find ourselves, because we are sinful and selfish, losing one part of the gospel for the sake of another, but with the different voices, we have a hope of becoming a community where iron sharpens iron and wounds from a friend can be trusted. We are called to that kind of life. We are called to be a family where the gospel retains both its doctrinal accuracy and its transformative potency, but we can live up to that calling only when we remain connected and in dialogue with each other.

> *Living out a transformative gospel as an individual in community means accepting the constant tension of dialogue with multiple people who are also being transformed.*

The gospel makes me humble, it makes me faithful, and both together remind me of my own propensities toward imbalance. I need other believers for my growth, they need me for theirs, and our dialogue needs to include even our understanding of the gospel itself.

THE NEED FOR GOSPEL DIALOGUE

Until recently, I never let myself feel the tensions in the gospel. My evangelical ecosystem grouped the implications of the gospel into four little packages: living lives of personal holiness (spiritual disciplines and the morality code), living in fellowship (church activity) with other like-minded believers, telling other people how to be saved (receiving Jesus through a prayer of confession), and then teaching them to repeat the process too (getting more people saved).

Nevertheless, as I continued to grow and learn, I discovered that other church traditions have different convictions that are just as biblical (or not) as my own. Some think imitating Jesus means promoting societal *wholeness* even if that takes a form I consider socialism. Some think imitating Jesus means promoting societal *holiness* even if that takes a form I consider Christian nationalism. Some think it means working for social justice or racial reconciliation. Some think it means performing miraculous healings. All of them have their own reasons for their perspective and traditions, and all of those reasons need to be challenged. But my own reasons need to be challenged too, and praise God, he lets it happen! The more I interact with other Christians from other traditions, the more my own thinking is challenged and the more I realize that my understanding of Jesus and the gospel is narrow in just the ways that serve me best. Their perspective doesn't distract me from the Bible. It drives me deeper into the Bible. Their perspective helps me see what's actually there as opposed to what I expect to find. I need their input to help me see Jesus, and myself, more clearly. Even though my church tradition has its way to understand and prioritize the fruit of the gospel, others do it differently, sometimes better, sometimes worse, and I need to be in dialogue with them.

The gospel is more than doctrine, and it's more than behavior. The gospel is a union of spiritual, personal, and social. Even as Jesus is *God* in *flesh*, so too the gospel is more than just one thing. Even as no individual Christian can be the *body* of Christ without the others, no individual Christian can fully comprehend the gospel. We have a long history of misunderstanding the gospel because we have a long history of misunderstanding each other! The gospel was a mystery to the angels (1 Pet. 1:12), Peter thought Paul was hard to understand (2 Pet. 3:15–16), and Paul himself said we see only a poor reflection (1 Cor. 13:12). It's certainly important for me to know what *I* mean by the gospel, but without dialogue with the larger body of Christ as informed by both Scripture and lived experience, my knowledge of the gospel will always be weak, and its integration in my life will always be shallow. If I want the gospel to be deeply integrated in my life, if I want it to bear the fruit in me it should bear, then I need to be in conversation with other Christians whose view of the gospel is *different* from my own and who will challenge me with that different perspective.

There are tough questions I will never be able to answer from my narrow view, questions about morality and priorities, and I shouldn't even attempt to answer these questions on my own. I'm too inclined to make decisions that benefit me. I'm too tempted to distort the gospel according to my own comforts. I *need opposition* from other believers. It's how I grow.

WITHOUT DIALOGUE

Sadly, the history of the church is filled with stories of dialogue ended rather than engaged, and the American church follows firmly in that flow of history. Evangelical Christians have often failed to take advantage of opportunities for conversation with those in other camps, but even among ourselves, we fail to maintain honest dialogue. Instead of using a gospel foundation to drive us closer to each other, we avoid the problem by avoiding the topics and keeping things vague. Nearly every evangelical church agrees that the role of the gospel-centered community is to do things like these: worship God, disciple people, fellowship with believers, and minister to the world in a variety of ways. But by using insider jargon and by keeping the words vague, we can pretend we are in agreement when we are not, and we can redefine the words whenever we want to strengthen the lines of division. I can use certain words when partnership with you is beneficial, but I can define those same terms in different ways when partnership with you becomes difficult. My comfort dictates whether I stay in dialogue with you or separate myself from you. What does individual ministry look like? What does corporate ministry look like? What does it mean to imitate Jesus and work for reconciliation as individuals and as churches in this world? What would multichurch cooperation even mean? These questions are difficult, and frankly, it's more comfortable to avoid them and avoid each other.

Without a commitment to dialogue, it's just too easy to slide into the comfort of division. In our siloed Christian enclaves, we can congregate with others who see the gospel the way we do, and we can come up with specific strategic answers to our own specific questions. What's more, our tribal divisions over the *methods* of the gospel reinforce our differences regarding the *meaning* of the gospel. As a result, cooperation between churches has always been limited to cooperation between like-minded churches.

Perhaps we should just embrace the mantra that everyone is entitled to his or her own opinion. Maybe we just agree to disagree, stay separate, never talk about our disagreements. Maybe I'll do my thing and you do your thing. It makes sense practically, but it's wrong. It is an affront to the lordship of Jesus who desires something more.

> "I have given them the glory that you gave me, that they may be one as we are one—I in them and you in me—so that they may be brought to complete unity. *Then the world will know that you sent me* and have loved them even as you have loved me."
>
> JOHN 17:22–23

The gospel is literally fleshed out by our *unity*, and it is wounded by our disunity. Therefore, a desire for gospel integration must drive us to bear *collective* fruit through cooperation. Even if we do not agree on all strategies or doctrines, we must press on for unity in the body. We must engage the dialogue even when it's difficult.

Already I can hear the murmurs of people critiquing me, dividing themselves from me, saying I am *watering down* the gospel (a favorite phrase among Christians who hold to a strict doctrinal idea of the gospel) or otherwise teaching a false gospel. I can hear the voices of fellow Christians and church pastors talk about the need to *build* walls of division because their definition of the gospel needs protection. I can hear them in my head now because I've heard them my whole life long. The language and emotions of Christian division are *pervasive*.

I grew up attending First Baptist Church of Apple Valley, and I went to school there too. Every day, on the way to school or church, we drove right past First Southern Baptist Church of Apple Valley. Then, from our church parking lot, I could look across the street to see First Church of the Nazarene. How dare these churches call themselves "First"! I clearly remember thinking that they probably weren't real Christians anyway, and for a time, I actually felt animosity toward them and any Christian outside our fellowship. My school was Apple Valley Christian, and I couldn't stand the kids from Hesperia Christian, or Victor Christian, or any of the other Christian schools in our league. I hated those kids.

This is the result of us not living in gospel dialogue. One perspective demonizes the other as watering down the gospel, while the latter accuses the former of having a dead faith. One perspective embraces an uncritical activism, while the other accuses them of being too political and shuts down further conversation. We must do better. The conversation, contentious as it may be, must happen. The integration of the gospel is too important a thing to be misunderstood, and the unity of the church is too important a thing to be lost. And the only way it will happen is if we bring our disagreements into the light and under the lordship of Christ.

We need to revisit the lessons of Acts 15.

THE ACTS 15 PATH

In Acts 15, we learn of a dispute that arose when some Christians from Jerusalem arrived in Antioch and began to teach the church that before a person could be a real Christian, that person needed to become a Jew. On the surface, they claimed gentile men needed to be circumcised to become Christians. Under the surface, it was a disagreement about the gospel itself. It was a dispute about how deeply the message of Jesus had changed things or should change things, and it was such a problem that Antioch sent a delegation to Jerusalem to confer with the elders of the church there. Barnabas and Paul went south, and a counsel was convened to address the issue. After much conversation, after strong words from Peter and Paul, and I'm sure many words from those promoting circumcision, James summarized the conclusion of the council this way:

> "It is my judgment, therefore, that we should not make it difficult for the Gentiles who are turning to God. Instead we should write to them, telling them to abstain from food polluted by idols, from sexual immorality, from the meat of strangled animals and from blood. For the law of Moses has been preached in every city from the earliest times and is read in the synagogues on every Sabbath."
>
> ACTS 15:19–21

Applying the gospel to the new reality of gentiles coming to faith led to a conflict of opinions. Some thought circumcision and living by the laws of Moses were central components of faithfulness to God. Others saw Jewish laws as peripheral or even canceled. What should the early church do? One option of course is to let everyone have his or her own opinion. There could be some churches that ask everyone to be circumcised, there could be other churches that don't. There could be some churches that say, "make your own decision if circumcision is right for your own family," and other churches that say, "here's what the Scripture says on the topic."

Is it really worth all the potential division to try to come up with one approach? Isn't it better to keep the "unity" of the Spirit by avoiding the argument? Shouldn't we let everyone just do their own thing? Or is it possible that some deeply practical issues, unaddressed by existing Scripture, should be directly addressed by deeply concerned people?

After a great amount of dialogue (arguing, I'm sure) and prayer, James gave a summary of three behaviors all Christians should embrace:

- Christians should abstain from food sacrificed to idols.
- Christians should abstain from sexual immorality.
- Christians should abstain from eating blood.

This prescription surprisingly left out circumcision but actually endorsed three other rules from Jewish law. Why these behaviors? Fortunately, they wrote down their reasons. According to them, these recommendations were because people everywhere (especially the Jewish Christians) already had consciences formed by the law of Moses and these three behaviors were a minimal concession toward people of that conscience. What you eat and with whom you consort are relationally significant, sometimes public matters, but whether a man is circumcised is generally private. The early leaders gave these recommendations because they knew some behaviors were only individually significant while others had relational impact, and they were living by a deeper principle of unity: We limit our personal freedoms for the sake of the community.

It's also important to note that these mentioned guidelines didn't last forever in the life of the church. Years later, as the gospel continued to progress throughout the ancient world, Paul reached areas that were not so dominated by a Mosaic conscience, and in those contexts, even though he reaffirmed the need for sexual purity, he said completely different things about Jewish dietary restrictions. In fact, he actually claimed they were bad rules—merely human rules:

> Such teachings come through hypocritical liars, whose consciences have been seared as with a hot iron. They forbid people to marry and order them to abstain from certain foods, which God created to be received with thanksgiving by those who believe and who know the truth. For everything God created is good, and nothing is to be rejected if it is received with thanksgiving, because it is consecrated by the word of God and prayer.
>
> 1 TIMOTHY 4:2–5

Paul was claiming that God had given a new word (probably through the teaching of Jesus and the vision given to Peter on the roof) that *consecrated* all food and therefore had undone the dietary restrictions of the Jewish law. In many other places, Paul rejected or reinterpreted the dietary commands. Still, he regularly reaffirmed the prohibition against sexual immorality. Of the three provisions in Acts 15, Paul later affirmed only that one. Therefore, our takeaway from Acts 15 must be something that goes beyond the specific rules. Our lesson must be found in the *values* undergirding those guidelines and their formulation. I'll offer four of those values.

THE VALUES OF ACTS 15

First, the early church recognized that some issues are central, and others are peripheral. Remember the motivating issue was circumcision, but the counsel didn't even mention it in the letter they sent out to the new gentile Christians. Instead, they mentioned other issues that were more important, issues that were more central. Clearly, they had an idea that some things were central to the Christian life (e.g., making it easy for people who are "turning to God"), and other things were peripheral.

Second, the early church leaders were unafraid to call some things sin while also realizing that some things are contextual. They never said eating meat sacrificed to an idol was a sin, only that it violated the widespread context of people who understood the law of Moses. They considered the dietary commands to be contextual. Paul made it explicit in Romans 14:22–23 where he said eating meat sacrificed to an idol was wrong only in certain contexts. Still, when it came to sexual immorality, there was no equivocation. Every New Testament writer agreed and reaffirmed that sexual behavior outside of a proper marriage (see 1 Cor. 5 and 7) is sinful every time in every context, and Paul was especially unafraid to be quite blunt about it. Some things are always sin, some things are contextual, and we should be clear about the difference.

Third, the early Christians saw themselves as part of a long heritage of proclaiming God's will to the wider world. Note that James wasn't worried only about *Jewish* people when he mentioned the guidelines. Instead, he spoke of the law of Moses as something universally known even among gentiles. Eventually, the world would come to learn the beauty of the Christian faith, but that hadn't happened yet. On the other hand, the Jewish law *had* been proclaimed all over, and therefore, even unbelievers had their consciences marked by that morality. The early church embraced that reality. They saw themselves as a *continuation* of God's earlier work, not a *revolution* against it. Moreover, they saw that deviating too much from the Mosaic law might actually make it harder for some people to come to faith in Jesus. Christians eating blood might make the *faith* unpalatable. *Outsiders* might be offended! That was unacceptable. The early church valued accommodating themselves to the consciences of unbelievers so they could more effectively witness to the gospel.

Finally, the early church understood the value of dialogue, consensus, and diversity. Even though Paul is sometimes quite feisty in his approach, and even though he sometimes aggressively opposes his opponents, he nevertheless fully endorsed the restrictions in Acts 15 for at least a time. Paul would later minimize two of those restrictions, but at the end of this council, he accepted them. He knew they wouldn't apply for all people at all times, but he still accepted them for that time; he *compromised*. He, along with the other leaders, demonstrated a willingness to hold fast to the message of Christ's death and resurrection and to prioritize the work of reconciliation over competing interests. Certain uniformities were rejected (circumcision), while others were embraced. They found ways to have both consensus and diversity. Even the early church knew that not every church would look the same and not every city would have the same kind of ministry, but those first Christian leaders understood that finding common ground for the sake of the gospel was essential.

The early church, faced with its very first dilemma over how the message of the gospel interacted with the realities of the world around them, gathered together and decided to find common ground in the midst of their normal divisions. Through their efforts at dialogue, they chose to prioritize what was central and allow the peripheral to fall away. They chose to clearly label sin as sin, when sin was sin, but to also recognize that sometimes sin depends on the context. They realized that their message was part of a long tradition of bringing the truth of God to the people of the world. And finally, they also realized the need for unity even at the cost of uncomfortable dialogue.

These four principles show us how those closest to Christ chose to live out their Christianity when cultures and values came into conflict. These four principles illustrate how a doctrine can remain the same while implementations and community morals can be more fluid. In our modern world, we are facing a similar clash of cultures, and therefore, we should employ a similar set of principles.

THE QUESTIONS WE NEED TO ANSWER

I'm sure the conference in Acts 15 wasn't always the most pleasant to experience. I imagine that Paul and Peter were each boisterous individuals in their own right, and I bet the Jewish believers were just as set in their ways. Nevertheless, they were convinced that they had a *transformative message* that made deep changes to both individual and society, so they did the hard work of dialogue, and God honored their decision. The church in America today—and I'm specifically singling out the evangelical camp here—needs to do this work again, but today it's not about circumcision and dietary restrictions. Today, our work involves a complex web of questions over the church and its relationship to morality, spirituality, psychology, politics, social justice, racial reconciliation, environmental concerns, and even evangelism! The church didn't suddenly get more complex, but the world around us is vastly more complex, and our dilemma remains the same: How should followers of Jesus interact with the world around us? Thankfully, the values expressed in Acts 15 can govern our response today just as well as they did back then. To guide our thinking in future chapters, I'll rephrase them each in the form of a question.

First, because some things are central and some things are peripheral, we ask,

Which values are central to the Christian life, and which are peripheral?

Second, because there is a difference between what is actual sin and what is a contextual concern, and because there is a difference between the expectations of a Christian and an unbeliever,

Which central values are internal to the body of Christ only, and which should Christians promote in the society at large?

Third, because the calling of the church is to be engaged in the world through the work of discipleship and reconciliation, but also because methods carry their own moral force,

How should we, individuals and churches, promote those values?

Fourth, because we value dialogue, consensus, unity, and diversity,

Where is there room for disagreement?

In the last section of the book, I'll use these questions to help us identify our idols, eliminate the wood, hay, and straw, and find a new path forward for the church in America, but that's going to be a tough conversation, and I need to build a bit more common ground with you before we go there. Before I offer you any recommendations for how we need to do better, before I offer you any words of challenge or instruction, I need to tell you a little more about me and where I'm coming from. Specifically, I need to tell you how I spent years giving people the wood of an overly narrow gospel, the hay of being vague on important truths, and the straw of staying silent over some truly damaging ideas.

CHAPTER 4

A Confession

OVER THE PAST FOUR YEARS, I've done a lot of thinking about my twenty plus years in pastoral ministry. It started the night I was sitting in a room surrounded by close friends and members of the church I started, men whom I invited, trained, and appointed to be elders in the church. Earlier that week, I had spoken out against then president Donald Trump, who had posed for a photo op in front of a church, awkwardly holding up a Bible, after ordering a crowd to be sprayed with tear gas so he could preach a message on TV about law and order. I was deeply aggrieved by his obvious use of Christian themes and symbols to gain the loyalty of his largely evangelical political base while using those very themes to disrespect the anguish of Black people in this country. I made a video as part of my daily devotional to the church, and I was blunt in describing him as a false teacher based on his fraudulent and performative claim to be a Christian leader. I didn't address his policies. I didn't tell people to not vote for him, but I said unequivocally that he was exactly the kind of false teacher described in 2 Peter 2.

My video offended many in the church and prompted the elders to request a meeting with me. That night, those men uniformly told me they did not want an "activist" pastor, and by the next day, all of them but one had resigned as elders, left the church, and cut off all communication with me. Others followed, also accusing me of being too political.

From my perspective, I hadn't become an activist, I hadn't become political. From my perspective, I was doing what I had always done.

I was calling people to see through the lies of the world and to put their trust in Jesus. I was calling people to read the words in the Bible, believe them, and put them into practice. I was calling people to act in love the way Jesus would. The only thing that was new was that I had specifically identified one of those lies, and I had passionately named the liar.

Actually, that's not true. I had previously identified lies, and I had previously identified liars, but this time, what was different was that the lie and liar I identified were directly tied to American conservative politics. Even though I didn't see this critique as being substantively different from my previous critiques, others saw it differently. To them, I had become something different. People who thought they knew me saw that moment as a *departure* from the pastor they had known before. How is it that I saw myself as the same, but they saw me as something different?

It took a great deal of reflection, but there was a clear and obvious answer.

I hadn't been honest with them. Or perhaps even myself.

I had previously presented a version of me that wasn't fully authentic, and they had adopted a vision of me that wasn't exactly real either.

That moment forced me to reconsider the pastor I had been before. How had I failed them in the previous fourteen years? How had I misrepresented myself over those years? More importantly, how had I misrepresented the teaching of the Bible so thoroughly that when I said something that came right out of the Bible, they chose to see it and dismiss it as political?

I'm now convinced that my failure was twofold. To begin, I personally held convictions that were nothing more than idols built of wood, and I passed those flawed convictions on to others as well. Then, my failure was also found in my silence. If my understanding grew or my convictions matured, I still kept silent unless I knew those convictions were compatible with the politics and presuppositions of my congregation. In my ministry, I taught the Bible with terminology that was just vague enough so as not to offend one political party or another. At times, I held back on giving any commentary about a societal sin because it was tied too closely to a political platform. At times, I preached about a biblical value in just such a way that confirmed the political leanings of the majority of people in my congregation without identifying the weaknesses of those perspectives. And at all times, I avoided mentioning anything that someone could interpret as political unless it was a political opinion already shared by the majority of my congregation. In my teaching, through ignorance, vagueness, silence, or avoidance, I allowed people to see me as someone aligned with their political ideology. Whether by promoting bad theology or failing to expose it, I've reinforced idols and need to repent of that failure.

I recognize that in my journey of faith over the past few years, I may have accidentally retained portions of a view that should be tossed aside, or perhaps I have allowed the pendulum to swing too far away from my origins and have tossed out something that should be retained. By putting these thoughts down on these pages, I'm intentionally inviting the criticism and evaluation of others so I might grow, but I do so for another reason too. I'm thinking through the implications of my origin story because I want you to join me in thinking through your own. We all have to address our biases. Some values we believe to be central actually aren't. Some things we think of as peripheral need to be brought closer to center. But until we see our biases clearly, we won't be able to see the difference between what is authentic and what is idolatrous. Since I can't speak for you, I'll just speak for me, but perhaps you will see a bit of yourself in my story too.

My failure has deep roots—deep in my upbringing and in my education.

I'M AN EVANGELICAL

I have freely used this word so far, but I should be more specific. *I was raised in, educated in, and am ordained as a pastor in the world of middle-class, white, evangelical, conservative North American Christianity*, and all those words are important.

- Middle-class, or even more accurately, upper middle-class. I went to private schools. The church I was raised in owned land, had multiple buildings, operated a school, and paid multiple full-time staff. The congregations in which I move are predominately populated by people who own their own homes, have full-time jobs with benefits like vacations and health insurance, drive multiple cars, and never question where their next meal will come from.

- White. The church circles in which I move are overabundantly populated by white people. Black people and people of any ethnicity other than what passes for white are a rarity in my church circles. This has significant implications that I'll address in a moment.
- Evangelical. The churches in my circle have a commitment to the proclamation of the gospel, which in Greek is the word *euangelion* and is the source word for our self-identification. The term gained prominence tied to a gospel-focused, socially active movement in England and has been embraced at various times in America for various reasons, but most evangelicals use the term today to mean Protestant and Bible centered.
- Conservative. The churches in my circle have a commitment to the integrity, authority, and infallibility or even inerrancy of Scripture. According to this viewpoint, since the Bible is the only true authority and since its truth is already written, true believers should be focused on conserving the already-given truth. In this context, "progressive" and "liberal" mean moving beyond the text and are often considered bad words. As a result, although "conservative" is supposed to communicate something specific about biblical interpretation and Christian doctrine it often carries its secular political meaning as well, and for these churches, political conservatism is assumed and endorsed while all forms of liberalism are disdained.

I don't have a problem implicitly with any of these words or the definition as a whole. It's not wrong to be middle-class. It's not wrong to be white or to have been raised in a predominately white environment. It's not wrong to have a high esteem for the message of the gospel or the authority of Scripture. Nevertheless, as you can already tell by the way I have described the terms above, I have come to realize that much of the Evangelicalism I'm steeped in has been built with wood, hay, and straw. There are flammable idols among us. Some arose directly from the doctrines of Evangelicalism, but even more grew out of the overall culture of Evangelicalism.

Furthermore, since I uncritically participated in all of it, I find myself complicit in the establishment and support of those idols. I took the approach that the evangelical point of view was the right one, and I thought of the gospel as a narrowly specific doctrine about how people get forgiven of their sin and go to heaven.[1] I never considered the social and societal implications of that doctrine or even whether the word "gospel" meant anything more than something to believe.

As you know by now, I consider my former perspectives to be insufficient, and I am beginning to move past their limitations, but I still need to acknowledge them and the other biases flowing from them, because I can't claim to have changed entirely, nor can I claim to have perfectly transitioned to something better. Part of my growth is an evolution of my previous perspective, part of my growth is a reaction to it, and part of my growth is a rejection of it. So, when I say "evangelical," I'm talking about me and the tradition from which I come even though it's also a tradition I am now trying to critique. Yes, this is a confession of how I've been wrong in my understanding of things, but it's also a confession of how Evangelicalism in America has itself been wrong, deeply and doctrinally, even down to its core. I and my fellow evangelical pastors are guilty of promoting real, doctrinal falsehoods that prop up real, insidious idols.

WITH A NARROW GOSPEL

Modern Evangelicalism depends on the teaching of the apostle Paul as understood by Martin Luther, John Calvin, and the other Reformers, filtered through the individualistic, revivalist religious dynamics of the past two centuries. I've discussed already how Paul's gospel should be understood as a reexplanation and contextualization of the same gospel taught by Jesus, but now, I want to confess that I and my fellow evangelicals have taken Paul's contextualization too far. I was taught and fully believed that the gospel as described by Paul and explained by the Reformers is the *real* gospel and that the "good news" spoken of by Jesus was only a foreshadowing of the actual gospel. The real gospel, I thought, is a doctrine of salvation from sin through the sacrifice of Christ on the cross applied to a person's life when they believe it. Evangelical pastors base their doctrine on verses like these:

> You see, at just the right time, when we were still powerless, Christ died for the ungodly. Very rarely will anyone die for a righteous per-

son, though for a good person someone might possibly dare to die. But God demonstrates his own love for us in this: *While we were still sinners, Christ died for us.*

ROMANS 5:6-8

For the *wages* of sin is death, but the *gift* of God is eternal life in Christ Jesus our Lord.

ROMANS 6:23

For it is by grace you have been *saved, through faith*—and this is not from yourselves, it is the gift of God—*not by works*, so that no one can boast.

EPHESIANS 2:8-9

For I resolved to know *nothing* while I was with you except *Jesus Christ and him crucified.*

1 CORINTHIANS 2:2

These verses are interpreted to say that the central message of Christianity is individual, personal salvation (forgiveness of sins, promise of heaven) that we obtain through placing our faith in what Jesus did for us on the cross. According to that perspective, nothing matters nearly as much as the *message* of the gospel, a proper *understanding* of the gospel, and individual *acceptance* of it as *true*. Among evangelicals, intellectual assent to a proper concept of the gospel takes practical precedence over everything else. Consider what Paul said in Galatians.

You foolish Galatians! Who has bewitched you? Before your very eyes Jesus Christ was clearly portrayed as crucified. I would like to learn just one thing from you: Did you receive the Spirit by the works of the law, or by *believing what you heard*?

GALATIANS 3:1-2

This comes in the context of Paul accusing the Galatians of leaving faith behind and focusing too much on observing the law, but the implied threat for all evangelicals is that certain attitudes and behaviors of Christians can lead them to diminish the significance of Christ's death. This is a real fear evangelicals have. This is a real fear I was raised to have. It's the fear that if I have *believed* an incorrect gospel, I will be subconsciously invalidating the work of Christ in my life and will therefore disqualify myself for salvation. One more passage will drive this home.

> For all who rely on the works of the law are under a curse, as it is written: "Cursed is everyone who does not continue to do everything written in the Book of the Law." Clearly no one who relies on the law is justified before God, because "the righteous will live by faith."
>
> GALATIANS 3:10–11

As a result of verses like this, read from within the framework that the gospel is primarily a doctrine to understand and accept, I believed with the majority of my evangelical brothers and sisters that faith is the important thing, that faith meant mental acceptance of a set of doctrinal claims about Jesus, and that if your doctrine was insufficient, then your faith was insufficient and your salvation was probably not real either. For most evangelicals, how a person lives is far and away less important than the set of doctrines that person believes.

I've already shown how this understanding of the gospel is simply too small, and I now confess it was wrong to hold it and to teach it as if it were the whole gospel. Not only did it downplay the literal words of Jesus but it also led to a great deal of other errors, as I'll address. I believe these verses, and I believe the doctrine is true, but I'm convinced it's only part of the story. I renounce the narrow gospel.

WITH A SELECTIVE MORALITY

We evangelicals say belief is most important, but spend any time under the teaching of a pastor like me, and you will hear a practical inconsistency (dare I say hypocrisy?) in that teaching. Specifically, if you listen to just a few of my sermons from my ministry, you will hear the strong implication that certain behaviors really matter, and they matter so much they can invalidate the spiritual effect of correct doctrine!

It's a problem for us because we are attached to a narrow, doctrinal view of the gospel, but we also know that Paul didn't teach doctrinal accuracy alone. He gave strong and clear moral instructions too. Now, if you push evangelicals on whether the moral code is as central to the faith as the gospel, they will likely deny it, but if you listen to how they talk about their faith and what it means to be a believer, the strength of Paul's moral statements will be clearly evident in their words. Passages like the following are deeply important to evangelicals.

> The acts of the flesh are obvious: sexual immorality, impurity and debauchery; idolatry and witchcraft; hatred, discord, jealousy, fits of rage, selfish ambition, dissensions, factions and envy; drunkenness, orgies, and the like. I warn you, as I did before, that *those who live like this will not inherit the kingdom of God.*
>
> GALATIANS 5:19–21

Passages like this allow evangelicals to talk about a gospel that saves you by grace while also talking about behaviors that invalidate you for salvation. Moreover, passages like this allow evangelicals to make lists of *which* behaviors are the most damaging to one's spiritual condition. I call this an inconsistency or hypocrisy simply because it empowers us to focus on certain behaviors and ignore others whenever convenient. If you advocate a behavior that I don't think is all that important, I'll say, "Actually, salvation is by grace!" But if you pull the grace card on some behavior I think is important, I'll flip and tell you, "Actually, if you were really saved, you wouldn't do that thing."

For nonevangelical church traditions, the apparent incongruity of Paul's message isn't a problem, because for them, the gospel has always been tied to behavior. The gospel is the news of what God has done for us (behavior) through the obedience of Christ (behavior) and an invitation for us to join in the work (behavior) and receive the blessings of that good news. For those church traditions, understanding the doctrine of Jesus is not a magic bullet that turns you into a Christian, understanding what Christ has *done* and then *following* him is what makes you a *Christ*ian.

However, I and my fellow evangelicals have been trained to reject that understanding of the gospel, calling it either "progressive" or "legalistic." We train ourselves and others to think of salvation as something brought about exclusively through a mental acceptance of doctrinal statements about Jesus (evangelicals call that *faith*) plus certain specific (and often culturally defined) behavioral changes that are supposed to result from accepting the authority of Jesus, like praying, going to church, reading your Bible, embracing internal moral purity, and following other norms like modesty, abstinence, and temperance. On the one hand, evangelicals claim all that matters is proper belief, but on the other hand, we really want people to get their act together.

I confess this individualistic, selective morality is wrong, and I'm trying to move away from it.

WITH A STRUCTURE OF HYPOCRISY

This combination of a doctrine-focused gospel and an individual-focused morality produces a truly self-serving structure of hypocrisy within Evangelicalism. As an evangelical pastor, I disagreed with other evangelical pastors over which specific behaviors are the litmus test of true Christianity. Amazingly, I always passed my own litmus test. For some reason, I did really well with the morality I selected for myself, and when others failed to uphold my morality, I had an excuse to separate myself from them.

I once had a conversation with a pastor who told me he had made a vow to his congregation that they would never cooperate with Catholics. You might ask, "Why would that pastor avoid Catholics?" It was because he considered Catholics to be legalistic. "Legalism" is a term that is supposed to mean "putting too much emphasis on following rules and not enough emphasis on faith in Christ," but in practical application, "legalism" is a term used by any evangelical to accuse some other Christian of getting the gospel wrong. He used it against Catholics. I, in fact, used it against him. Other pastors I knew used it against me. We all embraced it to some extent because it helped us define why we were different from some other church.

Evangelicals have two expressions we use when it comes to claiming Christian authenticity. *We* would never *water down* the gospel, and *we* would never slide into *legalism*. As I said, "legalism" is the term used when they think some other church is overly focused on the moral mandates of the Bible, but "watering down the gospel" is the phrase used when they think some other church is *insufficiently* focused on the moral mandates of the Bible. It's terribly convenient when you have expressions to convey that one Christian is too focused on moral living and another Christian is not focused enough. These terms empower each individual Christian, pastor, and church to think that they alone are getting it right, they alone are living in the Goldilocks zone of the gospel.

I confess I abused this way of thinking to preserve my own insufficient view of the gospel for far too long. This way of thinking was and still is not just practically divisive but spiritually destructive. Look at what Jesus said about people who use the words of God to point fingers at other followers of God.

> Jesus replied, "And you experts in the law, woe to you, because you load people down with burdens they can hardly carry, and you yourselves will not lift one finger to help them."
>
> LUKE 11:46

Using the words of God to burden other people invited harsh opposition from Jesus, but I, along with my other evangelical pastor friends, are skilled in it.

If you aren't familiar with the way an evangelical pastor thinks, allow me to go a bit deeper. It all comes down to creating a careful dividing line between the essentials and the nonessentials. On the essential side of my line is a list of doctrines regarding which you must agree with me, or else I'll think you're going to hell. Also on that side of the line is a list of morals that if you don't meet, I will doubt your authenticity as a Christian. Anything on the other side of that line is something I consider less important, nonessential.

However, some other pastor will draw his line differently. One of my good friends is a pastor of a Pentecostal church. According to Pentecostal doctrine, everyone who is actually saved will demonstrate salvation by speaking in tongues. Their tradition has speaking in tongues on the "essential" side of the line. However, I don't speak in tongues, and therefore, according to hard-line Pentecostal doctrine, I'm not saved. Happily for me, when I pressed my pastor friend on the issue, he broke with traditional Pentecostal doctrine and said he thought I probably was a Christian but just lacking in my Christian experience. We were able to have a relationship as fellow pastors particularly because he was willing to break with his tradition and draw a line that was favorable toward me.

WITH CIRCULAR DOCTRINES OF DIVISION

My Pentecostal pastor friend was a generous man to draw his line in a way favorable to me, but it doesn't usually work that way. Let me show you how this line-drawing usually plays out among evangelical pastors, churches, and believers.

Based on how we see the writings of Paul, we will say that people are helpless to live by the *law* because they are mired in sin. However, when we put our faith in Jesus as the gift of God who died for our sin, we are *justified* before God. Then, the Holy Spirit enters our life and does the work of *sanctification*, making us more holy and less sinful bit by bit over time. Finally, the mark of our sanctification is our adherence to a moral code. This is the basic evangelical framework for belief and behavior, and it's perfectly sound so long as you live in a fairly siloed community of people who deal with similar struggles in similar ways. However, as soon as one person begins to deviate from those community values, someone needs to do some explaining. If some Christian is failing to follow the morality defined by the community, that person is a counterexample to the entire framework. If they aren't being sanctified in the way we expect, maybe they never were justified in the first place. After all, *true* Christians will *behave* themselves.

There's some truth there, but don't be fooled. This is circular reasoning with diabolical results. I'll say it as plainly as I can, the way I actually thought it for far too long.

I believe what I believe is what Christians should believe, and I believe how I behave is how Christians should behave. I doubt those who don't. The only Christians I accept as true Christians are the ones who believe what I believe and behave the way I behave.

This is circular, divisive, and obviously self-serving. Time and time again, we have put some belief or behavior into that same circular loop as a way to justify ourselves and ostracize others. We claim our rules are biblical, but we've just selected the rules we like, and we point our fingers at those who don't follow our rules our way. We call them legalists or backsliders or even heretics.

Forgive me. I'm being simplistic and harsh in my criticism here. Yes, there really are behaviors that are consistent with following Jesus and those that aren't. Yes, there really are beliefs that matter. Yes, I really think the gospel should transform you. I'm not saying that framework is wrong. In fact, I think that basic framework is good and sound. However, there is one terrifically bad way we have applied the framework.

Too often, *I* am the standard I use to measure others. I draw the lines. I determine when you are guilty of "legalism." I determine when you are giving in to license. I do it against you, not with you, and certainly not for you.

That's sinful, and I'm guilty of it.

True Christians are those that look like *Jesus*. He's the standard, not me.

AND WITH A SCAFFOLDING OF WOOD

I'm beginning to see that a good amount of my previous perspective was built with wood, hay, or even straw. Most of it was constructed to serve me or my closest community. I focused on behaviors when that focus benefited me or beliefs when that focus benefited me. But biblical morality covers far more ground than I ever did. I successfully put the Old Testament through a sieve to determine which rules were overshadowed by Jesus and which ones persist today, but I often disregarded the socially focused divine morality underpinning both the Old Testament law and the polemics of the prophets. I focused on the mostly individualistic behaviors of Paul's moral code but not the social or societal *implications* of his code. The Scripture wasn't wrong, but how I considered it and applied it was.

I need to go deeper with this.

My interpretive scaffolds prevented me from seeing how Paul's moral instructions were based on deeper social realities. Paul often mentioned sexual immorality, improper speech, drunkenness, idolatry, and greed, but I chose to see them almost exclusively in individualistic terms. When he spoke against sexual immorality, I saw it only as a prohibition of extramarital sex. I never considered the social context—one person using their power to exploit or oppress someone else for their own benefit. I saw Paul's comments about greed as being about my personal thought life related to my possessions. I never considered greed in the context of a community of people who depended on each other's hospitality and generosity. Fearing both legalism and liberalism, I interpreted Paul's morality in the narrowest and most individualistic possible terms, creating a line for myself that I knew I was probably never going to cross.

It's not that my teaching and upbringing were wrong. Paul does speak against sexual immorality and greed. But an ill-formed, self-focused, individualistic viewpoint on those morals was a scaffolding of wood blinding me to the bigger picture. Because I saw sexual immorality as a prohibition against extramarital sexuality, I *couldn't* see the power dynamics present in the text or in the world around me. In fact, if I ever heard someone talking about sexuality in terms of power dynamics, I'd get upset feeling like that other person was being too liberal and not letting the text of Scripture speak for itself. That was wrong. I was the one who was blind.

Let's keep going. Because I had a strange relationship with the morality of Paul, I also developed a strange relationship with things Paul never spoke about. For example, Paul said nothing about tax brackets, public health measures, public schools, climate change, vaccinations, systemic racism, and more, so I said nothing about them either. Internally, I had my opinions shaped, as I thought, by the Bible, but because Paul never talked about them, I didn't either. I would talk about the smaller issues or the issues where I knew most of my hearers shared my perspective, but on other issues, I just kept silent. Why should I talk about systemic racism if Paul never did? I agreed with the majority of my evangelical friends that these things were private matters, matters of personal freedom, or political and therefore irrelevant for the life of the church. In many ways, my silence on these matters was another scaffolding of wood.

That isn't the whole story, though. Even though I labeled a lot of moral issues as peripheral because Paul never mentioned them, there are *other* moral issues never addressed by Paul that *did* find a central place in my morality. Paul never said anything about immigration, abortion, capital punishment, capitalism, or the proper size of government, and yet I along with many evangelicals took great pains to teach the Christian way one should think about those issues. No evangelical will admit that capitalism is a central component of their faith, but if you question capitalism in front of an American evangelical, you will quickly discover how important it really is to them. I, too, echoed these values, and whenever I did, I was reinforcing another scaffolding of wood. I built structures of silence and structures of opinion that collectively gave the impression that I was just as much a conservative as any other member in my congregation. Frankly, I was. The scaffolds had been in my heart long before I ever built them up in the people I led.

Things changed for me some years ago when I started talking with people who thought differently. I started talking to pastors who didn't agree with me on every doctrine. I started talking to pastors who questioned my own salvation. But mostly, I started talking to pastors who were Black.

In 2014, a police officer in Ferguson, Missouri, shot and killed Michael Brown, an unarmed Black man. In response, the city exploded in protests, rioting, looting, and other expressions of unrest. By God's grace, I had already come to know Pastor James Foster, the president of the African American Pastor's Alliance in Lafayette. He shocked me when he said the situation for Black people in Lafayette, Indiana, was not that different from Ferguson, and out of my shock, I determined to learn more. Over the next few years, I built a friendship with the pastors of the Alliance, and that friendship opened me up to new perspectives. Not only did I begin to see new social implications in Scripture, I also started to believe they should inform my preaching.

Don't get me wrong, I also disagreed with some of the preaching I heard from my friends, and I still think the main job of the preacher is to explain and apply the meaning of the text, but through those friendships, I learned that Scripture is much broader than the snippets of morality I was pulling from it. Yes, when Paul mentions greed, there is an aspect of individual application there, but there is also social commentary. For example, just consider what would happen if all American Christians actually eliminated their greed. Greed powers capitalism, and most Americans claim to be Christian. If Christians stopped being greedy, we might destroy our own economic system. If I really preached against greed, I'd be seen as undermining our national economy. People might get upset. I'd be called political and divisive. Maybe it's better to say nothing.

Then again, maybe we shouldn't stay silent about the contradictions between our culture and our morality.

Is it proper to talk about capitalism when the text never uses that word?

Yeah, I think so. Well, I think so, now.

The point is that we always add things to the gospel, and we always ignore things about the implications of the gospel. We, just like the Pharisees, are too often self-serving in what we believe and how we behave. We have built up structures of wood and hay and straw all around us, but the question we need to ask ourselves is this: Will I test these structures with fire, or will I defend them against the testing fire? I confess to playing defense too often.

I have only recently been able to see the hypocrisy in myself. Limiting my understanding of morality to what Paul explicitly said was too narrow. Limiting my teaching of Paul's morality to terms that fit the narrative of certain political leanings was terribly flawed. Only considering Paul's morality and not that of Jesus or James or the Old Testament prophets was too narrow. I confess my own narrow-mindedness, and I likewise confess its prevalence in the circles in which my faith and ministry have been formed. I have built scaffolding of wood, hay, and straw, and I have been hesitant to put it to the test, but I think it's time to set some of that scaffolding ablaze.

CHAPTER 5

Flammable Materials

WHAT YOU'RE ABOUT TO READ has lost me a number of friends. Well, actually, people have given me two responses. Some people heard these things and cheered for me. But other people heard these things and decided to end their relationship with me. The former were those who shared my perspective already and were glad that someone finally said what they thought needed to be said. The latter didn't share my perspective and felt betrayed. They accused me of being too political, too woke, too liberal.

You might rejoice at these things, or you might recoil at them, but my hope for you is different. My hope is that you might read this chapter to understand better where your presuppositions have been built on wood. My further hope is that you might find ways to light your own wood scaffolding on fire, and my eventual hope is that we might together start a new dialogue about what it means to be authentic followers of Jesus without such false convictions.

I'll start with a doctrine that perfectly illustrates the faulty wood scaffolding present in modern Evangelicalism. It's a flawed doctrine that comes from and empowers a specific way of viewing the Bible, a doctrine that deeply impacts the way Christians view their place in the world, and a doctrine that empowers some of our worst instincts as sinful selfish beings.

YOUNG EARTH CREATIONISM

For the past sixty years or so, conservative, Bible-focused Christians have promoted a literal reading of the Genesis origin story called Young

Earth Creationism. The YEC approach is nearly universal among evangelical Christians, and they have invested heavily in equipping their children with tools to reject evolutionary science. I was a beneficiary of that education. Having been raised in an evangelical church and having attended an evangelical Christian school from kindergarten through high school, I was taught in every science class that the Earth (and the universe as well) was a maximum of ten thousand years old, more likely only six thousand, and Christians had the science to prove it no matter what the secular scientific community had to say about it.

I remember the day in seventh grade when my teacher taught me about the shrinking of the sun. Paraphrased, the lesson went like this:

> The sun is shrinking by X feet every year. Scientists have done the math. At the current rate of shrinking, if we extrapolate back in time, at about ten thousand years ago, the sun would have been so large that the Earth would have been on fire. Therefore, there is no scientific way the Earth can be older than ten thousand years!

I wasn't just taught that; I believed it. I accepted the claim that scientists had proven a young Earth by extrapolating current measurements of the sun into the past. I was thrilled to know that Christians were better at science than non-Christians. It gave me a sense of pride to know that only people who believed what I believed could see the world clearly. The arrogance and hypocrisy of the argument were beyond me at the time, but I see it now. After all, extrapolating current measurements into the past is exactly how science determined long times for the age of the universe, the age of the Grand Canyon, and the age of fossils, but I, according to what I was taught, accepted only one extrapolation, the shrinking sun, because it came from Christians and favored the Christian perspective. It gave me a reason to reject all the other extrapolations done by the scientific community. When the extrapolation worked for my viewpoint, I accepted it, but when the extrapolation didn't work for me, I rejected it.

I accepted the statement of the sun shrinking as definitive proof of a young Earth for decades. It wasn't until many years later when I learned how stars actually work, how fuel, temperature, and gravity are always in a state of equilibrium, how the sun doesn't burn its fuel like a campfire, and how shrinkage of the sun simply doesn't happen the way I was told. I was lied to. More accurately, someone came up with a wrong idea and passed it on to someone who believed it and passed it on to others until it eventually got to me. It was still a lie, but it was so tantalizing a lie that I never thought to doubt it. Furthermore, lest you think I'm describing an archaic out-of-fashion thing that Christians don't actually think anymore, you should know my children were taught this very same sun-shrinkage proof in their Christian school not five years ago! When I saw their homework about it, I made a point to tell them (1) the proof was wrong and (2) they should keep silent and not argue with their teacher about it. Perhaps I should have encouraged them to speak up, perhaps I should have addressed it with the school, but I didn't. I kept silent too.

Here's another proof I was taught. Paraphrased, it went like this:

Carbon 14, and other forms of radiometric dating are unreliable methods for determining how old something is. Not long ago, a seal was found dead on the beach, and when scientists did carbon 14 dating on it, the numbers said it was thousands of years old! Clearly, carbon 14 dating methods are flawed, and therefore, we can't trust any radiometric methods for determining the age of fossils or the age of the Earth.

Anecdotes like that were frequently given to me, but they were always given without sources. Who were the scientists? Why did they decide to date a recently dead animal? Were they biased toward disproving carbon 14 dating? Did they even do the test properly? How does one bad result from one group of scientists using one method of dating (and coming from a biased perspective) prove all radiometric dating wrong? None of those questions were asked, and I wasn't encouraged to ask them myself. Instead, over and over, I was just given similar anecdotes and logical arguments that pretended to be science even though none of them were published in a scientific journal or recognized by any scientific community outside the Young Earth Creationism enclave. In fact, I was taught that the whole secular science establishment was just a godless hoax propped up by Satan to get Christians to toss out Genesis. I was told that science was an elaborate scheme by Satan to lead us away from God. In my science class! According to my teacher, the only science we could trust was science that came from another Christian, because that Christian had the proper presuppositions and the Holy Spirit to guide his thinking.

It always came back to Genesis. It always came back to Young Earth Creationism. Satan wanted us to toss out Genesis. Why? Well, according to these creationists, if we got rid of Genesis, we would have to toss out the rest of the Bible, and if we got rid of the rest of the Bible, we'd also have to toss out Jesus and all the teaching about him. The implication was clear even if never spoken: if God didn't make the Earth in 144 hours, six thousand years ago, we had no reason to follow Jesus.

For a good long time, I bought into it all too. I rejected the science about evolution. And as a side benefit, once you learn to reject one kind of science as a hoax, you are free to reject any science whenever it's inconvenient to you. Since I doubted the science of evolution, I also rejected the science of climate change, ecology, anthropology, paleontology, geology, cosmology, psychology, and anything else that disagreed with my presuppositions. I accepted science whenever it suited me. I spent money on refrigerators, bought a car based on its ratings for gas mileage and safety, went to doctors, took my medicine, and used a phone, but anytime science was in contrast with my own comfort, I could appeal to my supposedly biblical ideas. Now however, I confess that such thinking was hypocritical and self-serving.

Furthermore, I confess now that such thinking was arrogant.

Far from being thoughts in submission to God's word, these were beliefs built upon the assumption that I and my Christian brothers and sisters were simply more noble and more intelligent than the entire secular scientific community. Darwin, we concluded, was an evil man with an evil agenda, not a brilliant scientific mind who discovered a simple yet beautiful natural principle for all the biodiversity of the world. Only I and my Christian friends could see the truth through all the nonsense. The rest of the world was hopelessly duped.

Such thinking was and is arrogant and wrong. I am casting it aside.

But that raises the question: What should we do with Genesis 1 and 2?

There are four things you need to know about Genesis 1 and 2 that actually work *against* Young Earth Creationism.

YEC Isn't Required by Genesis 1 and 2

Before the twentieth century, Christians considered the age of the Earth to be an open question. In 1654, Archbishop James Ussher assembled some biblical events and genealogies to calculate the creation of Adam as happening in 4004 BCE. Others did similar work, but there was no consensus. In fact, the majority of Christians simply had no firm opinion on the age of the Earth or the interpretation of Genesis 1 until midway through the twentieth century (a story I'll tell in a moment).

One popular historical interpretation of Genesis 1 starts with the recognition that it's written as a Hebrew poem. Look closely, and you'll see a clear parallelism linking day 1 with day 4, 2 with 5, and 3 with 6. On day 1, God separates light from darkness (day and night), and on day 4, God creates the sun and moon to "rule" the day and night. On day 2, God separates air from water, and on day 5, God fills the air and water with birds and fish. On day 3, God separates water from land, and on day 6, God fills the land with animals culminating in people to represent himself whom he tells to likewise "fill the earth." The creation story of Genesis 1 is a trifold repetition of a good God creating a good environment and then filling it with something good until at the end, he commands humans to continue that work over all the Earth: subduing and filling his "very good" world. For centuries, the people of God took note of this parallelism and reveled in the majesty and goodness of a God who creates a good place and then fills it with order and beauty. In fact, that's probably the reason the text consistently puts "evening" before "morning" when talking about each day. Each day starts dark, chaotic, or empty and ends with something bright, orderly, and full. "Evening" and "morning" can refer to the rotation of the Earth, but they don't have to. Those words can represent the movement from chaos to order as much as they can represent the movement of the sun in the sky.

Here's the bottom line. Does the text require us to believe that God made flying birds before he made crawling lizards, or that he made green plants before he made the sun they depend on, or that he somehow made Earth with a day-night cycle before he made the sun? Not according to the centuries of people who read this text before us. They were not so specifically pedantic about the text. The young Earth interpretation is a largely new phenomenon.

YEC Is a Selective, Not Literal Reading of the Text

Second, Young Earth Creationism wants you to think it is the *literal* way to read the text, but they conveniently leave out some literal words in their interpretation. Consider these words of God:

> And God said, "Let there be light," and there was light.
>
> GENESIS 1:3

Did God make the light? Let me phrase it differently. *How* did God make the light?

The right answer to both questions is, "Yes, kind of, I don't know." Depending on whom you ask, they will answer these questions in all kinds of different ways. Sometimes the explanation will be that God "spoke the light into being," and that's an okay explanation, but the *literal* meaning of the text is that God declared what he wanted and it happened, and we are given no more information than that. How did he do it? How long did it take? The right answer is, "We don't know." That's just the tip of this iceberg. Something even more difficult to grasp appears in this parallel part of the story from days 3 and 6:

> Then God said, "*Let the land produce* vegetation: seed-bearing plants and trees on the land that bear fruit with seed in it, according to their various kinds." And it was so. . . . And God said, "*Let the land produce* living creatures according to their kinds: the livestock, the creatures that move along the ground, and the wild animals, each according to its kind." And it was so.
>
> GENESIS 1:11, 24

I've highlighted the words that literal interpreters usually skip over. What's the literal interpretation of "Let the land produce living creatures"? Is it more literal to say God made these things, or that God commanded the Earth itself to make these things? Shockingly, this is more in line with *evolutionary* thinking. The best *literal* interpretation of these verses is that Earth has been given life-producing power. Genesis tells us God spoke that power into it, but how did it work? How long did it take the land to produce plants and eventually animals? The right answer is, "We don't know."

But what about the whole "there was evening and there was morning, the ___ day" thing? Well, that's the third thing you need to know about this passage, how to understand "day" in the context.

YEC Misreads the Context

Those who claim to be interpreting this passage literally make an interesting choice when they literally stop their literal interpretation at verse 31. Remember the original text wasn't written with chapter numbers and verse numbers. Look at the boundary verses between those chapters, and you'll notice something modern translators have noticed for a while. The creation account of chapter 1 doesn't end until you are pretty deep into chapter 2. Here's how that transition happens. Without verse numbers, can you tell where chapter 1 ends?

> God saw all that he had made, and it was very good. And there was evening, and there was morning—the sixth day.
>
> Thus the heavens and the earth were completed in all their vast array. By the seventh day God had finished the work he had been doing; so on the seventh day he rested from all his work. Then God blessed the seventh day and made it holy, because on it he rested from all the work of creating that he had done.
>
> This is the account of the heavens and the earth when they were created, when the LORD God made the earth and the heavens.
>
> GENESIS 1:31–2:4

That last sentence is four verses deep into the second chapter. Scholars have noted that there's an important division between verses 3 and 4 because the name of God switches to Yahweh in Genesis 2:4, and therefore 2:4 seems to be the start of a new section, possibly with a different original author. Nevertheless, whoever the final editor of Genesis was, whether Moses or someone else, these two accounts were put directly next to each other for a specific reason, to communicate an overarching truth about God as the Creator, and because this is an intentionally crafted piece of literature, we need to embrace it fully with its context. However you understand the text, you can't be a literal interpreter unless you take verse 4 just as literally as the previous verses, but YEC interpreters stop their literal interpretation at Genesis 2:3 without the context of verse 4. This is important because verse 4 uses an important word. Here is verse 4 from the New American Standard Bible, a word-for-word-style translation.

> This is the account of the heavens and the earth when they were created, in the day that the LORD God made earth and heaven.
>
> GENESIS 2:4 NASB

The original Hebrew text of Genesis 2:4 says, "in the *day* that Yahweh God made earth and heaven," and 2:4 is referring to the *entire* process of creation, not just one component! There were *six* days in chapter 1, but the epilogue of the story transitioning us to the next story claims there was only *one* day! And the Hebrew word for "day" is the same in all those places. So which is the literal reading of the creation account? Is it six days or one? Those who claim to be interpreting Genesis 1 literally have a big question to answer. Which verses are the literal ones?

At the very least, you have to realize that "day" is metaphorical in 2:4. That's why most modern translations actually use other words in 2:4 (i.e., NIV: "*when* the LORD God made the earth"). But that raises a different problem for the YEC holdout. If the narrative of the creation account ends with a metaphorical use of the word "day," there's no textual reason to take it literally all the other times. One confirmed metaphorical use implies others. After all, there are metaphorical uses of the word back on days one and four. On those days, the word "day" is given to the period of light in contrast to "night," but of course, it also refers to the entire process of "evening and morning." Simply put, the Hebrew word *day* often operated the same way our English word does. It's a malleable metaphorical word that can mean any arbitrary period of time unified by something of singular importance. It can mean a period of time unified by a solar transit, but it can also be an unknown period of time unified by the purpose of God to establish something or to fill it.

Does the text require us to think of each day as a twenty-four-hour solar cycle?

No.

YEC Misses the Point of the Text

I said there were four things you needed to know about the creation account, and the fourth one is the most important. The creation account has a *purpose*, and it has nothing to do with the age of the Earth or the speed of creation. Every group of people has an origin story, but most origin stories in the ancient world talked about how people were made either as an accident by the gods, an intentional work of a nefarious god, or the self-serving work of a demanding god who wanted someone to do his work for him. What makes the Hebrew origin story different from all the others is the depiction that God is intentionally acting to create a beautiful and good world and to put human beings in it not as his slaves but as his deputies, his agents of authority in this world. No other ancient text gives such a unique vision of the goodness of the divine being, the goodness of his creation, and the dignity of the created people. The primary purpose of Genesis 1 is not to give a play-by-play account of the *hows* and *how-longs* of creation but to portray the wisdom, goodness, and power of God and to clearly portray the incredible position of humans: God's agents made in his image!

FOR MANY YEARS I BOUGHT into the doctrines, the misinterpretations, and the justifications of YEC, but even after I began to grow out of it, I continued to teach it or support it in at least two ways. First, whenever I spoke about Genesis, or whenever the topic came up in a public context, I took the approach of equivocation. YEC proponents are passionate about their position, and they are firmly convinced that undermining YEC is undermining the entirety of the faith. I knew that, and so I would always say two things at once. First, I would give the safe answer: "God is all powerful, and if he decided to create the world in *one* day, he could have done it, so I have nothing against the young Earth view." And then, I would give the more accurate answer: "But in fact, there's nothing in the text of the Bible that *requires* us to hold a young Earth view, and therefore, I'm personally okay with the modern scientific time line." On the one hand, I thought my approach was designed to maintain the unity of the Spirit, but in fact, my approach was a fear-based attempt to placate people who could accept only the narrowest reading of Genesis.

Furthermore, my approach, by validating a flawed reading of the text, enabled people to persist in further errors built on top of this flammable flooring. I confess that my approach was wrong. It was dishonest of me to speak as if the various positions were equally valid, but more than that, it was a construction of straw, not based on the foundation of Jesus. I bolstered a position that pretended a specific reading of the text led to salvation, not the literal death and resurrection of Jesus himself. They were propping up an idol, and my preaching did nothing to counteract it.

Still, if Young Earth Creationism hasn't always been the main interpretation of Genesis 1, and if *more literal* interpretations of Genesis 1 move us *away* from a six-day creation, then why is it so pervasive among evangelicals today? Why is it so powerful and held on to with such passion?

I didn't like the answer. The reasons are deep, emotional, and complex, but they all include one terribly uncomfortable historical truth.

YOUNG EARTH RACISM

When I began to look critically at the arguments of the Young Earth Creationists and the history of the movement, I was surprised to learn that Young Earth Creationism didn't take hold of conservative American Christians until 1961. Throughout most of church history, scholars disagreed on the age of the Earth, but many took Genesis metaphorically, and most taught that the age of the Earth was unknown. In fact, in 1859, when Darwin published *On the Origin of Species*, his seminal work, some Christians hailed it as a glorious exploration of how God's wisdom was wired into the natural world. Even the Christians who disagreed with the theory of natural selection had no problem with Darwin's proposed age of the Earth.

> By the late nineteenth century, even the most conservative Christian apologists readily conceded that the Bible allowed for an ancient earth and pre-Edenic life. With few exceptions, they accommodated the findings of historical geology either by interpreting the days of Genesis 1 to represent vast ages in the history of the earth . . . or by

separating a creation "in the beginning" from a much later Edenic creation in six literal days.[3]

So, if Christians did not universally believe in a six-thousand-year-old Earth even in the face of Darwin's theories, how did Young Earth Creationism come about? It started in 1961 when John C. Whitcomb and Henry Morris published a book called *The Genesis Flood*. Since the 1920s, the Seventh Day Adventists had been promoting a young Earth, but conservative-minded Christians rejected that doctrine along with everything else coming from the Adventist movement. However, when *The Genesis Flood* was published, a young Earth perspective rapidly won over American Christians. Why? What changed between the 1920s and the early 1960s that made American Christians more open to young Earth theories?

I can't give you all the answers to that question, but at least one reason Young Earth Creationism rose to prominence when it did was racial prejudice. Before you think I've gone crazy, you need to know that there are real doctrinal connections between young Earth thinking and racism, and Henry Morris, along with many other conservative white Christians, embraced them fully. I was shocked when I first considered the connections between YEC and American racism, but I shouldn't have been so surprised. In fact, I was taught them. I believed them. For many years, I taught them too. The linkage was right in front of me, but I was in denial.

It all comes down to the realization that human racial diversity couldn't arise naturally in only a few thousand years of time. Either human diversity developed slowly on its own over eons of time, or God made a decision to create specifically distinct races of people. Since Young Earth Creationism says God made the Earth and all the biodiversity on it in a short period of time, it requires the belief that God made separate races because his plan included *separate* races. The doctrine (not actually in the Bible but taught just the same) says that God made three basic races of humans by intentional choice immediately after Noah's flood. Noah's son Shem was the father of all the olive-skinned Middle Eastern people. Japheth was the father of all the white-skinned people who ended up in Europe. Ham was the father of all the dark-skinned people who ended up in Africa. Incidentally, no one in my evangelical circles ever tried to explain to me where the East Asian, Native American, Aboriginal Australian, or Inuit people came from. I asked once, but they didn't have any good answers. My racial education was limited to, "Red and Yellow, Black and White, they are precious in his sight," and I was happy just to know God loved the separate races of people.

The idea that God created different races by divine choice empowered a belief that these different races were intended by God to be separate, and therefore, Christians had a moral reason to *keep* them separate even if God found them equally precious in his sight. I'll admit, the first time I heard the phrase *separate but equal*, it made total sense to me. I thought it was *right* because it fit perfectly with a young Earth worldview.

But it gets worse. YEC doctrine originated with the belief that the different races are not actually equal. Ham, the supposed father of all dark-skinned people, once saw his father Noah drunk and naked and mocked him for it. Noah responded by cursing Ham's son Canaan and his descendants to be "the lowest of slaves" (Gen. 9:25), and early proponents of Young Earth Creationism latched on to that idea. Here's Henry Morris in his own words (originally published in 1977):

> Thus, all of the earth's "coloured" races,—yellow, red, brown, and black—essentially the Afro-Asian group of peoples, including the American Indians—are possibly to be Hamitic in origin and included within the scope of the Canaanitic prophecy, as well as the Egyptians, Sumerians, Hittites, and Phoenicians of antiquity. . . .
>
> Often the Hamites, especially the Negroes, have become actual personal servants or even slaves to the others. Possessed of a genetic character concerned mainly with mundane matters, they have eventually been displaced by the intellectual and philosophical acumen of the Japhethites and the religious zeal of the Semites.[4]

I believed this! Now, I went to Sunday School in southern California in the late 1970s and early 1980s, and none of my teachers ever said out loud that Black people were "mundane" or that white people were intellectually superior, but even so there was an unspoken implication that dark-skinned people were under the curse of Ham somehow. I remember the moment in Sunday School when I heard the story of Ham and had the actual thought: "Oh, so that's why Black people are slaves," before correcting myself, "*were* slaves."

It is no coincidence that in the early 1960s, just when the Civil Rights Movement was gaining traction, schools were desegregating, and activists like Malcolm X and Martin Luther King Jr. were putting pressure on white America, the young Earth doctrine took hold among conservative Christians—a doctrine that happened to also give biblical reasons for racial "purity." It worked that way in my own life.

Young Earth Creationism required me to reject the slow natural process of genetic diversification. Young Earth Creationism required me to believe that the races were *made that way* by God. It required me to believe that God designed those races to be separate. And because of the story of Ham, Young Earth Creationism is *directly* connected to a conclusion that Black people bear a generational curse. This is why evangelical Christians can so strongly support all the "separate but equal" forms of racism and the implicit biases that are pervasive and persistent in the United States. Young Earth Creationism doesn't include racism as a tenet of faith, but it's a doctrine that grew out of a racist society, and it continues to empower racism in its wake. Not only is it a scaffold of straw, but it's dangerous and damaging as well.

I've had pushback on this from many friends in the evangelical world. I'm not saying that Young Earth Creationism is directly racist. I'll put it back on me. All I'm saying is that Young Earth Creationism empowered racism in the past, and it also empowered racist biases in my own heart. Biases I couldn't see for a *long* time. Biases hopefully you don't even have. But biases I now confess.

RACIAL SILENCE

No one explicitly taught me that systems of segregation are God's will, but the teaching didn't have to be explicit. I got the gist well enough. A *white bias* dribbled into my own subconscious not by direct teaching but by implications of the Young Earth Creationism doctrine combined with the way my Christian subculture remained ignorant and silent regarding issues of racism. We never talked about the practices of redlining, the inequities in lending or in the GI Bill, the atrocities following Reconstruction, the dehumanizing days of Jim Crow, the hideous legacy of lynching, or the ongoing effects of implicit bias in the modern world. That is, even though I knew racism was bad, no one ever told me to consider the injustice of actual racism in our society. In the silence, I simply absorbed the perspective that racism wasn't a big deal anymore and that perhaps God wanted us to be separate. Sure, sometimes someone would refer to something in the New Testament about unity in the body of Christ and how the old divisions were now over, but it always came with the implication that white people were living in the normal or preferred culture and that other people needed to join in (assimilate). I was never taught *separate but equal*, but I adopted a strong unspoken belief in *separate or same*. There was only one proper culture, and it was the one into which I was born. We left the door open for others, but they had to choose to come in.

Such attitudes are more than racist. They are expressions of white supremacy.

I am ashamed that in the 1960s, 1970s, and beyond, evangelical Christians were busy creating activist organizations like the Institute for Creation Research but were avoiding or actively opposing the work for racial justice. The leading evangelical of the day, Billy Graham, assiduously avoided any connections with civil rights issues but was more than willing to denounce communism. Referring to Graham, Jemar Tisby wrote,

> During the civil rights movement, activists who courageously risked their well-being for black freedom were few and far between, but Christian moderates who were complicit with the status quo of institutional racism were numerous.[5]

In retrospect, I wish we had built an Institute for *Racism* Research or an Institute for Racial *Justice*! Instead, evangelicals used their energy to oppose evolution, communism, drug use, and more, all while ignoring racial injustice. We had many enemies, but we made a truce with racism, and it lingers to this day. Evangelicals regularly exercise activism in all manner of issues—among us can be found proponents of religious freedom, opponents of abortion, opponents of climate science, and opponents of a variety of public health measures—but the white evangelical voice is still largely silent on issues of racial injustice. Many of today's evangelicals often deny that racism even exists.

I confess that my participation in that worldview was ignorant, arrogant, and wrong.

Beyond that, my silence on the matter increased my guilt.

I recall the day Bishop O'Neal, an African American pastor in Lafayette, told me the story of him being pulled over by a cop and mistreated. That same day, Pastor James Foster said it had happened to him multiple times too. I trusted them, and I learned from them that their account was universally understood and felt by Black people throughout the country. That's when I really started believing that racism was alive and well. I studied what I could about historical racism, systemic racism, implicit bias, and more, but regardless, I said nothing about it on Sundays.

When Black Lives Matter became a part of the public conscience, I again kept silent. Christians all around me were finding ways to discredit the movement and to offer alternative "Christian" statements like "All Lives Matter" or even "Blue Lives Matter," but I said nothing. I was too afraid of the consequences in my own ministry to verbalize anything that sounded so political as to say, "Black Lives Matter." I'm deeply ashamed that I couldn't bring myself to say those three simple words before my breaking point in 2020. I avoided truly addressing the injustice of racism because I didn't want to offend the consciences of people in my church overmuch. Yes, Jesus literally died for *all* people, but he identified and pursued the *lost*. He said he came for the sinners. His heart was broken for the outcast. Why could I not say, "Black Lives Matter"? Sure, doctrine tells me *all* lives matter, but that only reinforces the fact that *Black* lives matter! To identify the one group that needs special attention is not to discredit the needs of the larger group. Jesus did it all the time. But I kept silent. Throughout it all, I kept silent out of fear that my ministry would be damaged.

Therefore, I confess that not only did I harbor latent, ignorant racism in my own heart for far too long, but I stayed silent about the injustice even after I came to accept it as fact. I was arrogant, hypocritical, afraid, and silent exactly in the wrong ways, and as a result, I've been complicit in the ongoing blight of racial injustice in our nation.

Continuing my work of confession, I turn next to the smoke screen I used to excuse my prejudices.

RELIGIOUS PRIVILEGE

In 1962, the US Supreme Court ruled that public schools should no longer practice the daily ritual of Christian prayer. To this day, Christians in evangelical circles point to that moment as a landmark tragedy in the history of our country. I can't count the number of times I've heard pastors and other Christians lament the "ban on prayer in schools" even though prayer is probably more common now than ever before. Prayer is expressed by students and teachers before school, after school, in club meetings, and individually at lunch tables. Still, for evangelical Christians, the issue of institutional prayer in schools is one of today's fundamental issues. "If only we could get prayer back in schools," they say wistfully, as if the reintroduction of ritual corporate prayer in public schools will somehow take us back to a golden age, restore God's blessings, and solve society's problems.

This same basic idea expresses itself in the evangelical desire to have monuments to the Ten Commandments, Christian nativity scenes, and the use of phrases like "Happy Easter" and "Merry Christmas" prominently displayed in public places and on the lips of public officials. However, just as before, even though evangelicals have embraced large-scale activism to reintroduce prayer and other expressions of Christianity in the public square, they still have yet to employ any large-scale activism to address issues of social justice. I could once again point out the sinfulness of that moral imbalance, but instead, I'll confess to a different kind of discrimination borne together with this religious activism. In our efforts to promote Christian religious freedom, evangelicals like me have largely disregarded and in fact opposed all public religious expression that is not Christian in nature.

Those who want prayer to come back to school are adamant that *Christian* prayer is what must return to schools. They don't want Muslim prayers three times a day or Baha'i prayers in graduation ceremonies. They don't want tribal songs in the morning school announcements or guided meditation over the loudspeakers at sporting events, but they definitely want prayers in Jesus's name in all those places at all those times. Likewise, those who want the Ten Commandments in front of courthouses want only the Christian concept of marriage to be reflected by the practices of those courthouses. Specifically, they want the courts to oppose same-sex marriages and to defend Christian discrimination against those who identify as LGBTQ+. This is hypocrisy. It speaks like a desire for religious freedom when it's really a desire for religious *favoritism*. Islam, Baha'i, secularism, and even homosexuality are all belief systems, regardless of whether they identify themselves as religions. Of course, they compete with the Bible in many ways, but they are alternate *belief systems* nonetheless and therefore fall together with Christianity under the protection of the First Amendment. Evangelicals benefit greatly from the protections offered us in the Constitution, but based on our actions, we desire those protections for ourselves only. Evangelicals claim religious freedom is a foundational concern, but we actively oppose extrabiblical worldviews even through political activism.

This is not the advocacy of religious freedom; this is the advocacy of Christian favoritism or even Christian nationalism, and I confess that I have been a participant in it. Inasmuch as I have supported religious exemptions or special treatment for Christians while opposing or remaining silent about similar exemptions or similar special treatment for people who hold competing worldviews, I am guilty of a hypocritical Christian nationalism that says Christianity, further, my version of Christianity, should be the predominant and controlling worldview and morality for this country regardless of how it affects those of other faiths, worldviews, or no faith at all. We should admit this is at least unconstitutional, but more than that, it is un-Christian, arrogant, and sinful, and I confess I have been guilty of it in my advocacy, my preaching, and my silence.

I need to explain this confession a bit more to prevent misunderstanding. I have had a number of conversations with evangelical believers who literally do want this country to embrace Christian nationalism. They will ask me questions like this: "Don't you want more and more people to turn toward God, to receive Jesus, and to walk as his followers in this world? Don't you want people to turn away from religious error and false doctrine and turn toward Jesus? Don't you want God's will to be represented in our country in the way people live their lives? Don't you want people to be *saved*?" My answer to all these questions is, "Of course, yes!" but I now firmly disagree that the *Christian* way to achieve these goals is through the leveraging of secular political power.

> Jesus said, "My kingdom is not of this world. If it were, my servants would fight to prevent my arrest by the Jewish leaders. But now my kingdom is from another place."
>
> JOHN 18:36

No one can read *anything* Jesus said and conclude that he wanted us to use violence, political power, or legislation to get people to obey God, to learn correct doctrine, or to follow him. Do I want people to become Muslims or to embrace the LGBTQ+ worldview? I'll be honest, no. But do I think people will become true followers of Jesus if the government outlaws Islam or transgender hormone treatments? Also no! And do I want to live in a country where one worldview is favored at the government level to the exclusion or detriment of others? Definitely no!

I have not always felt this way, though. For much of my life, I have embraced the hypocrisy. I have lived and labored with the idea that Christians should be activists whenever the issue in question is something that supports Christians and the Christian worldview. But I have opposed or ignored all issues that relate to the benefit of people outside my in-group. Though I still want to promote Christian morality and the Christian worldview in this world, and though I still want people to find and follow Jesus, I no longer think political activism to defend or favor Christianity is the right way to operate. In fact, I think it is sinful, and I repent of my involvement in it.

ANTIABORTIONISM (+RACISM)

In 1971, years before *Roe v. Wade*, the Southern Baptist denomination adopted a resolution stating the following:

Be it further RESOLVED, That we call upon Southern Baptists *to work for legislation that will allow the possibility of abortion* under such conditions as rape, incest, clear evidence of severe fetal deformity, and carefully ascertained evidence of the likelihood of damage to the emotional, *mental*, and physical health of the mother.[6]

The emphasis in this quotation is mine, because I think it's important to see the *activism* of the Southern Baptists in 1971 included *promoting* laws to *legalize* abortion in specific cases including when the mother's *mental* health was at risk. This one paragraph illustrates how in the early 1970s, conservative Christians saw the technology of abortion through the lens of the needs of the mother and the quality of life of the infant so clearly that the Southern Baptists, a huge and historically conservative denomination, thought it was important to be *activists* in the *promotion* of abortion rights. However, something changed, and by the end of the decade, regulating, limiting, and outlawing abortion became the foundational position of the Southern Baptists and evangelical Christians across the country. What happened?

As before, learning the history of that change has been painful for me.

There were two big issues that divided American Christians during the first half of the twentieth century. The first split came over how we understand the Bible, and it divided the Fundamentalists from the Modernists. The major denominations in the nation were increasingly embracing a modernist approach that interpreted the Bible as a living document with different meaning for each generation, but they were also declining in attendance. Meanwhile, revivalism was on the move largely among Christians who held to an inerrant view of the Bible along with other core doctrines they called fundamentals of the faith. The revivalist, conservative expressions of Christianity thrived. Then, by midcentury, conservative Christianity was confronted with a second divisive issue. In the South, where holding to the old ways was considered proper and right, Fundamentalist Christianity was both vocally and tacitly supportive of racial segregation, but many Christians in the north found the racism of the southern churches objectionable. These, taking a page from the abolitionist evangelicals of England a century before, called themselves neo-evangelicals, embracing the same basic doctrines as the Fundamentalists, but rejecting their perspectives on race.

Nevertheless, a reunification event happened in the late 1970s when the two groups found common ground over political activism. As the story goes, they were brought together in a coalition to oppose the recently legalized practice of abortion. They formed a bond under the simplified name "evangelicals" and began the activism of a unified pro-life movement that to this day still tightly grips the evangelical community. Nearly every evangelical pastor I know spends a Sunday or two each year on the sanctity of human life and the need to oppose the evil of abortion. I did it too.

However, the story I just told is partially false. The true force unifying evangelicals at the end of the 1970s wasn't a push against abortion. That's just the story we tell ourselves about the time. In his brief book *Bad Faith*, Randall Balmer argues that the real unifying cause was actually racism:

> Although leaders of the Religious Right in later years have sought to portray their politicization as a direct response to the Roe v. Wade ruling of 1973, Weyrich and other organizers of the Religious Right have emphatically dismissed this abortion myth. Green v. Connally served as the catalyst, not Roe v. Wade.
>
> More broadly, evangelical leaders, prodded by Weyrich, chose to interpret the IRS ruling against segregationist schools as an assault on the integrity and the sanctity of the evangelical subculture. . . . That is what prompted them to action and to organize into a political movement.[7]

The true catalyst bringing Fundamentalists and neo-evangelicals back together wasn't opposition to abortion. It was the desire among Christians to preserve tax exemptions for Christian *segregationist* schools. Churches across the nation were afraid of losing their special status with the government, and the fear was so strong that northern Christians set aside their previous opposition to racism and joined the cause of the southern Fundamentalists. Pro-life was the smoke screen issue of the movement, taxation was the effective cause, but racism was at the core. I've heard and delivered many sermons against abortion, but in all my years in Christian churches, I have never heard a (white) evangelical pastor address systemic racism or the legacy of segregation from the pulpit on a Sunday. It's amazing how the pro-life political agenda entirely whitewashed the evils of racism so as to achieve "unity" among supposedly Bible-believing Christians. Pro-life served as an incredibly effective way for white Christians to ignore and even deny our own complicity in this country's racism. You'd think the fall of *Roe v. Wade* might have changed that, but instead, antiabortion fervor among evangelicals has continued to increase, while talking about racism remains taboo. By going all in on an antiabortion agenda without even attempting an antiracism agenda, evangelicals like me are complicit in a terrible wrong.

Additionally, I must confess my own hypocrisy regarding my former pro-life stance. Although I once thought being pro-birth was the same as pro-life, I now see more clearly that life is about much more than birth. A truly pro-life perspective should take into consideration the life, health, and well-being of the mother, the financial security of both fetus and infant, the ongoing health concerns of the young family, the provision of care for the elderly, a rethinking of how we handle addictions, revisiting the death penalty, and more. My former hypocrisy now baffles me. For example, increasing access to adoptions, providing contraceptives to women, or providing health-care and day-care services to young mothers are all proven to reduce abortions and favor the life of the unborn, but I, along with other pro-life activists, regularly ignored such policies. The *active* message of the pro-life position is that getting babies *born* is a foundational concern but helping them *live* or caring for the *life* of the *mothers* is not. Again, evangelical sermons against abortion are frequent, foundational, and encouraged, but talking about subsidizing medical care, offering free contraceptives, expanding adoption, or subsidizing day care will all be labeled political. Such sermons are likely to get an evangelical pastor fired. God forbid he also mention systemic racism, police violence, or the statistics about how conservative policies actually increase abortion rates by making life more difficult for impoverished moms!

For some reason, evangelicals are comfortable with activism that opposes abortion. For some reason, that activism has been sanctified, but any activism related to racial equity, the elimination of the death penalty, the expansion of health care, adoption, or financial assistance to moms is disdained. Being antiabortion is being *biblical*. Being for any of these other life-affirming policies is being *political*. This is logically inconsistent, it is practically hypocritical, and I confess that I have been guilty of it too.

I confess that I am complicit in promoting an antiabortion Christian activism that failed to recognize or address any of the other issues that should be included in a truly pro-life stance. I confess that by talking about abortion like I did, I participated in whitewashing other societal ills that are equally immoral. Although I spoke about the dignity of human life whenever I could, I never said, "Black Lives Matter." The only real application I voiced from the stage regarding the dignity of human life was the opposition to abortion. I was afraid to say anything more than that for fear of the blowback. I knew there were people in my church who opposed all taxation, so if I said the government should use tax money to alleviate any of these issues, I'd hear about it. I knew my congregation was mostly Republican, so if I said anything about expanding health care, I'd hear it. People would leave my church if I said the government should offer contraceptives and day care. I kept silent, protecting myself, thinking I was protecting the church, but my silence enabled people to think I was on their political side and failed to challenge their presumptions. Because I verbalized only the policy positions they agreed to, I misrepresented myself and the teaching of the Bible, and because I made it seem like pro-life was a central Christian tenet, I helped them build houses of hay and straw that reflected the whims of the current culture war more than the life of Jesus.

I confess that I was wrong to teach what I taught while keeping silent on the other matters.

AND MORE

The problem within the nation, the church, and the culture is not so much that people fall for crazed and irrational conspiracy theories. The problem is that too many people who don't actually believe the things they are saying say them anyway, because they are afraid of the people who believe such things.[8]

That has been me. Through things I said and things I left unsaid, I have been complicit in propping up an evangelical culture of mistruth and misinformation that played to the prejudices of people rather than promoting the good reality of following Jesus according to truth.

I confess that in my advocacy for Christian religious freedom, I helped normalize a kind of freedom that empowers Christians to discriminate against others or treat people poorly whenever we have a religious excuse to do so. I confess that I have been a participant in a Christian culture so in love with this personal freedom that I have personally blamed victims of my harsh words for being oversensitive when I said something insensitive.

I confess my complicity with those who deny modern science and oppose public health measures even when they are proven to save or improve lives. During the COVID pandemic's second year, I didn't myself oppose vaccinations, but I had already contributed to a culture that empowered those who did. I had contributed by staying silent when people around me thought it noble to oppose science and when they elevated as a religious discipline the rejection of climate change, pandemic policies, or anything else that came from the general (secular) scientific community.

I confess I supported a culture that treats the government as an enemy and opposes it to the practical detriment of countless impoverished people whose lives could have been tangibly improved by better public policies.

I confess I supported a culture that also treats the government as a tool, a sword we can wield to accomplish our "godly" mission in this world.

I confess I supported a culture that uncritically embraces Republican politicians and rejects out of hand any and all Democratic policies and politicians. I have participated in communicating explicitly or implicitly that if a person thinks some Democratic policy is good, that person can be written off entirely and treated with disdain along with everything they say.

I confess I have empowered a culture that makes being politically conservative a foundational aspect of the Christian faith.

I'm sure I have more to confess as well.

TIME TO SEE CLEARLY

I'm not blaming anyone other than myself. These scaffolds of wood arose gradually from the good intentions of people doing their best with what they knew. But as we grow and learn, we need to address our former errors. That is where I failed. Despite our best intentions, these scaffolds are the result of a selective reading and an uncritical application of Scripture. I'll say it again. No one taught me to think these issues were on par with the gospel. No one in my circles told me these tenets were central to the Christian faith. However, they were always there, just under the surface, falsely supported and perpetuated by many prooftexts in Scripture, and that's the deception I'm attempting to leave. I never thought of abortion or Christian religious freedom as being central issues to my faith either. It took me a long time to start seeing how central they actually were in practice, how important they had become to me and to others in my tradition, and how effective they had been at blinding me to other important issues of the faith.

My journey to become aware of these biases has not been an easy one. Even after I resolved most of the inner struggle, I then had to face the opposition from close friends, people in my church, and fellow pastors. Nevertheless, I have become convinced that just because my tradition says something is peripheral doesn't mean it is, and just because evangelicals practically consider something foundational doesn't mean it is either. I'm grateful that God has led me down a path of seeing these things for what they are: wood, hay, and straw; misapplications of an overly narrow gospel. I'm sure many aspects of my culture are continuing to blind me, but I'm on a new journey that I don't intend to leave.

I OPENED THIS CHAPTER with a warning that you might cheer for me and my journey or that you might react negatively against my progression, and I told you that I wanted you to join me in the journey of self-reflection. I'll reiterate that. The road is difficult, narrow even, but I do invite you to join me. Perhaps you see a similarity between your story and mine. Perhaps you have been on a journey of discovery and are encouraged by what I have said. But perhaps you feel that some of the items I just mentioned are *supposed* to be foundational and you are feeling offended by my assertions that they aren't. Perhaps you were put off by my mention of racism or the way I spoke about creationism or climate change or anything else. If that's you, I invite you to take the position of the Bereans:

> Now the Berean Jews were of more noble character than those in Thessalonica, for they received the message with great eagerness and examined the Scriptures every day to see if what Paul said was true.
>
> ACTS 17:11

If I'm wrong and these things truly are essential parts of the Christian faith, you will find them clearly taught in the Scriptures, modeled by Jesus, and what I say won't change your mind. But if by chance you have misunderstood God's word, or a bias of yours is preventing you from seeing it clearly, you owe it to yourself to get clarity. More than that, you have an obligation to your Lord and Savior to understand his word rightly.

I'll be clear with you. I'm writing these words because I think you might have a speck in your eye.

> "Why do you look at the speck of sawdust in your brother's eye and pay no attention to the plank in your own eye? How can you say to your brother, 'Let me take the speck out of your eye,' when all the time there is a plank in your own eye? You hypocrite, first take the plank out of your own eye, and then you will see clearly to remove the speck from your brother's eye."
>
> MATTHEW 7:3–5

I understand it is a dangerous thing for me to point out a speck in your eye if I have a plank in my own, and that's one of the main reasons I have spent so much time in prayerful self-reflection considering my own biases and perspectives. I understand that as long as a plank is in my eye, I won't see God's *word* clearly, and I won't see God's *world* clearly, let alone my part in it. But, dear reader, I assure you that to the best of my ability, I am working on the planks I find. And here is the beauty of what Jesus taught in the parable, as I find the planks and remove the planks from my eyes, I gain a better handle on identifying what the wood looks like even when it's small. As I work on removing these planks from my life, I gain better insight in identifying them and helping others to remove even the specks they have. Moreover, according to Jesus, it is my responsibility to help others remove the speck once I have removed the plank. So join me in this process of seeing clearly. Join me in the process of identifying what is worthy and what is not, what it really means to follow Christ and what is merely wood, hay, and straw.

It's time we strip away all our failed good intentions and the misplaced priorities of misguided predecessors to get back to what the gospel actually requires of us in the context of this modern world. Let's dig into the text. Let's uncover the biggest truths. Let's see what it really means to build a life on the foundation of Jesus and what he's calling us to be and to do in this world. To do that, let's attempt to build a theology for practical Christian living, a theology of proper Christian activism.

We'll start with a story of heartbreaking beauty.

CHAPTER 6

The Dilemma of the Church

JESUS'S MINISTRY STARTED with him proclaiming good news, but the lived experience of Jesus's followers has not always been good. He claimed the kingdom of heaven had come, but their experience was filled with opposition from the kingdoms of this world. We have already considered the definition and the practical outflow of the gospel, but we haven't yet talked about the fundamental incongruity of the gospel. It's a promise that hasn't delivered yet.

From the earliest days of Jesus's ministry with his disciples, the disciples faced this incongruity. Their preconceptions of the Messiah were often in conflict with what Jesus actually did, so they were constantly asking an internal question that they didn't vocalize until much later:

> Then they gathered around him and asked him, "Lord, are you at this time going to restore the kingdom to Israel?"
>
> ACTS 1:6

They thought the kingdom of Jesus was a kingdom of this world, and they always expected Jesus to set that kingdom up, but he didn't. His actions repeatedly fell short of the messianic hopes of those first-century Jews. One day, he said the kingdom was coming, but when they tried to make him the king, he ran off. Another day, he rode into Jerusalem on a donkey, fulfilling the prophecy of the coming king, but when he entered the city, he went after the practices of the Jewish people in the temple rather than the puppet king in the palace.

Nowhere is this incongruity starker than in the story of John the Baptist in prison.

> When John, who was in prison, heard about the deeds of the Messiah, he sent his disciples to ask him, "Are you the one who is to come, or should we expect someone else?"
>
> MATTHEW 11:2–3

You might wonder why John experienced such doubt. After all, isn't doubt the opposite of faith? Maybe you even feel a bit antagonistic toward him for being so apparently weak in his faith. But John had every reason for his doubt. Jesus wasn't doing what the Messiah should be doing, and John knew it. John knew the words of the prophets. It was part of his origin story. When Gabriel predicted John's birth (Luke 1), he quoted Malachi 4:5–6, the very last verse of the Old Testament. John was to be the prophet like Elijah to prepare the way for the Messiah, and he fully embraced that role. Still, out of humility, he never called himself Elijah. He took his primary identity from Isaiah:

> Finally they said, "Who are you? Give us an answer to take back to those who sent us. What do you say about yourself?"
>
> John replied in the words of Isaiah the prophet, "I am the voice of one calling in the wilderness, 'Make straight the way for the Lord.'"
>
> JOHN 1:22–23

John knew Malachi, he knew Isaiah, and as the one setting the stage for the Messiah, he certainly would have known the prophecies about the Messiah, what he would be like, and what he would do. Here's a verse I think he would have known:

> The Spirit of the Sovereign LORD is on me, because the LORD has anointed me to proclaim good news to the poor. He has sent me to bind up the brokenhearted, to proclaim *freedom for the captives* and *release from darkness for the prisoners.*
>
> ISAIAH 61:1

And that's a verse Jesus claimed for himself at the very beginning of his ministry.

> He [Jesus] went to Nazareth, where he had been brought up, and on the Sabbath day he went into the synagogue, as was his custom. He stood up to read, and the scroll of the prophet Isaiah was handed to him. Unrolling it, he found the place where it is written:
> "The Spirit of the Lord is on me,
>   because he has anointed me
>   to proclaim good news to the poor.
> He has sent me to proclaim *freedom for the prisoners*
>   and recovery of sight for the blind,
>   to set the oppressed free,
>   to proclaim the year of the Lord's favor."
> Then he rolled up the scroll, gave it back to the attendant and sat down. The eyes of everyone in the synagogue were fastened on him. He began by saying to them, "Today this scripture is fulfilled in your hearing."
>
> LUKE 4:16–21

There's just one problem. The prophecy of Isaiah proclaims freedom for the prisoners, but when we see John in Matthew 11, he is in prison.

And Jesus wasn't doing anything about it.

What do you do when the Savior doesn't save? What do you do when the supposed Messiah doesn't do his job? Wouldn't you doubt?

How could Jesus be the Messiah promised by Isaiah if John, a faithful servant of God, was literally in prison and Jesus wasn't doing anything about it? Despite the prophecy of Isaiah and the clear and obvious claim that Jesus was the fulfillment, John was still in prison. Was Jesus a metaphorical Messiah, or was he the real deal? Or was he simply the wrong guy?

No wonder John felt his doubt, and no wonder he asked his question, but the answer Jesus gave to John tells us a lot:

> Jesus replied, "Go back and report to John what you hear and see:
> The blind receive sight, the lame walk, those who have leprosy are

cleansed, the deaf hear, the dead are raised, and the good news is
proclaimed to the poor. Blessed is anyone who does not stumble on
account of me."

MATTHEW 11:4–6

The first time I studied those words, I thought they were insensitive.
John asked a simple question based on Jesus's aforementioned mission
statement and the inconsistency of its application, but Jesus answered
by saying, "I'm doing the work I'm doing, and people who don't get it
don't get it." At least, that's what I used to think. More recently, though,
I have been able to see this answer in a new light, and I love it now.
I now see the compassion and the brilliance of Jesus's words. Jesus was
sending a message specifically coded just for John's encouragement.

Jesus was making a reference to Isaiah 35, and I bet John knew that
prophecy too.

"Be strong, do not fear; *your God will come*, he will come with vengeance; with divine retribution he will come to save you." Then will
the *eyes of the blind be opened* and *the ears of the deaf unstopped*. Then
will the *lame leap like a deer*, and the *mute tongue shout for joy*. Water
will gush forth in the wilderness and streams in the desert.

ISAIAH 35:4–6

Jesus echoed a number of the statements in Isaiah 35 in his message
to John. The blind see, the lame walk, the deaf hear (and were given
speech too). If you compare the two lists, you see that Jesus mentioned
almost everything from Isaiah's list, but you also see that Isaiah 35 is
talking about someone *even better* than the Messiah. Isaiah 35 said,
"Your God will come." These signs accompany the presence of God
himself! When Jesus told John he was opening the eyes of the blind, he
was actually saying he was *more* than the Messiah. Only someone who
deeply knew Isaiah would have been able to decode that message. Not
even Matthew, who frequently quoted the prophets, made this connec-
tion. But I think John might have seen it.

Still, Jesus put some things in his list that didn't come from Isaiah 35:
healing lepers, raising the dead, and proclaiming good news to the poor.

I'll come back to the first two in a moment, but the third one is supposed to make us think about Isaiah 61, the passage we already mentioned:

> The Spirit of the Sovereign LORD is on me, because the LORD has anointed me to *proclaim good news to the poor*. He has sent me to bind up the brokenhearted, to proclaim freedom for the captives and release from darkness for the prisoners, to proclaim the year of the LORD's favor and the day of vengeance of our God, to comfort all who mourn.
>
> ISAIAH 61:1–2

When Jesus answered John, he was referring to both Isaiah 35 and Isaiah 61. Two different prophecies from Isaiah that would have been meaningful to John. In doing so, he was saying, "John, I am the Messiah Isaiah spoke of, and I am even more. I am the Agent of the power of God to initiate the work of the kingdom." But Jesus was also saying something else in his message to John. He was saying something else by leaving something out.

Both prophecies promise the vengeance of God, but Jesus left that part out. Even when Jesus read the passage in the synagogue, he stopped reading before he got there. That's not all. In his message to John, he also left out the phrase "freedom for the captives." John spent years warning people of God's coming *judgment*, and he was now one of the *brokenhearted* experiencing incarceration in *prison*, but Jesus bypassed both issues. I'm sure it was intentional. Jesus was telling John, "John, I am the Messiah, but not everything prophesied by Isaiah is happening *now*. Some of it is *now*, but some of it will happen *later*. Trust me on this."

That's why Jesus said, "Blessed is anyone who does not stumble on account of me." Jesus knew his ministry was not going to check all the Messiah boxes. Jesus knew he was going to disappoint people, and he knew that some people would stumble *because* of that disappointment.

I imagine John might have felt that disappointment, but this is where Jesus's compassion and his brilliance shine through for me. Remember those additional comments about healing lepers and raising the dead? They weren't from Isaiah 35. They weren't from Isaiah 61. I think even more than the other items on the list, those items were a code specifically for John's encouragement.

Consider the statement about healing lepers. No Old Testament prophecy says anything about the Messiah healing lepers. Some prophets mention him being a healer, but they never mention leprosy. In fact, in the Hebrew Scriptures, there are only three cases of leprosy being healed. God directly heals Moses at the burning bush. God directly heals Miriam after her rebellion. The third time involves a prophet, the only prophet who ever heals leprosy. In that specific story, the leper was a foreigner named Naaman, and he is healed by following the words of the prophet Elisha who told him to bathe himself in the Jordan River. I'll say it again, the story is about a leper who was healed by being immersed in the Jordan River. That's where John was baptizing people! Do you think John would have known the story of Naaman, Elisha, and the Jordan? Do you think John would have caught the reference to himself and his own ministry? Sure thing! Do you think John would have been encouraged by the reminder? I think so. But what's deeper is that this leper was healed through the ministry of *Elisha*, and Elisha was the prophet who came after *Elijah*.

Remember what the angel said about John?

> "And he will go on before the Lord, in the spirit and power of Elijah, to turn the hearts of the parents to their children and the disobedient to the wisdom of the righteous—to make ready a people prepared for the Lord."
>
> LUKE 1:17

John knew his job. *He* was the one like Elijah.

And Elijah never healed leprosy.

But the one who came next did.

That's why this is language specifically for John. Healing lepers wasn't a thing the Messiah was supposed to do, but Jesus said it anyway, and by saying it, Jesus was telling John, "Yes, John, you have been Elijah, and I am the one who comes after."

I can almost hear him whispering the words to John, "Well done."

I see in Jesus's words something incredibly beautiful. He gave words that were encoded specifically to speak encouragement to John. I see such beauty and compassion and tenderness in the words of Jesus. I'm certain John would have been encouraged by that message. And yet, I'm also certain that Jesus's message would have been bittersweet. After all, the final thing Jesus had in his list would have been simultaneously encouraging and frightening to John. As John is languishing in prison, facing the possibility of execution at any moment, Jesus said, "the dead are raised." Like with leprosy, none of the old prophecies predicted the Messiah would raise the dead, but Jesus mentioned it anyway, and it would have been a bittersweet message indeed. Remember, Jesus left out "freedom for the captives" and he added "the dead are raised." In all this, Jesus gave John one final coded message:

Yes, John, I am the Messiah and even more. I do what the Messiah does with the very power of God. I am the one who was to come, and your ministry was everything you thought it was, but I am also more than you expected. I will not free you from prison. I will let you die there. Still, hold on to your faith, because I raise the dead.

JOHN'S DILEMMA IS QUITE SIMILAR to our own. He believed that the Savior was presently at work in the world, but he himself was also going through incredible hardship. Was he wrong about the Savior, or was he wrong about how the Savior's ministry would intersect with the lived experience of real people? Is the Savior's message merely spiritual or does it have real-world effects?

Jesus's answer to John is the same answer we need to hear today. His ministry is a combination of now and not yet. Some parts of the messianic kingdom play out in everyday living, while other parts of the messianic kingdom are for the future. Furthermore, the parts of the messianic kingdom that were most important to John and those that are most important to us just might be the parts left to the future.

I want to know the difference. I want to know which parts are now and which parts are not yet, but the Bible never gives me any clear dividing lines. Even the events of the church in Acts muddy the waters considerably. After Jesus had died, risen, and ascended, the early Christian church experienced *literal* liberation from prison. Peter, Paul, and Silas each were imprisoned at various times, and each experienced miraculous liberation, but others, James the apostle, Stephen, and countless other martyrs, were not so fortunate. Between the now and the not yet lies a vast expanse of the kingdom classified only as "sometimes."

What do we do with that incongruity?

How do we handle this in-between time?

ACCEPTANCE, AVOIDANCE, OR ACTIVISM

Much of evangelical doctrine is focused on training young Christians how to accept and live with the dilemma of an unrealized kingdom. In most cases, the training is all about delineating between what is now and what is future. However, while some aspects of the kingdom are clearly now and others are clearly future, there is a wide area of gray between the two, and in that area values often conflict. For example, we know that forgiveness has been made available to all through the death and resurrection of Christ. That's a now thing in some sense, but evangelicals still highly value the earthly justice of criminal prosecution—even lengthy incarceration or capital punishment. We've been trained that forgiveness is now*ish*. Additionally, we believe the presence of the Holy Spirit is available to all who receive the message of Christ, but we disagree strongly with each other regarding what it *means* to have the Holy Spirit in your life. Some think the work of the Spirit is mostly in the past, others think it's still active today, and so we leave it in the gray area of nowish. Pretty much the only thing evangelicals agree on as being truly future is the resurrection of the faithful and the joy of eternity.

We live in the middle, between now and not yet, in the blurry lines of today, in a place supposedly of hope and faith, but pragmatically, we tend to resolve our uncertainty with a good dose of resignation. I can pray for what I want, I can ask God to apply the kingdom to my present circumstances, but I usually need to resign myself to whatever answer God chooses to give. Sometimes God answers prayers in ways we desire and sometimes he doesn't. Sometimes this world looks like the kingdom is advancing and sometimes it doesn't.

For most of my life, I thought that if I just let go and let God, then the parts of the kingdom that are supposed to show up on Earth will, and the parts that are for later will show up later. In short, I accepted the incongruity of a now-but-not-yet kingdom by resigning myself to a mindset of inaction, nobly described as "patient endurance," a mindset that says, "I'll hold on; I won't fall away." I knew there were slivers of life where activism made sense: Getting people saved, voting for Republicans, opposing abortion, and more, but my mindset was focused on individual purity and patient endurance.

However, I see something now I never saw before.

John was in prison because he was an activist for the values of the kingdom in the present day. He *spoke* against the immorality of his governmental authority. He accused King Herod of adultery and theft, and he was thrown in prison because of it. John acted as if the principles of the coming kingdom were supposed to be *active* in the world today. John was in prison because he *called out* the leaders of his day to live out those principles, and while Jesus never repeated John's statements, he also didn't walk them back. In fact, Jesus claimed that *no prophet, indeed no human, had ever been greater than John*!

> "Truly I tell you, among those born of women *there has not risen anyone greater than John the Baptist*; yet whoever is least in the kingdom of heaven is greater than he."
>
> MATTHEW 11:11

Rather than hearing Jesus approve of John's actions, I always heard the second half of that passage as an encouragement toward *diminished* influence in the here and now and *increased* attention on the coming kingdom. *Just focus on the coming kingdom. Hang in there*, I used to think, but I have come to realize that John was on to something. Some parts of the *future* kingdom are to be *advanced* in our present world by the *activity* of its citizens. John called out Herod. Jesus called out the Pharisees. Jesus emptied the temple courts to reclaim that space for the gentiles. James railed against presumptive business practices. Christ-followers are called to a unique kind *activism*. The question is not how much we should expect God to do eventually but how much we should join God in doing now. It's the question of activism:

How much of the not yet are Christians to advance in our real world today?

Our challenge is to know our role as *witnesses* and *agents* of a heavenly kingdom while our feet still touch the dirt of Earth. I used to be happy and content to say, "God will do what God wants to do in the world, and I just need to live my own life with integrity and purity." But John wasn't interested in living his own life or minding his own business. John spoke the words of an activist against the religious and governmental authorities of his day, and Jesus called him the greatest person who ever lived. Perhaps there's a lesson there for us.

We are not just citizens of a different kingdom; we are agents of it.

Sometimes we will need to raise our voice against the broken parts of our world that do not yet represent the coming kingdom.

Sometimes we will need to take action to bring healing into the midst of that brokenness.

Sometimes we will need to endure the brokenness while we wait for the heavenly kingdom.

And if we ever have power and influence, we should use it wisely, as Christ would.

USING CHRISTIAN POWER

For most of my life, I adopted the practice of silent, patient endurance, waiting for Jesus to return, waiting for the kingdom to come. Partially from training and partially from disposition, I focused on the internal life of the mind, the internal spirituality of the heart, and the personal morality of purity with very little attention given to anything communal or societal. However, while my tradition focused on the individual and the private, other Christians have been wrestling with the questions of social justice and public-square activism for centuries. In the first century, members of the church sold their property so there would be no needy persons among them, and as a result, economic equity became a hallmark inside the church. Then, their activism started affecting things outside the church family too. The early church took action against the practice of infanticide by going to the outskirts of towns and rescuing discarded babies. Through the centuries, that same activism persisted. In the Middle Ages, the church responded to pandemics by remaining in towns overrun by plague and caring for the abandoned sick when others fled. This kind of activism, the activism of individuals and groups living out the principles of the future kingdom, was the main form of activism of the church through the early centuries.

But times have changed.

For the past few hundred years, democracy, industrialization, capitalism, and the Information Age have complicated Christian activism by giving Christians greater power to influence society. In modern twenty-first-century America, all individuals and organizations can have immense influence through books, blogs, podcasts, social media, investment decisions, political activism, and, of course, voting. All these powers exist for individual Christians, and by extension churches and their church affiliations. Christians today in the United States hold as much potential for influence as any other individual or organization, and because the United States is still the most influential society on a global scale, the power of American Christianity is truly staggering. How we steward that power will change the world.

Part of me wants to shrink back from that power. I have been steeped in a Christian environment that encouraged me to think of my faith in personal terms. My faith has always been individual, intellectual, spiritual, and moral above all else. It's comfortable to me there. But the historic Christian faith was always active in ways that aren't so comfortable. In light of my predecessors, in light of our great influence in this modern world, I must reconsider what following Jesus is all about. Individual, personal, intellectual, spiritual, and moral living is insufficient. Christians in America have immense influence, and we are called to steward it well.

In my forty plus years seeing Christian ministry from the inside, I have seen this question of stewardship repeatedly divide Christians. Instead of being a unified body of Christ, we have split ourselves up according to doctrines, policy opinions, and political teams, and today, these divisions are stronger than at any other time in my life. What's worse, these divisions are more consequential than ever because the power of American Christianity has never been greater.

But I'm hopeful.

A growing number of us are already doing the hard work of rethinking the meaning of the gospel and the implications of the gospel. We are starting to ask some hard questions, and we are beginning to consider ways we need to lay aside some bad theology, bad assumptions, and bad teaching. So that means we *can* move forward. Let's keep going in this work. Let's try to understand what the values of the kingdom really are and in the process determine which ones are for the people of God, which ones are for the wider world, and which ones are purely for the future kingdom.

CHAPTER 7

Christian Morality

THE GOSPEL IS A MESSAGE of transformation carried by transformed people. Transformation is core to who we are as followers of Jesus. Our job is to make a difference. Our job is to advance at least some of the not-yet kingdom of God into current reality. Our job is to steward our immense influence as agents of the coming kingdom. Nevertheless, knowing our job doesn't tell us how to do it. Knowing about our influence doesn't tell us how to use it. How much transformation should we be about, and how should we pursue that transformation? To answer this practical question, we need something more than we have seen already. We have a better understanding of the gospel, and we have some principles from the example of the early church, but we still need a fundamental, clear understanding of basic Christian morality. Back in the chapter about the gospel, I identified four questions that will guide us toward that understanding, so in this chapter, let's start with the first two:

Which values are central to the Christian life, and which are peripheral?

Which central values are internal to the body of Christ only, and which should Christians promote in the society at large?

Christians sometimes think a value is central to the faith when it isn't, and sometimes Christians think a value should be promoted outside the church when it's intended for the Christian community alone.

That's why these questions are so important. They force us to wrestle with our presuppositions, and they force us to consider when our activism might actually be moving in the wrong direction.

To answer these questions, I offer here a brief survey of the values I see repeatedly emphasized throughout Scripture. For each value, I will do my best to give biblical justification for why it should be morally binding on Christians today. Then, I will attempt to divide the values into their appropriate contexts, whether they apply to individuals, to the general Christian community, or to the broader society. Finally, at the end, I will briefly comment on a few peripheral issues that masquerade in cloaks of importance they don't deserve. Whether we misunderstand our values or apply them in the wrong way, we will accomplish the same goal: building our lives out of worthless materials. On the other hand, by applying good values in good ways, we will be the true agents of the kingdom we are called to be.

Let's begin by creating a list of those values that should be central to the life of any individual Christian. I'll start as I've done before, with the words of Jesus.

THE MORAL TEACHING OF JESUS

The Greatest Commandment

There's no better place to start than Jesus's answer when asked which commandment was the greatest in all of God's law.

> Jesus replied: "'Love the Lord your God with all your heart and with all your soul and with all your mind.' This is the first and greatest commandment. And the second is like it: 'Love your neighbor as yourself.' All the Law and the Prophets hang on these two commandments."
>
> MATTHEW 22:37–40

If Jesus thinks these are the most important commandments ever given, we would do well to put them into practice. So let's make these the starting point for all other Christian values. I'll formulate the first two values this way:

1. Christians demonstrate a life-consuming love for God, placing him above all other things in every aspect of their lives.
2. Christians demonstrate a practical love for the people around us, whether like us or not, near or far.

In the statement of the first value, I say our love for God should be life-consuming. By that, I mean it should flow through our heart, soul, and mind. It should touch every aspect of our being. It should be emotional, spiritual, and intellectual. Then, in the second value, I used the word "practical" and the phrase "whether near or far" because Jesus taught those attributes in the story of the good Samaritan, where one man crosses a cultural barrier and makes personal sacrifices to tangibly care for someone he doesn't even know, someone who would have seen him as an enemy. Note also from the parable of the good Samaritan that when Jesus spoke about love, he never meant we should try to feel love toward other people while doing nothing about their needs. Love for God is more than mere emotion, so love for our neighbors must be more than cordiality or a positive attitude. It needs to be pragmatic and practical. The love to which Jesus calls us must cross lines of category, culture, and geography.

Since Jesus says that these two commands summarize everything God ever wanted, we could just leave it here and say Christians have only two central values, but our problem as sinful humans is that *we don't think like God*, and therefore our understanding and application of love are weak and misguided. Thankfully, God's word has a lot to say about what it means to love God and what it means to love others, so let's continue our exploration by considering more of Jesus's words. There's no better place to continue than the Sermon on the Mount in Matthew 5–7. (Since I won't be quoting the entire thing here, it might be helpful for you to have it opened next to you as you read this next section. Actually, it might be good for you to read Jesus's words first, before you read mine.)

The Sermon on the Mount

There's no way we can live as agents of the King and citizens of his kingdom without actually understanding the governing principles of the kingdom. Matthew 5–7 is the equivalent of a national constitution, describing what the kingdom of God is like, and the words of this sermon should drip from our mouths and ring in our ears anytime we say or think the word *should* in any context whatsoever.

Four clear themes rise to the surface in Jesus's masterful teaching, so let's add them to our list.

3. Christians live in humility before God, realizing our spiritual poverty, our need for forgiveness, and our utter dependency on our Father.

4. Christians live as agents of Christ and his kingdom, sprinkling the salt and shining the light of God's goodness into a dark and tasteless world for the sake of others and the glory of God.

5. Christians live in holiness, keeping God's word in both thought and deed, neither adding to it nor working around it, and not for earthly recognition but for eternal rewards.

6. Christians embody service, sacrifice, and forgiveness, deferring to those around us even if they accuse us, strike us, ask of us, steal from us, hold something against us, or otherwise sin against us. We are intentional losers living in a world obsessed with winning because our Father in Heaven is generous, just, and good.

If I were making a detailed and exhaustive list of everything Jesus taught here and elsewhere, I would have to mention the importance of having faith, how to give to charity, how to hold your tongue, and how to pray. I would add something about the need for endurance until the final judgment, the need for spiritually abiding in him, and more. Because I'm biased and because I have my own favorite stories, I'm tempted to add additional items, and of course I've left out things someone else would want to add. Nevertheless, I'm convinced that everything Jesus taught can fit within one or more of the above values. Everything, that is, except for three needed additions.

The Work of Faith and Followership

The first addition is actually the one many evangelicals would consider the most important teaching Jesus ever gave. Three passages illustrate it.

Jesus answered, "I am the way and the truth and the life. No one comes to the Father except through me."

JOHN 14:6

Jesus answered, "The work of God is this: to believe in the one he has sent."

JOHN 6:29

Then he said to them all: "Whoever wants to be my disciple must deny themselves and take up their cross daily and follow me."

LUKE 9:23

For evangelicals, nothing is as important as the value of putting your faith in Jesus, and I don't disagree. But Jesus never says, "Believe this thing, and then live how you want." Jesus says he is the only way. That claim demands total allegiance. For him, faith means following. There is no Christian morality of any kind that disregards the exclusive lordship of Jesus and our responsibility to surrender to him, obey him, and imitate him. I'll state it this way:

7.   Christians embrace exclusive allegiance to Jesus himself as our only Savior, true Lord, ultimate authority, and model for life.

The New Command

The second addition comes from Jesus's words *before* he went to the cross. Looking at his followers at the table of the Last Supper, he said to them,

"A new command I give you: Love one another. As I have loved you, so you must love one another. By this everyone will know that you are my disciples, if you love one another."

JOHN 13:34–35

Although he had previously told them they needed to love *everyone* around them like their neighbor, he said it this time with deeper and greater emphasis. He even called this a *new* command. It's new because it has a new target. The previous command was to love your *neighbor*, and the good Samaritan parable proved that Jesus wanted our love to cross boundaries, but this was a command for believers to love *one another*. It's also new because this command has a new standard. The previous command was to love your neighbor *as yourself*, but this command was for the disciples to love *as Jesus loved them*, and his love would soon prove to be *sacrificial* in a totally new way. I mention this value separately because it clearly identifies a unique relationship Christians have with each other that's different from the relationship we have toward the rest of the world. All the Law and the Prophets don't hang on this command. This one is for followers of Jesus alone, and it was so important to Jesus that he repeated the idea in his final prayer in the garden before his death.

> "My prayer is not for them alone. I pray also for those who will believe in me through their message, that all of them may be one, Father, just as you are in me and I am in you. May they also be in us so that the world may believe that you have sent me. I have given them the glory that you gave me, that they may be one as we are one—I in them and you in me—so that they may be brought to complete unity. Then the world will know that you sent me and have loved them even as you have loved me."
>
> JOHN 17:20–23

His final prayer before going to the cross was that his first followers and those to come after them would embrace the unity of sacrificial love for one another. It would be the ultimate evidence to the world that they are citizens of a different kingdom.

8.   Christians embrace a sacrificial love for one another that sets them apart from the rest of the world.

The Great Commission

Finally, the last thing I need to add comes from the passage we call the Great Commission. Thematically, it falls under value number four, but since Jesus made it his parting words to his followers, I think it deserves special recognition.

> Then Jesus came to them and said, "All authority in heaven and on earth has been given to me. Therefore go and make disciples of all nations, baptizing them in the name of the Father and of the Son and of the Holy Spirit, and teaching them to obey everything I have commanded you. And surely I am with you always, to the very end of the age."
>
> MATTHEW 28:18–20

> "But you will receive power when the Holy Spirit comes on you; and you will be my witnesses in Jerusalem, and in all Judea and Samaria, and to the ends of the earth."
>
> ACTS 1:8

Our Great Commission as a value statement is this:

9. Christians spread the influence of Jesus around the world by living how he lived and taught, sharing the message of his life and teaching, and leading others to do the same.

Not only does Jesus call us to live lives of love for God and others, lives that are marked by holiness, humility, service, sacrifice, and forgiveness, lives that reflect the kingdom of God, lives of dedication to him alone above all other authorities, and lives of unity with other believers, he also calls us to spread his message and to multiply his representatives around the world.

With this list of values, I think we have adequately covered everything Jesus said regarding the moral obligations of his followers. There are certainly other ways of phrasing them or other details we could include, but these are the umbrella values. These values encompass the others and yet are specific enough that we can grasp their practical significance. However, we are sinful people. We are prone to see these values through lenses that benefit us, and that's why God gave us the rest of the New Testament. How did the earliest followers of Jesus actually live out these values, and what did they say about them? By examining the examples and teaching of the first-century believers as recorded in the rest of the New Testament, we will discover a few more values that will clarify and intensify those we have already seen.

THE EXAMPLE OF THE EARLY CHURCH

In the first half of the book of Acts, we see the first Christians liquidating assets to prevent poverty in their midst, and we see the crowd of Christians not fighting back in the face of persecution even when that meant Peter was put in prison or that James and Stephen were killed. From this example and from teaching reaffirmed elsewhere in the New Testament, we have two more values to consider, *sacrifice* and *submission*. Early Christians didn't invent these values. They had seen Jesus live them. They saw Jesus submit to authorities even when it cost him his life. They saw Jesus live a life of sacrifice for others even when they didn't appreciate it. They heard Jesus teach repeatedly about living for others, serving others, praying for enemies, blessing those who hurt you, and on and on. The early Christians had seen it, they had heard it, and they probably didn't want to do it because they saw the consequences of living like that. Nevertheless, they were compelled by the message and model of Christ, and they were constrained to obey their Lord, and so they did it. They lived sacrificially. They lived in submission to one another and even to the governing authorities. For the early Christians, living according to those values was painful and difficult, it hurt them when famine struck, and it eventually cost them their lives. Honoring their example, we add the following two statements to our list of values:

10. Christians sacrifice their own resources to care for the poor, especially those in the family of God.
11. Christians submit to earthly authorities in everything that doesn't conflict with the lordship of Christ.

Additionally, the early Christians had to blaze new ground in certain doctrines and practices. For example, Jesus never taught directly about circumcision or how to include gentiles in the life of the church, so when the issue came up, the early church had to use the Old Testament together with the teaching of Jesus to find their answers. We already discussed Acts 15, but now we can draw some tangible value statements from it. Recall that it was a gathering of the early church leaders, and the issue was whether the church could welcome uncircumcised gentiles fully into the family of faith. During that council, the early church leaders identified two guiding principles for applying Old Testament teaching to the community of Christ. Those two principles should inform our values:

12. Christians discard Old Testament commands that were specific to ancient Israel (circumcision) or that were superseded by Christ's direct teaching or his example (capital punishment for adultery, food restrictions, the temple, and the sacrificial system) but do so in ways and timings that respect the sensibilities of others (recall their guidelines in Acts 15).

13. Christians retain Old Testament commands that were confirmed by Jesus as expressing the heart of God for his people (like avoiding both idolatry and sexual immorality).

Through their example, the early church helps to clarify for us even today what it looks like to build with gold and silver, and their writings do even more. To be sure, there are values to be gleaned from James, Jude, Peter, John, and the writer of Hebrews, but the capstone of didactic writing in the New Testament is obviously the work of Paul, so for the third time, let's return to his letters.

THE TEACHING OF PAUL

As the most prolific and most comprehensive writer from the early church, Paul brings clarity to these principles while also emphasizing a few new values we should add to our list. Also, because he specialized in applying the message of Jesus to various cultural contexts, and because he was committed to viewing the Old Testament through the lens of Jesus, he helps us greatly in figuring out how our values should be contextualized.

Previously, I said it was inappropriate how evangelicals have embraced Pauline morality as they have, and you might have gotten the picture that I didn't like Paul, so let me clarify. The problem isn't in accepting Paul's morality. The problem is when we accept *only* his morality and only *certain parts* of his morality. Kept in context with the teaching of Jesus, and taken in context with how Paul lived and all that he wrote, the values we glean from Paul are wonderfully instructive.

Walking in Humility

As a prisoner for the Lord, then, I urge you to live a life worthy of the calling you have received. Be completely humble and gentle; be patient, bearing with one another in love. Make every effort to keep the unity of the Spirit through the bond of peace.... Do not let any unwholesome talk come out of your mouths, but only what is helpful for building others up according to their needs, that it may benefit those who listen. And do not grieve the Holy Spirit of God, with whom you were sealed for the day of redemption. Get rid of all bitterness, rage and anger, brawling and slander, along with every form of malice. Be kind and compassionate to one another, forgiving each other, just as in Christ God forgave you.

EPHESIANS 4:1–3, 29–32

Therefore if you have any encouragement from being united with Christ, if any comfort from his love, if any common sharing in the Spirit, if any tenderness and compassion, then make my joy complete by being like-minded, having the same love, being one in spirit and of one mind. Do nothing out of selfish ambition or vain conceit. Rather, in humility value others above yourselves, not looking to your own interests but each of you to the interests of the others.

In your relationships with one another, have the same mindset as Christ Jesus: Who, being in very nature God, did not consider equality with God something to be used to his own advantage; rather, he made himself nothing by taking the very nature of a servant.

PHILIPPIANS 2:1–7

Notice how Paul's instructions are directly in line with Jesus's teaching from the Sermon on the Mount and the example he lived. Jesus exemplified humility. Paul made humility tangible and gave us lists about it. He identified practical ways Christians should live out the value of humility, and his practical instruction can be phrased as a helpful value statement:

14. Christians reject selfishness, pride, and all their fruits—greed, sexual exploitation, unedifying speech, foolish arguments, defending one's own rights, flaunting one's own liberties, and more.

The Christian Community

Let the message of Christ dwell among you richly as you teach and admonish one another with all wisdom through psalms, hymns, and songs from the Spirit, singing to God with gratitude in your hearts.

COLOSSIANS 3:16

Now to each one the manifestation of the Spirit is given for the common good.

1 CORINTHIANS 12:7

So it is with you. Since you are eager for gifts of the Spirit, try to excel in those that build up the church.

1 CORINTHIANS 14:12

Much has been written about the role of the Spirit in the life of the church and in the life of an individual Christian, but once again, Paul's main point is clear. He's just taking the "new command" Jesus gave his disciples and making it practical. What does it mean to love one another? Use whatever God gives you to be a blessing to the people around you, and also trust God to bring blessing to *you* through *them*. The clear implication is that the first building project of the church is to build each other up using the gold, silver, and precious stones of worship, teaching, fellowship, and blessing each other with whatever the Spirit of God has given to us!

15.   Christians love each other through worship, teaching, fellow-ship, mutual edification, and mutual submission in the family of believers—this is the Spirit's work.

Christians and the Surrounding World

The last things we will glean from the work of Paul are three principles often misunderstood but more often simply ignored. Few Christians debate the earlier two values from Paul's teaching, we know the value of humility regardless of whether we do it, and we know the value of Christian community, but Paul had specific things to say about our relationship to the world around us, and *those* lessons are frequently distorted or ignored. Because of that, we'll have to spend a bit more time on these. To start with, let's consider a passage that is widely quoted, but often misapplied.

> Finally, brothers and sisters, whatever is true, whatever is noble, whatever is right, whatever is pure, whatever is lovely, whatever is admirable—if anything is excellent or praiseworthy—think about such things. Whatever you have learned or received or heard from me, or seen in me—put it into practice. And the God of peace will be with you.
>
> PHILIPPIANS 4:8–9

Just think of how truly expansive this command is. The key word is *whatever*, and that's important. Elsewhere, Paul spoke of spiritual fruit, or deeds of the flesh, or acts of the church, but in this one verse, he expands his moral code into something far bigger than any religious behavior. Our problem is that we see this list—noble, right, pure, lovely, admirable, excellent, and praiseworthy—and we subconsciously replace all the words with "spiritual" as if Paul's point were to have us regularly think about spiritual things all the time. But that can't be what he meant. He says this mindset drove his every behavior. He says, "Watch all the *whatevers* of my life and do likewise." Paul is describing an ethic that reaches beyond what we call spiritual and into everyday life. Nothing in direct Christian teaching covers how you eat at a dinner table, what type of shoes you wear, whether you let a specific word be in your common vocabulary, whether you make eye contact with people when you talk, or whatever, but there are good and beautiful ways to do even these mundane things. Good and beautiful doesn't always have to be religious.

Allow me to be blunt. Some non-Christian things are true. Some non-Christian things are noble. Some are right, lovely, admirable, and in some senses even pure. Christians and the Christian faith are not the only sources of these virtues. These things can be found inside and outside the context of what is religiously significant, and Christians for centuries have believed that. Historically, things like beauty, truth, and justice have been key components of the Christian value system regardless of whether they originated inside the church. The Christians of the Renaissance believed it was godly to rejoice over a scientific discovery that's true or a work of art that's beautiful regardless of where or how it originated. Here are just three examples taken right from the Bible.

Psalm 19 rejoices in the beauty and regularity of nature's laws:

> The heavens declare the glory of God; the skies proclaim the
> work of his hands. . . .
> *[The sun] rises at one end of the heavens and makes its circuit to*
> *the other; nothing is deprived of its warmth.*
>
> PSALM 19:1, 6

Proverbs extols the wisdom that comes from observing ants:

> Go to the ant, you sluggard; consider its ways and be wise! It has no
> commander, no overseer or ruler, yet it stores its provisions in summer
> and gathers its food at harvest.
>
> PROVERBS 6:6–8

And Paul quotes secular philosophers to teach Christian doctrine:

> The God who made the world and everything in it is the Lord of heaven
> and earth and does not live in temples built by human hands. . . . "For
> in him we live and move and have our being." As some of your own
> poets have said, "We are his offspring."

Therefore since we are God's offspring, we should not think that
the divine being is like gold or silver or stone—an image made by human design and skill.

ACTS 17:24, 28–29

The psalmist had spent time gazing at the stars and noticing the
regularity of the path of the sun. Solomon had spent time considering
the ways of the ant closely enough to know that ants store food in the
summer to sustain them through the winter. Paul had literally memorized lines from secular Greek philosophers and was able to quote Stoic
and Epicurean philosophers to make a point about God! The testimony
of Scripture and the explicit instruction of Paul is that truth, excellence,
and rightness are valuable no matter where they are found. Yes, there
are spiritually flammable things in the world around us, but there is
also *gold*. Therefore, when I say we should rejoice in what is true, noble, right, pure, excellent, and praiseworthy, and when I say we should
embrace things like artistic expressions, scientific discovery, and even
philosophical reasoning whenever they are true, noble, right, pure, excellent, or praiseworthy, all I'm really saying is that we should see all of
creation through the lens of an all-knowing, wise and good Creator!

16.   Christians rejoice in what is true, noble, right, pure, excellent,
       and praiseworthy, seeing all of creation through the lens of the
       Creator and experiencing peace by trusting his goodness.

Still, not everything in the world is true, excellent, or praiseworthy.
There is plenty of sin and brokenness all around us, and there is much
that we should reject and avoid. Paul had a lot to say about that too:

Do not be yoked together with unbelievers. For what do righteousness
and wickedness have in common? Or what fellowship can light have
with darkness? What harmony is there between Christ and Belial? Or
what does a believer have in common with an unbeliever? What agreement is there between the temple of God and idols? For we are the
temple of the living God. As God has said: "I will live with them and
walk among them, and I will be their God, and they will be my people."

Therefore, "Come out from them and be separate, says the Lord. Touch no unclean thing, and I will receive you." And, "I will be a Father to you, and you will be my sons and daughters, says the Lord Almighty."

Therefore, since we have these promises, dear friends, let us purify ourselves from everything that contaminates body and spirit, perfecting holiness out of reverence for God.

2 CORINTHIANS 6:14–7:1

Therefore, I urge you, brothers and sisters, in view of God's mercy, to offer your bodies as a living sacrifice, holy and pleasing to God—this is your true and proper worship. Do not conform to the pattern of this world, but be transformed by the renewing of your mind. Then you will be able to test and approve what God's will is—his good, pleasing and perfect will.

ROMANS 12:1–2

A number of Christian groups throughout the centuries have used passages like these to claim the true nature of the Christian church is to be completely separate from the world, completely separate from the surrounding culture, but doing so ignores the way Paul himself lived out these principles:

Though I am free and belong to no one, I have made myself a slave to everyone, to win as many as possible. To the Jews I became like a Jew, to win the Jews. To those under the law I became like one under the law (though I myself am not under the law), so as to win those under the law. To those not having the law I became like one not having the law (though I am not free from God's law but am under Christ's law), so as to win those not having the law. To the weak I became weak, to win the weak. I have become all things to all people so that by all possible means I might save some. I do all this for the sake of the gospel, that I may share in its blessings.

1 CORINTHIANS 9:19–23

Somehow, Paul holds these two principles in tension. On the one hand, he passionately desires to fit himself into his cultural context to minimize the hindrances to the message of the gospel to those who need to hear it. On the other hand, he declares the utter difference between the mentality of the people of the world and the proper mentality of the people of God. He holds these things in tension *for the sake of the gospel*. He doesn't want anything to hinder the advance of the gospel. He doesn't want anything to distort the view of the gospel. Therefore, taking our lesson from him, a Christian must keep proper distance from the world wherever the principles of the gospel are not the principles of the world, lest the people of the world and the people of the church misunderstand the difference between the two. However, that Christian must also keep himself or herself embedded in the world to make sure people who need the gospel have a chance to see it and hear it authentically.

17. Christians must be culturally astute so they can engage the culture around them with an authentic expression of the gospel without adopting, absorbing, or aligning themselves with that culture.

Finally, one of the greatest temptations that Christians have is to view their own Christianity and their pursuit of purity as somehow empowering them to be agents of judgment against the people of the world rather than agents of grace. Therefore, before we leave the New Testament and the teaching of Paul, there is one final value so important and so often misunderstood that it requires special attention.

I wrote to you in my letter not to associate with sexually immoral people—not at all meaning the people of this world who are immoral, or the greedy and swindlers, or idolaters. In that case you would have to leave this world. But now I am writing to you that you must not associate with anyone who claims to be a brother or sister but is sexually immoral or greedy, an idolater or slanderer, a drunkard or swindler. Do not even eat with such people.

What business is it of mine to judge those outside the church? Are you not to judge those inside? God will judge those outside. "Expel the wicked person from among you."

1 CORINTHIANS 5:9–13

I already mentioned that avoiding sexual immorality is a component of Christian humility and submission to the authority of Jesus, and on the surface, this passage appears to be about it too, but if you look closely, you can see this passage is actually using sexual immorality as a way to teach a larger lesson. The real lesson here is about how Christians judge other Christians and also how Christians judge the morality of non-Christians. In short, Paul commanded the Corinthians to exercise firm moral judgment regarding people *inside* the church but to intentionally *refrain* from using that same judgment with people *outside* the church. A Christian can share a meal with a sexually immoral *unbeliever*, but not a sexually immoral *believer*. To fellowship with one who claims to be a *believer* while living in unrepentant sin is to tacitly endorse the sin. *That* will taint the gospel with license. On the other hand, to eat with a sinner who doesn't claim to be a believer is to tangibly offer grace and forgiveness. It's doing what Jesus did with the tax collector friends at Levi's house. It's what he did at the home of Zacchaeus or Simon the Pharisee. According to the teaching of Paul and the example of Jesus, we are to *judge believers* but *not unbelievers* even over the same exact behavior. Also, anyone who repents of their sin and turns to the family of believers is to be welcomed with forgiveness and open arms. Jesus illustrated it with his famous story of the prodigal son, and Paul made it explicit when he said this about a repentant person:

> Now instead, you ought to forgive and comfort him, so that he will not be overwhelmed by excessive sorrow. I urge you, therefore, to reaffirm your love for him.
>
> 2 CORINTHIANS 2:7–8

Putting these concepts together as a value statement, we have this:

18.   Christians should apply Christian values to those who claim to be believers, should not condemn unbelievers, and should always offer forgiveness and reconciliation to anyone who repents.

At this point, we have pretty well summarized all the moral teaching for Christians recorded in the New Testament. To be sure, there are details we are leaving out, like some specifics regarding mutual submission in the life of a church, how to exercise charismatic gifts, or how much alcohol is permissible. However, all those details in the New Testament are given in the larger context of another value we have already listed. Let's turn our attention to the Old Testament.

OLD TESTAMENT PRINCIPLES

There are at least two values expressed in the Old Testament that we haven't seen yet, because they aren't explicitly mentioned in the New Testament. However, in light of Acts 15, we know that some Old Testament commands remain in force even if not explicitly reaffirmed in the New Testament. The principle from Acts 15 was this: we disregard Old Testament commands that were specific to ancient Israel or that were superseded by Christ, and we retain Old Testament commands that were confirmed by Jesus as expressing the heart of God for his people. Do any such commands teach values we haven't already seen? I think there are at least two. These two values are obviously foundational to the will of God, are fully in line with the rest of the New Testament, and also bring something new to the table. Therefore, I consider them ongoing central Christian values as well.

Regarding Nature

First, on two separate occasions, Jesus confirmed the importance of the first chapters of Genesis. When asked about divorce, he quoted from Genesis 1 and 2:

> "Haven't you read," he replied, "that at the beginning the Creator 'made them male and female,' and said, 'For this reason a man will leave his father and mother and be united to his wife, and the two will become one flesh'? So they are no longer two, but one flesh. Therefore what God has joined together, let no one separate."
>
> MATTHEW 19:4–6

Elsewhere, he made a shrewd reference to the image of God present in humans by saying this:

"Show me a denarius. Whose *image* and inscription are on it?"
    "Caesar's," they replied.
    He said to them, "Then give back to Caesar what is Caesar's, and *to God what is God's.*"

LUKE 20:24–25

These are two references by Jesus, one explicit and the other implied, to the first and second chapters of Genesis. By making these references, Jesus confirmed the importance of those early chapters in understanding the moral obligations of humans in this world. Therefore, we should consider what the creation account has to say about humans:

So God created mankind in his own image, in the image of God he created them; male and female he created them.
    God blessed them and said to them, "Be fruitful and increase in number; fill the earth and subdue it. Rule over the fish in the sea and the birds in the sky and over every living creature that moves on the ground."

GENESIS 1:27–28

God created human beings to bear his image, to represent him on the Earth, and even to have massive authority over the Earth. Back in Jesus's day, no one could have conceived of how much power humans would have over the world. They knew they had power over animals in some ways, but during Jesus's day, they hadn't subdued electricity, knew nothing about computational logic, and hadn't burned an ounce of fossil fuel. They had no idea how good at subduing we humans could be. Still, the text is clear. God gave human beings the power and the responsibility to take dominion over the planet and to exert authority over it. It has taken us a long time, but we are finally reaching the ability to obey this original command. We are now achieving our original God-given potential to influence and eventually completely control the entirety of our global environment. But if we are now able to achieve our potential, we must remember the *purpose* of our power. God created us to *bear his image* in the way we subdue the Earth. Therefore, even though the Bible doesn't give any explicit commands regarding *how* to care for the Earth, the command we had from the beginning, to subdue it in his image, is still in force. We need to add it as a value:

> 19.   Christians exercise dominion over the Earth not for our own benefit but as those who bear God's image, valuing both what and whom he has made.

Yes, I am claiming that a kind of environmentalism should find a central place in Christian morality. Burning up the planet is clearly poor stewardship. Stripping the planet for our own comfort or benefit is to disregard that we are agents of a higher authority. Environmentalism is a core component of God's first command to human beings, and it is uniquely Christian for us to embrace this as a value. No earthly agency or secular perspective can fully explain why we should care for the planet or why we have such power, but Christians know both answers.

Regarding Justice

Finally, there is a second value present in the Old Testament and heavily implied by the words and the life of Jesus, but it's a value that isn't addressed often by evangelicals simply because it's a value espoused by people we consider political enemies. It has to do with social justice, and even though it has become a political flash point, it was a biblical idea long before any social group ever tried to embrace it. The whole notion of social justice arises from the fact that we are image-bearers and other people are image-bearers. Remember that Jesus launched his ministry by quoting a very social justice sort of passage.

> "The Spirit of the Lord is on me, because he has anointed me to proclaim good news to the poor. He has sent me to proclaim freedom for

the prisoners and recovery of sight for the blind, to set the oppressed free, to proclaim the year of the Lord's favor."

Then he rolled up the scroll, gave it back to the attendant and sat down. The eyes of everyone in the synagogue were fastened on him. He began by saying to them, "Today this scripture is fulfilled in your hearing."

LUKE 4:18–21

Too often, evangelical Christians overspiritualize this passage. Based on the teaching of Paul, we understand that "freedom" can mean freedom from sin, and since Jesus never literally freed anyone from any literal imprisonment, it makes sense for us to see this entirely in a spiritual or metaphorical way. However, no one in Jesus's day, no one when he read those words, and no one in the centuries before Jesus thought this was a spiritual passage, and Jesus himself literally did bring sight to the blind. Surely, this passage has deep spiritual meaning, but it is not exclusively spiritual either. When Jesus read this passage, he wasn't just claiming to be the messianic answer to the condition of the oppressed and the poor, he was also endorsing the words and work of the ancient prophets who incessantly advocated, under the direct empowerment of the Holy Spirit, for the cause of justice. These were the first activists who deeply criticized their governments and pleaded with people to change their behaviors so that God would be glorified in and through his image-bearers. Here are a few of those prophetic statements:

"Then you will call, and the LORD will answer; you will cry for help, and he will say: Here am I. *If you do away with the yoke of oppression*, with the pointing finger and malicious talk, and *if you spend yourselves in behalf of the hungry* and satisfy the needs of the oppressed, then *your light will rise* in the darkness, and your night will become like the noonday."

ISAIAH 58:9–10

"So I will come to put you on trial. I will be quick to testify against sorcerers, adulterers and perjurers, *against those who defraud laborers of their wages*, who oppress the widows and the fatherless, and *de-*

prive the foreigners among you of justice, but do not fear me," says the
LORD Almighty.

MALACHI 3:5

If those highlighted phrases don't bring conviction and motivation
to you, you've believed a lie about the heart of God for the people in
this world. According to Jesus, his messianic work includes bringing
fulfillment to these proclamations of the prophets, and whether the
fulfillment ever gets fully realized before he returns in glory, the endorsement of the *message* is abundantly clear. The life and words of
the prophets express a righteous *activism* that Christians should still
embrace regarding the needy and oppressed among them. Let's state
the value like this:

20.   Christians bear the burden and take up the cause of the needy
      within our sphere of influence, especially orphans, widows,
      foreigners, and others who are impoverished or oppressed.

This is a good and mostly safe way of phrasing the value, and it is
fully in line with the direct teaching of the Bible, but it's important to
realize that oppression and impoverishment manifest themselves in
many ways today. Toward that end, when I speak of the cause of the
needy today, I am including the threatened unborn, the unjustly incar-
cerated, those who are political refugees, minorities, social outcasts,
and others. Plus, because our influence today is global, I want to reiterate that our concern should be for people everywhere, not just in our
own city, state, or country.

WHAT ABOUT THE OTHERS?

Again, I'm sure I have missed a specific command that is important
to you or someone else reading this. I didn't say anything about the
right or wrong way to worship God. I didn't say much about the evils
of divorce, the problems with deception or violence, and I have spoken
often in general terms, but for the most part, I'm convinced these values
adequately encompass all the relevant teaching from Jesus, the New

Testament writers, and even key portions of Old Testament teaching that are still applicable to Christians today.

I also want to affirm that in making this list, I have tried my best to be governed only by clear biblical teaching and not by any modern political perspective. Although aspects of modern political positions might overlap with these values, these values themselves as outlined above are first and foremost biblical and, more specifically, Christian. I also want to reiterate that what we have considered so far is really only about the morality God desires for his *own* people and not what he desires for a society at large. To that, I turn next.

CHAPTER 8

Christian Morality, Translated

WE CHRISTIANS FREQUENTLY ATTEMPT to translate our values directly
to the wider society. After all, if God is the same God over all people,
then his moral code should apply equally to all people too, right? It's an
attractive thought; however, it fails to account for many things. Many
of the Christian values we've mentioned only make sense within the
sacrificial framework of a Jesus-follower. Remember that Paul prohibited judging outsiders according to standards of Christian morality.
We have to acknowledge that perhaps only a few of the above values
can be directly translated from the church to the society. Complicating
matters, all the values mentioned in the previous chapter were given in
contexts very different from today's. In fact, all the biblical values were
delivered in only one of two contexts. Either they were given to a people
who had very little social power to affect the broader society, or they
were given to a people who were actually building a totally theocratic,
monocultural society.

In the days of the Old Testament, there was no such thing as a secular
society. The commands to Israel were given to God's people who were
forming a single-culture theocratic society—a holy nation. The Israelites and their national structure belonged to God, and the other nations
belonged to their gods. The idea of a secular society just didn't exist. As
a result, we must see the Old Testament commands through the lens of
this theocratic expectation. All cultures were theocratic, and therefore
the Old Testament commands were specifically designed to set the the-
ocracy of Israel apart from all the others. Many commands in the Mosaic

law were intrinsically divisive, antagonistic even, regarding the wider world. Leviticus and Deuteronomy are especially focused on making Israel *different* from the people around them, avoiding interaction with them, and sometimes defeating them. Yes, there were commands about social justice and treating foreigners well, but they were limited in scope to people who were within the borders and under the umbrella of the kingdom God had established. In the Old Testament, the commands were given in the context of a thoroughly religious society and an earthly kingdom in opposition to the world outside its borders.

In the New Testament, however, the relationship between God's people and the surrounding society was dramatically different. From one perspective, it can seem like an antagonistic relationship similar to that of the Old Testament—the Romans were antagonistic toward the Jews, the Jewish people were antagonistic toward gentiles, and both Jews and Romans were antagonistic to Christians. However, Jesus never spoke of the surrounding society as if it were an enemy to be fought or opposed. When Jesus talked to his followers about their role in the broader society, he taught them to be salt and light—sources of flavor and illumination. When he told them to love their neighbor, he also told them to expand the borders of their neighborhood. When people wanted him to establish a kingdom to defeat the current kingdom, he rejected it, declaring his kingdom to be not of this world. He commanded his followers regarding how *they* were supposed to behave but said nothing about controlling the behavior of others. His followers were supposed to have influence in their society as agents of a different kingdom, but he never told them to wield control over that society. Jesus wouldn't even allow Peter to defend him with a sword in the garden of Gethsemane. For the first followers, all of this made sense, because they had no societal power anyway. In fact, all of the New Testament commands were given to people who were essentially powerless to directly influence the workings of their society.

Times have changed again. Christians today, especially in the United States, experience a world far different from that in either the Old Testament or the New Testament. This world is unlike that in the Old Testament because we have a secular, pluralistic society. This world is unlike the one in the New Testament because in our society individual people, both Christians and not, have immense social and political power. Therefore, translating biblical values from the original context to ours is a difficult challenge. Making matters worse, neither the Old Testament nor the New Testament gives instructions about how one should use political and social power, because none of the people of God in either Testament ever had secular political or social power. But all is not lost. The Christian values themselves give us clues. In them, we get a very clear picture of how God wants people to treat each other in general, at all times, and without regard to religious perspective. So it isn't that much of a stretch to also conclude how he wants a society to operate. We just need to remember the distinction between what God expects of all people and what God expects of *his* people.

A quick aside: I have spoken to many Christians who firmly believe there is no distinction between what God wants for his people and what God wants for society at large. I have spoken to Christians who firmly believe that the exact same value system should be employed inside and outside the church. It should be obvious so far that I do not share that sentiment, nor do I think it can be supported biblically, but I will delay addressing it until a future chapter when I discuss cultural conservatism.

For now, I'm going to revisit the value statements from above to identify which statements apply beyond the confines of the Christian community. I'll list them and do some exploratory work with them, but I'll save the work of application to the next chapter.

THE OLDEST VALUE

Let's return to the list of values mentioned in the previous chapter. Scanning through them, we see that some were given in contexts that predate the nation of Israel or in contexts that specifically cross contextual lines. Recall that the first command God gave to any person was the command to steward the Earth, and that command was not tied to nationality or faith but to the mere fact that all humans were created in the image of God. Therefore, this responsibility exists for all humans of all time, not just believers, and we can state it as a universal value:

All people should care for creation: the Earth and its inhabitants.

And Christians should do so as an act of stewardship and worship.

THE CULTURE-CROSSING VALUE

Staying with the Old Testament, God commanded that his people should care for the poor and oppressed, as we have seen, and even though this was a command given inside the context of ancient Israel, it was given as an explicitly cross-cultural value. Much is said about God's command for the Israelites to clear out the wicked people from the promised land, but few people remember God also commanded the Israelites to be a blessing to the benign foreigners living in the land. In Israel, foreigners (even if enslaved) were to be treated with as much dignity and concern as fellow Israelites, and in most cases, whatever economic benefits were provided to needy Israelites were also to be provided to needy foreigners.

> "When a foreigner resides among you in your land, do not mistreat them. *The foreigner residing among you must be treated as your native-born. Love them as yourself,* for you were foreigners in Egypt. I am the LORD your God."
>
> LEVITICUS 19:33–34

> *Do not eat anything you find already dead.* You may give it to the foreigner residing in any of your towns, and *they may eat it,* or you may sell it to any other foreigner. But you are a people holy to the LORD your God.
>
> DEUTERONOMY 14:21

Don't get distracted by the part about eating roadkill. Rather, notice the principle from these two passages. The *benefits* of the community were to be applied equally to both Jews and foreigners, but the *restrictions* were often not. Many of God's rules for the Israelites were supposed to be upheld by foreigners also, but the commands about preserving holiness (i.e., dietary restrictions) were not. That is, social *benefits* should cross social lines even when *responsibilities* do not.

It's not only in the law of Moses. We see it in the words of the ancient prophets, too. Many Christians know what the prophets said about Israel's idolatry, but we shouldn't forget all they said about issues of social justice. The words of Amos are especially damning.

This is what the LORD says: "For three sins of Gaza, even for four,
I will not relent. Because she took captive whole communities and sold
them to Edom, I will send fire on the walls of Gaza that will consume
her fortresses."

AMOS 1:6–7

This is what the LORD says: "For three sins of Israel, even for four,
I will not relent. They sell the innocent for silver, and the needy for a
pair of sandals. They trample on the heads of the poor as on the dust
of the ground and deny justice to the oppressed. Father and son use
the same girl and so profane my holy name."

AMOS 2:6–7

Justice is a cross-cultural value because it includes instructions
for treating foreigners, but it's also cross-cultural because it applied
both inside and outside Israel. God's wrath was against Israel for taking advantage of the poor and against Israel and Gaza alike for selling
slaves! We must conclude that God's desire for justice applies to the
entire world.

In our modern world, this value is best expressed by the phrases
"human dignity" (every human life has incalculable worth and intrinsic
value) and "economic equity" (every person should have the opportunity to fully participate in their society). These principles are broadly
represented in the words of the prophets, but they aren't exclusive to
the Old Testament. When Jesus was asked about the greatest commandment, he said, "Love your neighbor as yourself," as a quotation
from Leviticus 19—a passage about caring for *foreigners*—and then told
a story of a foreigner Samaritan showing love to an Israelite. This value
crosses cultures and should be promoted by all people of all time. As a
universal value, then, we have the following:

All people should value human dignity and economic equity.

*And Christians should elevate the cause of others even to their own
detriment.*

THE COMPATIBLE VALUE

By "compatible," I'm saying there is one value Jesus taught us that in some ways depends on the existing value system of the world. Jesus told his followers to behave in such a way that the world, evaluating them by its own standards, would call their behavior good. I mentioned the value previously without quoting the context, so here's that context now:

> "You are the salt of the earth. But if the salt loses its *saltiness*, how can it be made salty again? It is no longer good for anything, except to be thrown out and trampled underfoot.
>
> "You are the light of the world. A town built on a hill cannot be hidden. Neither do people light a lamp and put it under a bowl. Instead they put it on its stand, and it gives light to everyone in the house. In the same way, let your light shine before others, *that they may see your good deeds* and glorify your Father in heaven."
>
> MATTHEW 5:13–16

There are many ways Christians have misunderstood or misapplied this passage. For my part, there was a time when I thought the job of a Christian was to be a preserving agent in the world, because salt can be a preservative against rot. I thought Christians were the salt that was supposed to slow down that process of rotting. Therefore, I thought the application was to conserve the old ways and prevent the progress of rot. Likewise, I thought that being a light meant acting like a spotlight pointing out all the ways people around me were failing to live up to God's standards. However, I was misguided on both metaphors.

Both of those ideas can be drawn from the metaphors Jesus used, especially if you live in a society where spotlights exist and microbiology is understood, but neither of those things falls in line with the mindset of Jesus's audience or the actual application Jesus gave for his own metaphor. When Jesus told us we were the salt of the world, he referred to our saltiness as the indicator of good salt. He didn't make any reference to anything preservative or preventative. In fact, if you toss salt into the street, it will retain all of its preservative properties, but the flavor will be drastically less palatable. Salt thrown into the street can still prevent weeds, but you tossed it out because it was doing no good in your kitchen. Clearly, Jesus was talking about the salt's *flavor*. Additionally, when Jesus told us to let our light shine, he mentioned a glimmering and beautiful city up on a hill, which draws you in with its inviting glow. He said being a light meant that people could *see* our "good deeds" and even rejoice at them and thank God for us. In both cases, he's talking about something that makes life better, more palatable, more pleasant, warm, inviting, comfy, tasty. In both cases, the focus is on how people other than you experience what you bring to the table!

This should be obvious, but the only way a society can rejoice over our good deeds is if our deeds somehow line up with something the society already considers worthy of praise, something the society considers good. In other words, according to Jesus, sometimes and somehow the activity of Christians should coincide with the world's existing perception of "good deeds." Or perhaps the good deeds of a Jesus-follower might open the eyes of the world to see a thing as good because they have now tasted it. Being salt and light isn't about restraining the progress of the world or being a spotlight on sin; it must be about being tasty and pleasant in a way that even unbelievers can experience as good.

This concept is so often ignored that I want to say it again: *The only way our society can rejoice over our good deeds is if our good deeds somehow line up with something our society will rejoice over.* There must be some compatibility between at least a portion of the Christian ethic and the ethics of the world, and Jesus isn't the only one who taught this. Paul did too.

> Be wise in the way you act toward outsiders; make the most of every opportunity. Let your conversation be always full of grace, seasoned with salt, so that you may know how to answer everyone.
>
> COLOSSIANS 4:5–6

> Make it your ambition to lead a quiet life: You should mind your own business and work with your hands, just as we told you, so that your daily life may win the respect of outsiders and so that you will not be dependent on anybody.
>
> 1 THESSALONIANS 4:11–12

Now the overseer is to be above reproach, faithful to his wife, temperate, self-controlled, respectable, hospitable, able to teach.... He must also have a good reputation with outsiders, so that he will not fall into disgrace and into the devil's trap.

1 TIMOTHY 3:2, 7

According to both Jesus and Paul, the Christian ethic includes having a good reputation with unbelievers, but according to many Christians these days, that doesn't seem possible. Christians have so often focused on the verses that draw lines of division between us and the world that we completely ignore this deep compatibility between the Christian value system and the value system of the world. How should we understand the borders of that compatibility? Consider this passage again:

Finally, brothers and sisters, whatever is true, whatever is noble, whatever is right, whatever is pure, whatever is lovely, whatever is admirable—if anything is excellent or praiseworthy—think about such things.

PHILIPPIANS 4:8

Paul never isolated those words to Christian values only. The definition of truth, nobility, excellence, and so on can be found in any dictionary, and therefore, there should be many times when the values of true, noble, right, pure, lovely, admirable, excellent, and praiseworthy are equivalent between the Christian world and the secular world. Put into a simplified value statement, we have this:

All people should value what is true, good, and noble.

And Christians should often find common ground with the world on those things.

WHAT ABOUT THE OTHERS?

Again, you might ask, what about the others? What about giving "truth" a spiritual definition? What about warning people of hell? What about the limits of environmentalism? I won't address those issues here.

I think many of those questions are really an attempt to justify ourselves like the man who asked Jesus, "who is my neighbor?" Of course, there are so many ways we could be more precise in our language, and there are ways we can cover more ground, but it's more important that we start living it out. Stop asking who your neighbor is, and start showing love to the person next to you. Stop asking what the limits of truth are, and start showing love, joy, peace, and patience to the people in your life. Stop asking how to make unbelievers act more like believers, and start acting like believers toward them.

Our list of values translatable to the world is far shorter at this point than our list of Christian values, but that's the way it should be. For example, among our Christian values, we have the value of winning people to faith in Jesus, but that's a value about helping people transition from a worldly mindset into the family of God. As a value of transition, it can't be a value for the secular society itself. Also, we have the value of holding allegiance to Jesus above all other things, but that's a value that can apply only to people who have declared allegiance to Jesus. There are the values of submission and sacrifice, living in holiness, and loving God, but again, these values can apply only to a person who is standing under the authority of Jesus who lived and taught these things. The list of translatable values must be limited to these three: caring for creation, promoting human dignity and equity, and valuing truth, goodness, and beauty. To reinforce this, let's consider two ways that Christian values definitely cannot translate to the surrounding secular society.

TWO LIMITS ON CHRISTIAN INFLUENCE

First, as we have noted already, Christians are commanded to *avoid* passing judgment on those outside the church, but it's also important to remember the context in which Paul gave the instruction. When Paul prohibited passing judgment on the world, he specifically mentioned the sins of sexual immorality, greed, swindling, and idolatry. Why is it, then, that Christians today frequently judge unbelievers on their sexual morals? Why are we so willing to obey Paul's guidance when it comes to overlooking greed and idolatry in our society, but when it comes to sexual ethics, we suddenly feel the need to stand up and be the voice of truth against the evils of the world? This is a major failure among modern Christians. Paul instructed us to *not* judge the sexual ethics of the people in the world, and Romans 1 tells us that God himself avoids restraining the sexual behaviors of unbelievers.

Sexual ethics as well as many other core Christian ethics are not translatable to the broader secular society, and therefore, in light of Paul's clear teaching, *it is absolutely not part of the Christian mandate to enforce sexual ethics and other aspects of Christian morality on the broader world*. We may promote them by persuasion and example, but enforcement is out of line. That's our first limit.

Second, we are not to fight any culture wars. In one of the most misunderstood and therefore disregarded passages in the New Testament, Paul encouraged the Corinthian Christians to *embrace* certain aspects of their surrounding culture even in their worship gatherings. Specifically, he actually commanded Christian men in Corinth to cut their hair and keep it short. Let's take a look at his words on the matter.

> Judge for yourselves: Is it proper for a woman to pray to God with her head uncovered? Does not the very nature of things teach you that if a man has long hair, it is a disgrace to him, but that if a woman has long hair, it is her glory? For long hair is given to her as a covering. If anyone wants to be contentious about this, we have no other practice—nor do the churches of God.
>
> 1 CORINTHIANS 11:13–16

This passage has confused Christians for centuries especially because it is part of a section in 1 Corinthians that discusses other gender norms in the Christian church. If you are curious about the practice of veiling in the ancient world and why Paul would encourage women to cover their heads, others have done a better job than I could.[9] However, I want to focus on the question of hair length. According to the NIV translation of this passage, Paul says, "the very nature of things" teaches us that it's glorious for women to have long hair, but also, "the very nature of things" teaches us that it's disgraceful for a man. In our modern society, we might agree, saying, "that makes sense." After all, we still consider long hair to be a glorious expression of femininity.

However, all of that misses the point. The passage said all the churches of God follow the same practice, but the early Christians *didn't* encourage men to have short hair. According to examples in Acts, Christian men in Jerusalem still followed Jewish customs regarding vows and hair, sometimes shaving it off and sometimes letting it grow out. Among Jewish men, it could be *noble* to have uncut hair; it made you look like Samson! Was Paul mistaken? Had he forgotten his education in Jerusalem? Was Paul, who opposed male circumcision, now saying that short hair was a requirement for Christian men? Why did he say, "all the churches" did things this way? To understand what's going on, we need to know three very important cultural realities.

First, we need to remember that Paul was extensively trained as a Pharisee in Jerusalem, and in the Jewish religious context, only men did public praying, and when they did so, they would often *cover* their heads with a scarf or shawl of some kind. In other words, Paul's command to the people in Corinth that women pray with heads covered and men pray with heads uncovered stood in stark contrast to the Jewish tradition he had practiced for most of his life, a tradition that was possibly still practiced among Christians in Jerusalem. Against that tradition, Paul was *allowing* women to pray in public worship, and against tradition, he was also saying *they* should cover their heads while the men should *not*. Therefore, Paul's command is not coming from the background of any Jewish religious practice, nor is it coming from anything in Jewish Scripture.

Second, as I said before, in the Jewish culture, it was actually quite common for men to grow their hair long. Like in the story of Samson, long hair was associated with vows of commitment to God. When a Jewish man took a spiritual vow, the law required him to not cut his hair for the duration of the vow. I bet some Jewish men would have allowed their hair to grow long even when they weren't in the midst of a vow just to get the social capital that would come from it. Therefore, once again, we have clear proof that Paul's command in 1 Corinthians 11 is not based on any Jewish *cultural* norms either.

These first two points let us know that Paul's statement about hair length for men and women has nothing to do with his own Jewish context, nor was it a statement that all Christians everywhere have short-haired men and long-haired women. A third cultural reality will help us see what Paul was really getting at. Paul was writing to Corinth, a city steeped in Greek history but eager to represent Roman cultural values. That's important because the Roman society was perhaps the first society in the ancient world to have clear norms regarding hair length for men and women. Have you seen the statues from the time? There's one really significant difference between the Greek sculptures and the Roman ones. It's especially stark when you compare the statues of the Roman emperor to the statues of the Greek gods. Greek gods, male and female alike, have long flowing hair. Statues of Roman emperors, on the other hand, have tightly trimmed, short hair. However, Roman sculptures of *women* retain long flowing hair. The people of Corinth, receiving this letter from Paul, were living in one of the first societies to associate hair length with gender norms, and this is the only time Paul ever wrote anything about hair length even though he claimed it was a universal Christian practice.

Again, it is not a coincidence that the only New Testament reference to hair length went to this very Roman city. Can you see it? Paul was giving the people of Corinth the *universal* instruction to *accommodate* their public worship to at least *some* cultural norms of their society. Even though Paul himself was a Jew, he encouraged Christians in Corinth to willingly adopt (even during worship) *Roman* cultural norms that didn't violate Christian faith. Rather than telling Christians to spread their church norms to the surrounding society, Paul encouraged the opposite (at least sometimes).

Therefore, in light of Paul's command to Christians to accommodate their worship to the cultural norms of their society, we have to conclude that cultural norms are peripheral to Christian living. They should be adopted when appropriate, but they are to be neither controlled nor conserved. *It is absolutely not part of the Christian mandate to prescribe our cultural norms on the surrounding society, nor is it part of our mandate to preserve cultural norms that are beginning to fade from society.* So long as the cultural norms are outside the aforementioned translatable values, they are effectively outside the Christian mandate altogether.

SCRIPTURE CALLS US to a very clear morality, and portions of that morality apply only to followers of Jesus while other portions of that morality apply to everyone. However, we too often mix them up. We promote uniquely Christian morals to people who are not Christian, and we ignore universal morals because they seem tied to political agendas we don't support. Nevertheless, if Scripture calls us to embrace a different morality, it is also calling us to a different kind of moral action. Especially in a society where the people of God have influence, we must steward our influence well.

CHAPTER 9

Christian Activism

THE HALLMARK OF EVERY evangelical pastor in every evangelical sermon is this: What should we *do* with what we have now *learned*?

Our move in that direction will involve a discussion not only about what it means to properly live as *agents* of God's kingdom in this world, but it will also require us to unlearn a number of things. Specifically, we will need to identify and tear down some of the false idols we have built for ourselves. We will need to set our scaffolds of wood, hay, and straw alight and then spend quite some time sweeping up the ashes. We are almost ready to do so, but there's still one more thing we need to address. Specifically, I want to address what Scripture mandates for followers of Jesus when it comes to using our influence in the world.

In this chapter, I'm going to lay the groundwork for a new perspective on Christian activism. Activism has always been a core component of Evangelicalism. David Bebbington's definition of Evangelicalism contains four components: *Biblicism* (the Bible is the top authority), *Crucicentrism* (Christ's death for sinners is the primary message), *Conversionism* (individuals need a conversion experience), and *Activism* (faith should be accompanied by works).[10] Evangelicals have been activists for a long time. The question is whether our activism has been properly Christian. Let's begin by revisiting some of the activism of the recent past.

RETHINKING RECENT ACTIVISM

In the last hundred years, the evangelical church tradition has worked hard to promote some uniquely Christian values to the broader society through the implementation of laws and public policies.

First, one of our fundamental Christian values involves living lives of personal holiness. When Christians in the early twentieth century promoted this value to the broader society, they did so in the form of a temperance movement that led to Prohibition. Getting an amendment added to the Constitution was a major accomplishment for these conservative believers, and even though Prohibition was eventually repealed, the overall temperance movement continued in activism. It just morphed from opposing alcohol to opposing other mind-altering or mood-altering substances. The political peak of that activism was the evangelical support of what was called "the war on drugs" in the 1970s. With the encouragement and activism of evangelicals in partnership with the Republican party, laws were enacted to inflict serious penalties for the use, abuse, possession, and distribution of addictive substances like marijuana and cocaine. These have been massive political successes, but at the same time, they point to deep hypocrisies in the church.

On the one hand, the evangelical argument is noble in addition to being religious. We claim some substances are dangerous and removing them from society will benefit the society. Since these substances tend to blight impoverished communities the most, we claim their restriction is an act of social justice. However, it's clear that our activism isn't entirely motivated by health and safety or by economic justice. For example, our activism supported laws against some harmful substances, like marijuana, without addressing others, like tobacco. Additionally, harsher laws for certain forms of cocaine over others led directly to harsher sentences for people of color over white people, but we haven't addressed that injustice. The bottom line is that regardless of our motives or aims, evangelical Christians have been instrumental in forming our nation's current laws regarding regulated substances, and the end result has been a mixed bag at best. A deeper look into these things is certainly warranted, but my point here is just to illustrate the prior achievements of Christian activism.

Second, evangelical Christians have been and continue to be activists for individual responsibility specifically as it relates to what is called the social safety net—welfare, unemployment, Medicaid, Medicare, and Social Security. Evangelicals are at the forefront of efforts to reduce these programs and put the greater burden of responsibility on individuals to help themselves. In the late 1970s, the Republican rhetoric against the so-called welfare queen and others who might take too much advantage of social programs resonated with evangelicals, and that alignment was a major reason Reagan won each of his two presidential victories by large margins. Evangelical Christians have proven their power to pick presidents!

Third, evangelical Christians have a long history of being activists for personal and religious freedom. We've joined Republicans in supporting lower taxes and reducing regulations wherever possible, but our activism is the strongest when it comes to religious freedom. In 1993, Bill Clinton signed a law known as the Religious Freedom Restoration Act that was designed to put religious liberty slightly ahead of other liberties. Evangelical Christian groups have since pressed their states to enact similar laws with the primary aim of protecting Christians from antidiscrimination lawsuits. Companies like Hobby Lobby, wholly owned by an evangelical Christian family, have litigated cases to ensure companies can run their businesses according to the religious convictions of the owners. Whether it's a web designer sued for refusing to make a website for a gay wedding or a coach fired for leading prayers after games, evangelical Christians are warriors for religious freedom, bringing these cases before the Supreme Court and regularly winning victories.

And finally, I'll mention one more way the activism of evangelical Christians has been successful. Largely motivated by their opposition to abortion and their desire to have an antiabortion president, evangelical Christians were instrumental (and perhaps the deciding voting bloc) in the election of Donald Trump. Trump promised to put justices on the Supreme Court who were committed to overturning *Roe v. Wade* and allowing states to make abortion illegal. That one promise was enough to gain the support of many evangelicals. He was elected, and he kept his promise, appointing a total of three highly conservative justices to the court and completely transforming it. In 2022, that heavily conservative court overturned *Roe v. Wade*, giving evangelicals what they had pursued for over fifty years.

These are but four examples of how the evangelical church has been active and apparently successful in the political or social arena, but the fact we have been *successful* doesn't mean we have been *right*. The questions we regularly fail to address are whether our activism in the public arena is proper and whether it is actually Christian.

It's taken me many years, but I have come to see that most of the things I was encouraged to support in the public arena are actually things Scripture tells me I should hold *personally* and in the context of a *church* but not in the context of my activism. That is, most of the things I have been encouraged to support in the public arena are actually things Scripture tells me are *internal* to the people of God. Neither the Old Testament nor the New Testament tells me to work toward the creation of a society that values individual responsibility. Nothing outside the laws governing ancient Israel tells me to advocate for a society of personal holiness. And when it comes to personal (or corporate) freedom, Jesus actually tells us to embrace persecution rather than trying to achieve or maintain our own freedom. In other words, in the last decade or so, I have come to realize that the things Christians have been trying to *legislate* in the broader society are the very things we should be promoting only *among ourselves*, and the things we are called to *promote* in the public arena according to the values of Scripture are actually the things we have been *ignoring*!

Modern evangelical Christianity has gotten its political involvement exactly backward.

RETHINKING POLITICS

As I talk about *Christian activism* in light of our translatable values such as environmental concerns, social equity, and the pursuit of truth and goodness, I am frequently labeled a *political activist* by other evangelicals. In using the word "political" this way, they give themselves permission to disregard my perspective. It was the word used by antebellum Christians to dismiss the abolitionists. It was the word used by white pastors to dismiss and criticize Martin Luther King Jr. and other civil rights workers in the 1960s. "Politics" has been for a long time the label we use for anything potentially divisive that we don't want to talk about right now. For example, among evangelicals, pastors who promote expanding welfare or alleviating poverty are labeled political, but those who accuse Congress of spending too much money are just preaching "truth." Talking about granting immigrants a pathway to citizenship is called political, but talking about enforcing the laws at the border and deporting the undocumented is called moral. Talking about government-sponsored health care is political, but talking about government-prohibited abortion is moral.

Actually, this is one area where I think Christians are perfectly in line with mainstream America. I think all of us, Christians and non-Christians alike, have a double standard when it comes to terms like "political" and "moral." We use "moral" to defend our own ideas and "political" to attack someone else's, but the division is arbitrary, and we should admit it. All issues that affect groups of people are simultaneously both. The process of accomplishing moral goals for a group of people is a political process, and the political processes of a society have moral implications.

The concern for a Christian shouldn't be whether something is political but whether something in our world needs to be informed by the translatable Christian values. For example, although my activism about stewardship of the Earth might sound the same as a non-Christian politician who uses the language of climate concern to win votes, there is a category difference between what the two of us are attempting to do morally.

Why is this important? The hypocrisy around these concepts is just one way idols get established in the Christian community, and in the interest of tearing down those idols, we need to directly confront it. In fact, we should be honest with ourselves. American Evangelicalism is guilty of something worse than hypocrisy. We are guilty of syncretism, adopting aspects of the current political landscape as if they are central tenets of the faith, and allowing the values of that landscape to infect and at times even supersede our own uniquely Christian values. This is false teaching, and we should call it out.

If we will ever be able to formulate a concept of *proper* Christian activism, we need to clearly understand our attraction to improper syncretism. In the interest of clarity, and in the interest of identifying our syncretism, here are some political opinions that exemplify the problem.

On Capitalism and Socialism

Have you heard a Christian say, "capitalism is good, and socialism is bad"? Have you heard a capitalist justify their capitalism with Christian words? I certainly have. But capitalism is not Christianity, and Christianity does not presuppose capitalism. In fact, capitalism, socialism, and any other economic system are philosophies peripheral to the Christian faith. Inasmuch as capitalism champions individual freedom, responsibility, and the potential for advancement, capitalism can be a tool to promote the dignity of individual people, and therefore can, in that way, align with the moral values of Scripture, but we're foolish if we say capitalism is the only tool to promote the dignity of individual people. Consider socialism. Inasmuch as socialism champions the cause of the many, it can be a tool to promote economic equity for people, and therefore aligns with at least one moral value of Scripture, but we're foolish if we say socialism always promotes equity for people. Christian morality requires us to be champions of *both* dignity and equity, and both systems have their reasons for being, but neither economic system can be considered actually Christian. Furthermore, like all systems of power, any economic system can be used by the advantaged to take advantage of the disadvantaged. *Christians must remember that we advocate for the human dignity derived from the image of God and not for the temporal systems that may or may not at times protect that dignity.*

On Secularization

Although the United States of America enjoyed nearly two hundred years where Christianity was the assumed worldview held by nearly everyone and where Christian quotations, principles, and behaviors were displayed in the public square, it should never be assumed that the nation was ever a Christian nation. Just because people label themselves Christian doesn't mean they are. Just because they use Christian terminology doesn't mean they follow Christ, and since Jesus is the King of an eternal kingdom, no earthly government can ever be called Christian unless Jesus is literally on its earthly throne. Also, there's abundant evidence proving this nation has never been a Christian nation in any sense of the word. The perpetuation of slavery and segregation, the massacres and forced relocations of indigenous peoples, the internment of the Japanese during World War II, and our continued systems of racial injustice prove that the country as a whole has never been Christian in any way Jesus would endorse. Even the First Amendment, by guaranteeing freedom to all people to express any religion they wish, proves that the United States has never been a specifically Christian nation. And finally, I must reiterate that no New Testament writer ever encouraged Christians to create such a Christian nation or even to advocate that the broader society embrace uniquely Christian morals or behaviors. The apparent secularization of our society is entirely not our concern as Christians. Even if the surrounding society were to become atheistic or overtly hostile to Christianity, we are still not instructed by anything in Scripture to ever fight against such a turn. *Christians must remember that we are citizens of a heavenly kingdom, called to make disciples, not nations.*

On the Morality of Political Parties

The specific interests of political parties and their platforms are completely peripheral to the Christian faith, and the idea that one party is more righteous than another is simple naivete. The proper amount of taxation, the size of the government, the amount of freedom afforded to states, the existence of or height of a border wall, the number of immigrant visas granted in a year, and the level of regulation regarding guns are all political platforms adopted by parties for their own aims and are, in their formulations, peripheral to the church. Each of these platforms may touch on an issue of concern to Christians, because each of them may touch on an aspect of a central value, like defending the cause of the weak or embracing truth over falsehood, but the platforms defined by political parties are peripheral to the church. Furthermore, even if one party has a platform that violates a principle of Christian morality, such a violation doesn't make the entire party evil, nor does it make rival parties righteous. *No political party deserves Christian loyalty.*

As one example, let's consider the issue of immigration. In the United States, our political parties are relatively strongly divided on the issue. One side argues for better enforcement of the laws to protect the rights of citizens, while the other side argues for more humanitarian treatment of the immigrant. Christians should find themselves in the middle. Proper Christian activism says we should concern ourselves with the issues of human dignity and equity on both sides: *both* the plight of those fleeing hardship or oppression in their own country *and* the plight of those who might lose jobs because of expanded immigration in this country. Simply put, neither party is entirely morally right about this issue. Policies proposed by the parties will have varying degrees of compatibility with Christian morality, and each Christian has the right to advocate for or against a specific policy according to that morality, but we must remember that the policy details and especially the party platforms are peripheral to Christianity. Again, *Christians should bear no loyalty to any party, platform, or politician.*

On the Morality of Political Policies

Finally, it's important to recognize that some public *policies* do directly conflict with a central translatable value and should therefore be addressed by Christians using their voice and whatever influence they have. I have just commented on the moral implications of immigration policies, but for a starker example, consider slavery. The chattel slave industry in this country was a legal public policy that was an affront to human dignity and therefore deeply immoral. It should never have been accepted by or even ignored by Christians. Also, the dehumanizing policies of the Jim Crow South or the economic disenfranchisement of Black people throughout the nation should never have been considered acceptable or even peripheral. For over two hundred years now, Christians have failed to be consistent and united in opposing that injustice, often calling it a "political" issue.

It's easy to find examples of immoral policies in the past, and it's often hard to see them in the present, but that's no excuse. Our calling is to be a voice for dignity and justice, and therefore, *Christians should not be afraid to label unjust public policies for what they are even if it means other Christians accuse them of being improperly political.*

Here's the point: our activism will sometimes look or sound political because the line is blurry between a culture's politics and its morality, but that doesn't mean we are dependent on those political power structures. Our activism should be the kind that simply lives out the life of Christ in this morally messed-up world, that speaks up against the injustices surrounding us, that takes action to alleviate suffering and hardship where we can, and that motivates others to join us. We must not rely on the power structures of the world, but we must make the most of every opportunity to love our neighbor in Jesus's name.

PROPER CHRISTIAN ACTIVISM

Proper Christian activism is different from the activism of the past; it's not tied to any political perspectives; it is uniquely Christian; and it involves promoting certain Christian values to the surrounding culture. Therefore, our activism, to be properly Christian, must be enacted by people who personally express the *internal* Christian values while promoting our *translatable* values to the rest of the world. This is not an easy task. It's hard enough to live the Christian values—it's the reason God gives us his own indwelling Spirit—but it's even more difficult to know when and how to promote our translatable values to the rest of the world.

On the one hand, by Paul's instructions, we know we should not judge the people of the world outside the translatable values, we know we should embrace at least some expressions of the culture around us, and we know we should avoid the temptation to control that culture. On the other hand, we know that some Christian values *are* translatable to the society, and we know we are called to be transformative agents for the sake of the gospel and the kingdom of God in the world around us. Therefore, great care must be taken as we consider what it means to be transformative in this world. To disengage from the world, or to interact with the world only in the effort to get people saved, would be to avoid our calling to be transformative agents of reconciliation. However, to embrace an uncritical activism promoting all things Christian to the broader society and working toward the development of a Christian kingdom in the here and now would be to overstep our biblical boundaries.

The calling of Christians is to live in *this* world as agents of a *different* world, a different kingdom. Some of our values are translatable, and some are not. We are called to be transformative but not to establish an earthly kingdom. Therefore, the two extremes of disengagement on one side or Christian nationalism on the other are equally erroneous, and we must find a middle way. This middle path I call *proper Christian activism*, and we can begin to define it by reminding ourselves what our translatable values are. Here they are again, rearranged in order of biblical prominence:

> All people should value human dignity and economic equity.
> All people should value what is true, good, and noble.
> All people should care for creation: the Earth and its inhabitants.

Wherever Christianity has spread throughout history, these values have followed, and because the Western world was built largely in tandem with the growth of Christianity, each of these values can be found in our modern society. However, the growth of Western society and the spread of Christianity was deeply tied to colonialism and exploitation, and therefore, these values appear partially present and often warped. Additionally, Christians in America have a chaotic and stained history when it comes to social engagement, frequently falling to the errors of ignorant disengagement or aggressive nationalism. We need to do better.

Let's get serious, and let's get practical. Here, I'm going to take each of our translatable, universal values and restate them as four action statements. I'll share them briefly now, but I'll give a fuller description and application for each in the next chapter.

The Activism for Human Dignity

Because all people should value human dignity and its related economic equity, and because Christians have the strongest motivation for it,

> *Christians should use whatever voice or influence they have to take up the cause of the weak, marginalized, disregarded, or oppressed in their society to ensure all people are treated with dignity and justice, moving toward equity, without regard to the moral condition of those people.*

The Activism for Truth and Beauty

Because all people should value what is true and beautiful, and because Christians have the strongest motivation for it,

> *Christians should use whatever voice or influence they have to promote what is true, noble, right, pure, excellent, or praiseworthy, including art, science, journalism, and social policies even if it includes promoting something unfamiliar or unpleasant.*

Sometimes truth isn't pleasant; sometimes what's excellent isn't familiar. I'll expand on this in the next chapter.

The Activism for Environmental Stewardship

Because all people should care for creation, and because Christians have the strongest motivation for honoring God in this way,

> *Christians should use whatever voice or influence they have to address the environmental concerns that reflect our stewardship of this planet and unjustly impact the weakest members of our world both now and in the future.*

The Boundaries to Our Activism

Finally, because Christians are tempted to use our influence to go beyond these values, we need to remember our boundaries:

> *Christians should not waste their influence to advocate for or against any cultural trends, social groups, political worldviews, or public personalities unless such advocacy is required by one or more of the previous mandates.*

WHAT ABOUT SAVING SOULS?

In my description of proper Christian activism, I haven't said anything about witnessing or proselytizing. I haven't mentioned the need for Christians to live out the Great Commission and make disciples, but there's a reason I haven't. Sharing the gospel doesn't fall in line with what I'm calling Christian activism. To be sure, some Christians think that the job of a Christian in the public sphere is only to promote the name of Jesus and salvation in his name at any and every opportunity, but that completely misses the model Jesus demonstrated and the instructions Jesus gave regarding sharing the gospel. Here is just one we forget:

> "A new command I give you: Love one another. As I have loved you, so you must love one another. By this everyone will know that you are my disciples, if you love one another."
>
> JOHN 13:34–35

According to Jesus, one way the gospel spreads is through the unspoken witness of the Christian community walking out the love of Christ. The idea that Christians need to "get people saved" even through antagonism or threats is outside anything Jesus taught or demonstrated. Still, I have heard Christians advocate for that exact approach. I have known Christians who focused on accusing people of their sin before offering them grace. I have known churches that refused to partner with local food banks and shelters because those specific shelters wouldn't let the church give a gospel presentation before the dinner service. We can do better. There is no biblical problem with giving people the *love* of Jesus first while waiting for an opportunity to share the *message* of Jesus later.

This love-first principle can apply much more broadly, and I'll illustrate it with one of the first miracle stories in the Gospel of Mark:

> A few days later, when Jesus again entered Capernaum, the people heard that he had come home. They gathered in such large numbers that there was no room left, not even outside the door, and he preached the word to them. Some men came, bringing to him a paralyzed man,

carried by four of them. Since they could not get him to Jesus because of the crowd, they made an opening in the roof above Jesus by digging through it and then lowered the mat the man was lying on. When Jesus saw their faith, he said to the paralyzed man, "Son, your sins are forgiven."

MARK 2:1–5

Jesus eventually healed the man, but two things happened before the healing. First, Jesus saw their faith, and second, he offered forgiveness. This sequence is often misunderstood. I have heard a number of Christians use this story to say we need to bring people to a point of *faith* so that they can have *spiritual* healing *before* we bring them material healing. These people actually say that if you bring the gospel to a person, it doesn't matter if they die because you have saved their soul. The subtext of this Christian belief is that if you give a man a fish, you feed him for a day, but if you get him to pray the sinner's prayer, you can just let him die. Maybe I'm being too harsh, but there's a sad truth underneath my sarcasm.

Evangelicals misunderstand this passage because we have defined faith in the narrowest possible terms: belief in the atoning sacrifice of Jesus for my sins and trusting Jesus as my Savior and Lord. But the man and his friends knew nothing of all that. All they knew was that the healer was inside the house. They knew Jesus was powerful. They believed Jesus was good. And that made it worth the effort to dig through the roof. That was the extent of their faith.

When Jesus saw that, he was moved. He required nothing of the man on the mat in front of him. He merely looked at the man and his friends, saw they had mustard-seed faith, and declared with no strings attached that the man was forgiven—forgiven *before* he repented of sin, prayed a prayer, affirmed Jesus's lordship, or anything else. Literally the only thing the man does in the story is obey Jesus when he says, "Take up your mat and walk."

What if we did that? What would it be like if we offered *forgiveness* to people as early and easily as Jesus did?

Don't rely on this story alone. Look throughout the Gospels. Find any story where Jesus encounters a person, and see what he requires of them before showing them some tangible love. Zacchaeus? Nothing. Levi? Nothing. The woman caught in adultery? Nothing. The man born blind? The man with the crippled hand? The woman with the alabaster jar? The man whose daughter lay dying? The woman who touched his robe? The disciples afraid of the storm? The hungry crowd? The man filled with a legion of demons? Nothing, nothing, nothing. It's the way God works.

> But God demonstrates his own love for us in this: While we were still sinners, Christ died for us.
>
> ROMANS 5:8

Sure, Jesus calls people to repentance, to put their trust in him, to follow him, but he *always* offered tangible love *before* offering any call to spiritual or moral transformation, and our practice should be the same. We should definitely use whatever voice or influence we have to share the message of the good news of Jesus, but such proclamation should come *after* we have earned the right to speak such words, *after* we have demonstrated the good news of the kingdom. That is, before advocating for Christian morality, Christians should be demonstrating the *grace* of Jesus and the exceptional *goodness* of his lordship!

Serve people. In Jesus's name. In that order.

CHAPTER 10

Christian Activism, Applied

IT'S TIME FOR US to deal candidly with some difficult topics. In this chapter, I'll take the translatable values mentioned before, phrased in light of proper Christian activism, and I'll apply them to just a few very specific current issues. My applications will be in stark contrast to contemporary evangelical assumptions, and that's as it should be. Frankly, we have done the work of application wrongly for too long. We have misapplied our values, and we have misapplied the gospel of Jesus. We have gone too far and also fallen short in our activism. Turning that around will not feel comfortable or natural, nor will it even make sense the first time we think about it. Nonetheless, the application of our moral values in this world is a requirement of us being the salt and light Jesus told us we are.

PROMOTE DIGNITY AND JUSTICE

Christians should use whatever voice or influence they have to take up the cause of the weak, marginalized, disregarded, or oppressed in their society to ensure all people are treated with dignity and justice, moving toward equity, without regard to the moral condition of those people.

Dignity and Equity as Applied to Same-Sex Marriage

Let's start with a big one. Same-sex marriage was and still is a hot-button issue for conservative Christians. When the Supreme Court legalized same-sex marriage in the nation, the way most evangelical pastors addressed the issue at the time was to talk about how same-sex unions were not endorsed by God and that God, who created marriage, should have the final say about what gets called a marriage. This was moderately hypocritical, because for decades, those pastors and their churches required couples to receive governmental endorsement of their marriage before the church would recognize it as a marriage. Those churches told couples they shouldn't be living together until they were married, and when they said "married," they always meant legally recognized marriage—the process of getting a certificate filed with the government codifying their union. In other words, the churches wouldn't recognize a marriage as a marriage until the state recognized it as such. Inconsistently, evangelical churches looked to the state to endorse marriage but then got upset when the state chose to endorse marriages that didn't fit the biblical mold. Their activism then shifted to convincing the government to follow the Bible or at least tradition and to withhold the rights of marriage from same-sex couples.

The logical inconsistency of that position is only part of the problem, though. The more significant problem is that by opposing secular same-sex marriage, the evangelical church was actually violating two biblical principles we have already seen: (1) Christians are not to judge the sexual morals of people outside the church, and (2) Christians should be in favor of justice and human dignity for all regardless of their moral or spiritual condition. If you are an evangelical, you might accept this first principle. You might be comfortable with the idea that Christian morality should be kept inside the church and not legislated in the broader society. However, you might have a problem with the second principle in this context. That principle sounds like I'm about to say same-sex marriage is an issue of justice and human dignity. It probably sounds to you like I'm about to suggest Christians should *support* secular same-sex marriage.

I'm sorry to confirm your fears, but yes, we should, and here's why.

If a government maintains a certain social contract for the benefit and protection of its people, that government has the right to extend that contract to whomever it wishes, but for the sake of human dignity and justice, it *should* apply that social contract equally to all people regardless of their religious perspective or spiritual condition. If the government doesn't apply this beneficial protection to all people regardless of their religious perspective or spiritual condition, then that government has become a government of preferential treatment for some and is no longer promoting human dignity and justice for all. If one religion or worldview thinks that contract should be limited to only heterosexual monogamous couples, and another religion or worldview thinks differently, the government should not offer preferential treatment to one perspective over another unless it has a compelling nonreligious reason to do so. The government should make its decision purely on the basis of human dignity and justice. Likewise, Christians, following our translatable Christian values, should use whatever influence we have to advocate for universal human dignity and justice and for the universal application of those government benefits and protections, even if those benefits are tied to a social contract called "marriage."

That puts Christians like me in strange and uncomfortable moral waters. It requires us to support governmental policies that allow or even endorse immoral behavior. Don't get me wrong. I'm convinced the Bible presents an ethic limiting sexual behavior to the context of a monogamous heterosexual lifelong covenant. I still teach that ethic as a central moral value for Christians, but a commitment to universal human dignity in the secular world actually requires that I support the government's equal treatment of all people, regardless of whether those people adopt my sexual ethic. Supporting equity and dignity requires that I speak up for those who are prevented from full participation in our society. What am I to do? How should I handle it when a *translatable* value leads to conclusions that violate an *internal* value? More generally, what voice (if any) should I have in a culture where a concern for dignity and justice leads to conclusions that are outside the boundaries of Christian morality? More than that, what do we do when a person joins their sense of *identity* and dignity to something we see as sinful? Should Christians ever actually *advocate* for sinners to have the opportunity to sin more freely?

Although it is sure to be controversial, again I think the answer should be "Yes."

Remember that the tree of knowledge of good and evil was put in the garden by God himself. God actually created the opportunity for the first sin. He didn't do the tempting, but he made the tree and didn't build a fence. Romans 1 goes further, saying that God has given unbelievers over to their sin, and Romans 3 reminds us that God is still in the business of withholding punishment, at least for a bit longer. Giving people the freedom or opportunity to sin is not itself sinful.

Back to marriage. In this country, marriage comes with a number of benefits that no other contract has. There are financial benefits, including the elimination of gift taxes and estate taxes between spouses. There are legal benefits. Married couples automatically have power of attorney over each other in many areas of life, including medical and financial decisions. Married couples also have a number of social benefits both tangible and intangible. In other words, the social contract our government calls marriage provides a kind of *dignity* to people that is available only to those within that contract. When the government decides who is allowed that privilege and who is not, it becomes a question of *justice*. Therefore, this truly is an issue of dignity and justice, and from the perspective of this value, it is *right* for Christians to *support* the extension of marriage to same-sex couples.

Now, I'm a pastor, and I perform weddings. I have not and will not officiate over a same-sex wedding, because I don't see any scriptural endorsement of such unions. You need to remember that I'm an agent of the kingdom of God and not an agent of the state. I don't represent the state in a wedding. I represent God. Therefore, I don't have the authority to officiate over a union not endorsed by the text of Scripture. In other words, the definition of marriage I endorse does not match the government's definition. It was nice when the secular social contract of marriage appeared to line up with the one Jesus gave, and it's convenient for Christians that the government will accept a pastor's signature in place of a judge's, but in truth, the secular social contract of marriage has never lined up with the definition of marriage outlined by Jesus. Jesus's definition of marriage is more restrictive than any government's, and our country has never written his definition into law.

That doesn't mean Christians should give up the notion of Christian marriage or endorse the *morality* of homosexual behavior or the unions arising from it. Even though some modern churches embrace homosexual behavior as a fully viable lifestyle, I maintain that the biblical limits on sexuality are incompatible with homosexual behavior. Additionally, the Bible speaks repeatedly about the problems a person faces when they engage in sexual sin, and the church shouldn't keep silent about it, but as we have seen, the church is supposed to *live* that morality in the public arena and internally hold each other accountable to it without wasting energy pointing fingers at the broader society. In this way, it is completely reasonable for a church or a pastor to support a governmental expansion of marriage while maintaining a more limited, narrow, independent, and *internal* definition of marriage.

Dignity and Justice as Applied to Social Welfare Programs

I want to consider another area where the church should advocate for dignity and justice in the broader society even when doing so appears to conflict with some internal values of the church. Let's consider social welfare programs. One of the most important verses to evangelicals when it comes to social welfare programs is this one:

> In the name of the Lord Jesus Christ, we command you, brothers and sisters, to keep away from every believer who is idle and disruptive and does not live according to the teaching you received from us. . . . For even when we were with you, we gave you this rule: "The one who is unwilling to work shall not eat."
>
> We hear that some among you are idle and disruptive. They are not busy; they are busybodies. Such people we command and urge in the Lord Jesus Christ to settle down and earn the food they eat.
>
> 2 THESSALONIANS 3:6, 10–12

Christians in my tradition have adopted this verse and a few others like it from the apostle Paul to conclude that social welfare programs are evil or that they at least enable people to be lazy busybodies who leech off of others. There may be some actual reasons to think that social welfare programs enable laziness, but the thing evangelicals frequently forget is that here, too, in the teaching of Paul, the instruction is for *inside the church family* and not a statement about what a secular government should do for its people or how the church should approach the needs of the world around it. In fact, there are many reasons why a secular government might want to provide social welfare programs even if people take undue advantage of those programs. As an illustration, every child in every family lives under a parental welfare program until they move out of the home, and many of those children take undue advantage of the generosity of the parents. No child offers to the parents equitable compensation for the services they receive, and we all think that's okay. Moreover, we consider that *right*. We all believe it is the responsibility of the responsible parent to meet the needs of the irresponsible child while attempting to nurture that child toward responsibility.

I'm not saying a government should treat its citizens like children. Nevertheless, there might be good reasons for a government to provide social welfare even for irresponsible citizens, and if a good reason exists, it might be good for Christians to support it too. Remembering that Christians are not supposed to judge the unbeliever, we can set aside moral judgment regarding those who might take undue advantage of those programs. Then, we can begin to think about what a society would look like that elevates the dignity of those who live within its borders even if some abuse that generosity. In fact, we should go further. If a society *can* elevate the dignity of those who live within its borders, then Christians in that society *should* promote actions that result in such elevation.

To be sure, there are caveats upon caveats here since we never know what a change to one part of our economy might do to another part of the economy and whether elevating one group of people might work to the detriment of another group of people, and whether too many will just exploit it without ever becoming responsible citizens, but Christians should not be overly concerned by such worries or fears. If Christians can help their society become more aware of and attuned to issues of dignity and justice, then whenever one action creates a problem, the society will already be primed to see and address any new disparity as well. With Christians as a consistent voice for *dignity* and *justice*, the entire society will grow more *dignified* and *just*.

PROMOTE WHAT IS TRUE AND GOOD

Christians should use whatever voice or influence they have to promote what is true, noble, right, pure, excellent, or praiseworthy, including art, science, journalism, and social policies even if it includes promoting something unfamiliar or unpleasant.

The New Testament contains some unpleasant facts in even the most important places:

> Now Peter was sitting out in the courtyard, and a servant girl came to him. "You also were with Jesus of Galilee," she said.
> But he denied it before them all. "I don't know what you're talking about," he said.
>
> MATTHEW 26:69-70

> Trembling and bewildered, the women went out and fled from the tomb. They said nothing to anyone, because they were afraid.
>
> MARK 16:8

> When they came back from the tomb, they told all these things to the Eleven and to all the others. It was Mary Magdalene, Joanna, Mary the mother of James, and the others with them who told this to the apostles. But they did not believe the women, because their words seemed to them like nonsense.
>
> LUKE 24:9-11

Before Jesus died, Peter denied even knowing him. Unpleasant.

On the day of the resurrection, the first witnesses were women (considered untrustworthy witnesses in the ancient world), who were so scared, they told no one. Unpleasant.

When the women finally reconnected with the disciples, they did share their story, but no one believed them because it sounded like nonsense. Unpleasant.

If you were writing the founding documents of a new religion, how would you portray the leaders of that religion? If you were trying to portray the single most important event of that religion, how would you paint the story? Would you tell the story as, "But they were too afraid, it all seemed like nonsense, and no one believed it"? Would you have made the first witnesses of the event a culturally untrusted group? Why would the gospel writers tell such an unflat-tering, unpalatable story?

Because that's the way it happened. Because the writers of the Gos-pels were more concerned with telling the truth than with painting their group in a positive light. Truth matters even when it is uncomfortable or unpleasant. The early Christians were committed to the truth of their story, so committed that they told it the way it happened, unflattering parts and all. Christians today should be just as committed to truth, but not only in our testimony. Our commitment to what is true and good should extend to all aspects of life, even in disciplines of science and art, even when that pursuit leads us to uncomfortable places.

There was a time when Christians were at the forefront of science and art. Christians like Rembrandt, Bach, and Newton produced the most beautiful works of intellect and artistry in their day, and they did it because of and for the glory of God. Isaac Newton developed calcu-lus and an entire system of physics because he wanted to understand God and the order he wired into creation. Consider this quotation from the end of Newton's *Mathematical Principles of Natural Philosophy*:

> This most beautiful system of the sun, planets, and comets, could only proceed from the counsel and dominion of an intelligent and powerful Being. . . .
>
>   This Being governs all things, not as the soul of the world, but as Lord over all; and on account of his dominion he is wont to be called Lord God. . . . The Supreme God is a Being eternal, infinite, absolutely perfect. . . . And from his true dominion it follows that the true God is a living, intelligent, and powerful Being; and, from his other perfec-tions, that he is supreme, or most perfect. He is eternal and infinite, omnipotent and omniscient; that is, his duration reaches from eternity to eternity; his presence from infinity to infinity; he governs all things, and knows all things that are or can be done. He is not eternity or infin-ity, but eternal and infinite; he is not duration or space, but he endures and is present. . . . We have ideas of his attributes, but what the real substance of any thing is we know not . . . much less, then, have we any idea of the substance of God. We know him only by his most wise and excellent contrivances of things, and final causes: we admire him

for his perfections; but we reverence and adore him on account of his dominion: for we adore him as his servants.[11]

I'm astonished by the reverence Newton held for the Almighty God. He saw the pursuit of science to be exactly the same discipline as the pursuit of God. The more he learned of the world, the more his worship grew. Throughout the centuries, Christians drove science forward because every discovery empowered their worship. Even today, many Christians motivated by love for God and for their neighbors are pursuing the sciences of biology and medicine to bring relief to millions around the world. Christians are employing this science to eradicate polio, HIV, malaria, and more through education, vaccination, medication, and other public health measures.

However, in the past century or so, despite the long tradition of compatibility between intellectual pursuits and Christian faith, an antagonism has developed from members of the evangelical Christian community against the broader world of science. Compounded by doctrines like Young Earth Creationism and its claims about geology, anthropology, and evolutionary science, an antiscience sentiment has taken deep root among evangelicals. This manifests itself in a rejection of public health measures, opposition to vaccines, and a fascination with homeopathic medicines.

The evangelical skepticism of science has also produced a dangerous opposition to modern psychology and therapeutic counseling. Much of Evangelicalism depends on the belief that correct doctrine is the way to be saved. But if *doctrine* is the solution, then *bad doctrine* must be the problem. Simplifying all problems into this dichotomy, great swaths of evangelicals believe that psychology is a Satanic lie, that mental health problems are really just *sin* problems and *knowledge* problems. They accuse the sick person of ignorance or rebellion and declare the solution to be *learning* the Bible better and *doing spiritual exercises*. Many people are wounded by this improper belief.

A similar thing happened in the arts. As artistic endeavors were taken up by more and more people unmotivated by Christianity, more and more artistic works displayed values repulsive to Christians, and more and more Christians rejected those artistic enterprises entirely.

Abandoning the mainstream world of artistic endeavor and isolating ourselves into Christian echo chambers, we built our own music labels, media outlets, publishers, theaters, museums, and more.

As a result, conservative evangelicals today have a generalized disdain for or at least skepticism against any art or science that didn't originate from within the Christian community. Furthermore, the pursuit of truth among evangelical Christians has often dwindled into an exclusive focus on biblical truth. Attention is given to the truth of God's word to the rejection of truths found in God's *world*. Truths obtained through journalistic or scientific methods are rejected unless they confirm previous biases built up through sermons heard or passages taken out of context. This is arrogant and wrong. Believing that you are the only person who clearly understands the world is arrogant. Believing that your group's source of truth is the only source of truth is arrogant. Anyone who reads Psalm 19 or Romans 1 and still concludes that the Bible is the *only* source of truth is displaying either ignorance or hypocrisy.

It's time for evangelicals to reclaim what their institutions of higher learning have claimed to believe for decades: "All truth is God's truth." It means we can praise God for truth wherever we find it. No longer should we wage war against scientific or humanistic pursuits. It's time for evangelicals to embrace everything in God's world that is true, noble, right, pure, excellent, or praiseworthy even when those things are unfamiliar or uncomfortable.

Let's get practical. There are at least two ways modern evangelical Christians need to rediscover a love for what is true, good, and beautiful.

Christians Need to Be Competent with the Methods of Science

Christians should be comfortable with and competent in understanding the principles and methodologies of science.

I'm always surprised when I encounter a Christian who doesn't have a basic understanding of the principles of science. I shouldn't be. I was guilty of it once too. For example, from the time I was in middle school all the way through college, I had one basic answer to anyone who tried to promote evolution to me. You might already know my number one rebuttal. You might have used it yourself.

It's only a theory.

If you are an evangelical, I'm sure that you have said that phrase at some point in your life. I know I did. I said it a lot. I said it for two reasons. On the one hand, saying that phrase was my attempt to diminish my opponent. They thought something was true, and I wanted to toss it back in their face. "Oh, you believe in the theory of evolution? Well, you do know it's only a *theory*!"

The second reason I harped on the word "theory" is that I didn't understand what a theory was. I remember my seventh-grade science teacher telling us all the difference between a theory and a law of science: Gravity was a law; evolution was only a theory. Theories were something any seventh-grade student could develop. My science-fair project required me to develop a theory by using the scientific method: think of a question, make a hypothesis, do some experiments, and then describe your theory. If evolution were only a theory, that meant it was nothing more than Darwin's own science-fair project.

How naive I was! Real scientists don't call my science-fair-project conclusions a theory. Maybe an idea on the way to a theory, maybe a refined hypothesis, but certainly not a theory. More than that, real science doesn't follow the method I just outlined. Real science works more like this:

- A person or group of people are unsettled by some observed reality.
- They come up with an idea, develop tests, run experiments, describe what they think is going on, and then try to convince other people to spend money repeating those tests and experiments.
- Other people run the same tests and experiments, and if they succeed, they try to convince other people to do the same.
- Eventually, other people come up with new tests and experiments trying to disprove whatever the first group thought was going on. If they fail to disprove it, they try to convince other people to do better.
- If someone finds a better way of explaining what's going on, they start over at the beginning with their own idea.
- Repeat.
- Repeat.
- Eventually, when everyone who cares has tried and confirmed the current idea, and when everyone who cares has failed to disprove the

current idea, and when no one can think of new ways to test it, or new ways to disprove it, and no one has been able to start the whole process over with a different idea, then the community of people sort of give up the attempt to prove, disprove, or reformulate, and they agree to accept the idea as the current theory.

- From that point forward, college students spend hours on hours running through the same tests over and over again reconfirming the current idea, and PhD students suffer greatly trying to find some new nuance or problem with the theory just so they can have a topic for their dissertation.

Put simply, the entire process of science boils down to this: tons of people trying to make their mark by proving wrong someone else's idea while trying to develop a better idea in the process. So, what is a theory? It's an idea that has been confirmed so many times by so many people that no one has the time, resources, or willingness to try disproving it again.

Doesn't that sound like a really good way to figure out what's true?

More evangelical Christians should understand the rigor that goes into developing even the simplest of theories. They should know how the scientific method actually works, because there are profoundly important conclusions that have come from it. They should know the process and the conclusions. They should understand the mountains of evidence and detailed work that has gone into our current scientific knowledge, and they should understand the constant back-and-forth process of incremental revision that goes on in science. Calling something "just a theory" is more an expression of ignorance than anything else.

I'm not saying Christians should blindly accept all the conclusions of science, because blind acceptance is actually antiscience. Scientists themselves don't blindly accept all the conclusions of other scientists. The whole point of the scientific method is to test and retest assumptions and to evaluate and reevaluate conclusions. But the scientific method also depends on the willingness to rely on the expertise of others when that expertise has been well established. No biologist has time to reproduce all the physics experiments that led to the development of the electron microscope they use in biology every day. They rely on the work of others the same way you rely on the people who built the chair you're sitting in now. Everything in science is subject to change, but still, there is a baseline in science for what things can be mostly trusted and what things need to be skeptically and repeatedly retested.

Christians also need to understand that a changing perspective doesn't mean a faulty perspective. One of these days, you'll get a better chair, but that doesn't invalidate the job your current chair is doing now. Likewise, if scientists say the universe is 13.5 billion years old one year and then change it to 13.8 the next year, Christians shouldn't use that as proof that all cosmology is wrong and disdain its conclusions as being only a theory. If a doctor advises you not to wear a mask to avoid a deadly virus one week, and the next week tells you that actually, you probably should wear a mask, that isn't proof that the doctor hates you and your freedom. It might just be that an experiment was done in the intervening week that taught him new information! Christians should rejoice over the process of increasing knowledge. As people who are supposed to love the truth, Christians need to be competent in the topics they discuss, and they should understand the real meaning of terms they use (i.e., "theory"). If Christian activism requires us to be advocates for the truth, our first point of application is to become knowledgeable of the truth and the methods employed for its discovery.

All of that is just good sense, but Christians are actually called to something higher. We can appreciate science for reasons the world can't know. We can see the development of medicines and medical technologies including psychotherapeutics, vaccines, and public health measures that protect life and promote human flourishing and thank our heavenly Father. We can take the discoveries of science even when they are hard to imagine or understand—our universe is unimaginably old, the history of life on this planet is hugely diverse, and the mechanism employed for the development of species is beautiful in its simplicity—and rejoice. We can worship in spirit and truth because the methods of science have revealed to us an unimaginable world made by an unimaginable God.

> Oh Lord, my God
> When I, in awesome wonder

Consider all the worlds Thy hands have made
I see the stars, I hear the rolling thunder
Thy power throughout the universe displayed
Then sings my soul, my Savior God to Thee.
How great Thou art, how great Thou art![12]

Let's go beyond science, though. Scientific truth is not the only truth we need to embrace. We also need to understand other methodologies of truth like journalism and historical study.

Christians Should Be Competent with Methods of Journalism and History

Christians should be comfortable with and competent in understanding the basic principles of journalistic practice and historical study.

I'm always amazed when a Christian demonstrates disdain for journalists or historians. Our very Scriptures are given to us by journalists and historians. Our faith is based on a historical claim that Jesus rose from the dead. Our understanding of that claim comes to us through the writings of eyewitnesses and researchers. These facts should drive us toward a better understanding of how good history works, how to decipher legitimacy in the writings and testimonies of other people.

For decades, Christian apologists have been appealing to principles of journalism, historical study, and even archaeology to verify the legitimacy of the Scripture texts we value, but those same principles can and should also be employed in our efforts to understand truth in secular journalism today. If there are proper methods of journalism when it comes to Christian topics, then there are proper methods of journalism when it comes to non-Christian topics too. Furthermore, we do not need to feel threatened when a new academic paper arises challenging some preconception we had about the past or present world. Absolute truth is our bedrock, and we don't already know all the absolute truths. Maybe some of the truths we think we know actually aren't absolute at all. If we are to be people who love whatever is true, then we should be people who are eager to discover new truths, even if that requires us to interact with difficult academic methods or challenging historical analyses.

We need not fear sociological theories of religion, psychological theories of the soul, or critical theories of modern life. We shouldn't fear these things because we are people of the truth pursuing the truth. If some Christian goes on some broadcast telling you the evils of critical race theory or any other thing in the world, you can be the kind of person who says, "Oh, I've not heard of that. I should probably learn about it. If there's truth in it, that truth is from God, and if there's no truth in it, I can still learn something about the people made in God's image who think it is true."

Christians Need to Be Competent with the Methods of Subjectivity

Finally, on this topic of valuing the methods of truth, it's also important to remember that not all truth is *objective*. There is truth to be found in *subjective experience*. We've all felt it. There's a kind of truth that touches us differently than head knowledge. It's a truth we often call *beauty*, but it's just as profound and meaningful as any fact you ever memorized. In fact, for most of us, we don't actually accept things as true until our heart connects them to something beautiful. It's why we find it so easy to learn subjects we enjoy and difficult to learn what we don't like. We are wired to accept truth through the experience of beauty. Beauty is a gateway to truth.

Sometimes a work of art is visually beautiful, sometimes it is mentally beautiful because of what it represents or what preconception it challenges, but often it is both at the same time. One of my favorite artists is Piet Mondrian. I remember when I first saw one of his paintings, I consciously thought that I could do just as well, and I disdained him for it. However, I was curious too. His famous paintings were of red, yellow, white, and blue rectangles with thick black lines separating them, but the subtleties in his paintings captivated me. I was driven to learn more about him. I eventually learned that his paintings of grids and rectangles began as a series of drawings he did trying to express the beauty of trees. His beautiful drawings grew increasingly abstract as he experimented more and more until he finally embraced the utter simplicity of geometry and color. I found his journey as captivating as his destination. Surely, there is a vast difference between Mondrian's *Tableau I* and Van Gogh's *Starry Night*, but I find each of them compelling for their own reasons and each of them uniquely beautiful. Some works of art present themselves to me as immediately beautiful, and some require more of me, but I've become a person willing to do that work. Whether the art is abstract expressionism, a book describing some sinful behavior, or a song with offensive lyrics, there can be truth and beauty buried there. I know I can't read every book, learn every song, and study every work of art, and I know some things might be objectively not worth my time, but I want to be open. Beauty might not present itself to me immediately, but if something captivated someone's heart, someone who was made in the image of God, and if I can grasp a little of that, I will have learned that much more about my Creator and the people he loves.

AS CHRISTIANS, OUR GOAL should not be to preserve some form of art we find palatable, some form of history we find comfortable, or some ideas in science that we learned long ago. Christians should be those who rejoice in the truth wherever it may be found. Our faith is based on a truth claim that Jesus rose from the dead, delivered to us by poets, journalists, and historians, verified to us by archaeologists and chemists, and preserved and translated for us by scholars, linguists, writers, and other scientists. If we are people who don't appreciate and understand the work of scientists, writers, linguists, scholars, chemists, archaeologists, historians, journalists, and poets, then we are people who don't understand how to find and evaluate truth claims. And if our faith is not based on a historical truth, then as Paul said,

> *And if Christ has not been raised*, your faith is futile; you are still in your sins. Then those also who have fallen asleep in Christ are lost. If only for this life we have hope in Christ, *we are of all people most to be pitied.*
>
> 1 CORINTHIANS 15:17–19

We should be people of truth. We must understand it. Also, we must promote it.

Christians Should Speak Up for Truth

Once we have established a competence in the disciplines of truth, we then must embrace our responsibility to be advocates of truth in the broader society. This is especially important today. We are living in a world where misinformation is spreading like wildfire, and research shows that misinformation always spreads farther and faster than truth. Christians should not participate in that, and furthermore, the Christian voice should advocate against the spread of false information. Sadly, I saw firsthand in the early days of 2020 that evangelical Christians were among the leading voices spreading false information. Throughout the COVID pandemic, famous Christians and pastor friends declared restrictions against church gatherings to be governmental overreach. Churches and pastors I knew opposed mask guidelines because misinformation said masking was dangerous. Friends of mine opposed vaccines because a friend of a friend knew someone who had a bad outcome or because some online post said they didn't work, contained microchips, would make your blood magnetic, or contained the mark of the beast. I sat in school board meetings where well-meaning board members were berated by Christian parents who invoked Jesus's name and pronounced eternal judgment against them—all because the board supported COVID mitigation protocols. These were my experiences, but they were multiplied across the country as misinformation was shared on social media and spoken in pulpits.

This is a sad violation of our calling as representatives of Christ. We should be a group committed to advocating for truth. Our Lord called himself "truth" and told us to worship God with "truth"! And that isn't exclusive to *spiritual* truth. Scientific truth can be part of our advocacy too. For example, Christians should openly talk about the efficacy of vaccines in preventing deaths and promoting public health. Sure, there are unknowns with any medical treatment, and we shouldn't give people medical advice out of our ignorance, but our questions and unknowns shouldn't outweigh established truths. To be blunt, during COVID, Christians should have behaved differently. We should have stood with the professionals who invest their lives in public health issues and not the social media posts written with anecdotal evidence even if those posts came from a person using Christian words or claiming to be a prophet.

Additionally, since Christians need to understand the principles of journalism and historical study, we should also speak up in favor of those principles too. We should be proponents for truth in journalism. If a team of journalists reports a president-ordered drone strike that unjustly killed children, we should accept the truth, mourn the tragedy, but also rejoice that the truth is coming out even if we voted for that president. If a team of journalists reports a story regarding a president withholding aid from an ally in exchange for political favors, we should accept the truth, mourn the tragedy, and rejoice that the truth is coming out. If a report reveals sexual misconduct by a pastor in a church, we should accept the truth, mourn the tragedy, and rejoice that the truth is finally coming out.

We Christians should be people of truth, promoting truth, rejoicing in the truth even when one or more of those truths adversely affect our own aims. Whether journalism uncovers unjust police practices against minorities, inhumane family separations at the border, or repulsive practices at Planned Parenthood, Christians should rejoice equally at the discovery of truth. If new historical analysis leads us to rethink the origins of our nation or the racist underpinnings of our legal system, Christians should rejoice in truth. We should rejoice in the truth even when it is newly discovered or disagrees with our previous assumptions. *We are they who rejoice in the truth*, and we should use our voice to promote the truth.

PROMOTE ENVIRONMENTAL STEWARDSHIP

> *Christians should use whatever voice or influence they have to address the environmental concerns that reflect our stewardship of this planet and unjustly impact the weakest members of our world both now and in the future.*

On the heels of the evangelical rejection of mainstream science lies the evangelical rejection of mainstream *climate* science. The reasons for this are many. Some Christians, embracing the young Earth doctrine, deny the reality of large-scale climate change and presuppose all geological processes are short-term, brief processes. Not all evangelicals are Young Earth Creationists, but even when they are willing to accept geological science, it's often impossible to get them to accept climate science. In some cases, it is because climate science has become synonymous with liberal politics. In other cases, it is because environmentalism is linked in their minds with pagan Earth worship. And in other cases, it is because conspiracy theorists portray climate science as a hoax perpetuated by the elite so they can have more economic control over us.

Whatever the reasons, evangelicals have a presupposition that climate science is somehow flawed morally and therefore somehow flawed scientifically too. Then, this skepticism spreads because scientific literacy is so poor for so many evangelical Christians. Well-meaning Christians doubt climate science not because they have read any of the papers on climate change but because they have heard too many *other* Christians say the science is "debated" or "still out" on the matter, or that it's "just a theory" (see above).

I want to address this directly. Contrary to the evangelical rhetoric about climate science, the actual scientific community shares overwhelming consensus. According to the statistics compiled by *The Consensus Project*,

> 97% of published climate papers with a position on human-caused global warming agree: Global warming is happening—and we are the cause.[13]

The consensus among scientists is strong that climate change is real, that human activity is the main contributor, that the effects are accelerating to the point of soon being irreversible, and that major economic investments must be made now to prevent extreme damage to sensitive ecosystems and impoverished communities. Christians who have embraced the previous point of loving the truth even when it's difficult should likewise accept the undeniable scientific consensus that our world is currently in the midst of a growing climate catastrophe.

Then, once the climate science is understood and accepted, the Christian responsibility becomes clear. Because Christians believe that all humans bear the image of God and that our first job on the planet as humans is to represent him (not ourselves) in exercising dominion over the Earth, we should be the lead advocates for greater environmental concern.

Finally, when we consider that species, ecosystems, and even groups of indigenous or impoverished people are in danger of extinction from climate change, the passion of Christians to make a difference should

increase. When we consider that a changing climate will disproportionately impact the weakest members of our world, it becomes even more
clear that Christians should embrace climate advocacy as an issue of
human dignity. Though some environmentalists hold to a pagan kind
of rationale, Christians need not discard environmentalism because
of that. Christians have better reasons than they. We have a mission
given us by the Creator God himself to act on his behalf in guiding and
shaping this planet for the good of the planet itself, for the good of the
people on it, and for the glory of him who made it.

What should we do about it? Well, that's where things get tough for
everyone. It's hard to know what to do even though it's easy to recognize that something must be done. Climate data is convincing that we
need to make some changes and take dramatic action, but no one can
predict what will be needed to truly change things. No one can predict
what will have the biggest benefits with the lowest costs. Mitigation protocols are going to be changing constantly as we get more information
and as we take actions and see the results. Nevertheless, Christians can
begin to think and talk in ways that demonstrate a concern for honor-
able stewardship of this beautiful planet. Christians can behave with
more conscious thought to the implications of their choices, Christians
should inform themselves regarding the various mitigations that are
currently being proposed, we should talk about the matter with other
Christians, we should make personal changes to reduce our individual
environmental impact, and we should support public policies that address these environmental concerns. It's time for Christians to simply
step up to the Adam and Eve mandate and claim that what happens on
this planet is our responsibility. We have the power and authority to
make it better for the glory of God.

DON'T WASTE YOUR INFLUENCE

> *Christians should not waste their influence to advocate for or against any
> cultural trends, social groups, political worldviews, or public personalities
> unless such advocacy is required by one or more of the previous mandates.*

Finally, it is abundantly important that Christians recognize the total
impermanence of all earthly ways of thinking and living. Nothing on

this Earth deserves our perpetual, unquestioned allegiance, and since our calling is to neither judge the world around us nor fall in love with it, we should not overly concern ourselves with the temporary and transitory aspects of our society.

Against the popular thoughts in modern Evangelicalism, I want to say again that it is not our calling to fight a culture war. It's not our calling to create a culture or restrain the culture. It is not our calling to oppose transgenderism, antidiscrimination laws, so-called cancel culture, or the mainstream media. It is not our calling to align ourselves for or against any political party, platform, or public individual. It is not our calling to get books banned. It is not our calling to defend our rights. It is not our calling to fight against critical race theory, wokeness, evolution, or even socialism. In fact, in some of these cases, it might be our calling to actually embrace one of the so-called progressive moves in our society.

Never forget that our kingdom is not of this world.

In this world, we are ambassadors, not kings.

Ambassadors. Not kings. Not even judges.

To be sure, in our advocacy for Christian environmentalism, for the dignity of individuals, or for the advancement of beauty and truth, we may take positions that sound like they are for or against a specific political system or party, but do not mistake that position as alignment with or allegiance to that political system, that party, or some person. For example, Christians may oppose a tax increase because of the undue burden it would place on impoverished people, but that doesn't make us Republicans. On the other hand, Christians may support rules limiting corporate carbon emissions, but that doesn't make us Democrats. As Christians, we rise above such petty, temporary, earthly allegiances because we have a higher calling for a higher purpose from a higher authority.

CHAPTER 11

Idols and Temples

I ENDED THE PREVIOUS CHAPTER with this sentence:

"As Christians, we rise above such petty, temporary, earthly allegiances because we have a higher calling for a higher purpose from a higher authority."

That's a strong statement, and it's biblically true, but I'm not seeing many Christians actually living it out especially in the political climate of the current day. Do we actually believe God is the highest authority, or have we adopted the fear that other authorities have a competitive chance? Have we embraced our earthly allegiances because they evidently represent the eternal voice of God, or is it because we are simply afraid of our enemies? By listening to the wrong voices or by giving them too much authority in our lives, we have allowed peripheral matters to be treated as if they were central, and we have constructed our worldviews out of worthless and flammable materials. So far in this book, I have called us to reconsider the true nature of the gospel and the central moral principles in Scripture. I have confessed the ways my own understanding of Scripture was flawed, how I taught those flawed ideas to others, and how I turned to silence when my own thinking matured. In my own confession, I addressed some difficult topics, but I haven't yet mentioned the big ones.

Even though I've mentioned things like Young Earth Creationism and antiabortion sentiments, even though I've commented on same-sex marriage and religious freedom, I haven't touched on the biggest, deepest issues plaguing evangelicals these days. I've avoided them because in my experience, the issues we are about to tackle are too deeply ingrained in the hearts of too many people, and I thought it would be better to give you more time before I reached this point. I thought we needed to ease into this discussion slowly. However, I think the groundwork has been done, and it's time to press on.

In this chapter, I'm going to address the seriously destructive misalignments between the moral opinions of modern evangelicals and the actual teaching of Scripture. I'll frame everything from the perspective of my own experience in the evangelical church tradition, so there is no guarantee that you have personally experienced all these things I'll discuss, but I assure you they are real and should be confronted by those who love Scripture more than the whims of modern society or religious tradition. Additionally, the criticism I'm about to offer my own tradition is based not on things expressly *taught* in evangelical churches (in most cases) but on the *values* that arise from the way central doctrines have been explained and illustrated. Not many churches in my tradition teach these issues as central, but in practice, they are treated as central, so central and so deceptive in fact that I believe they are rightly called "idols."

Let me be clear about that word.

WHAT IS AN IDOL?

Recall that an idol is not necessarily another God. An idol is a *representation* of a god, even of the one true God. When Aaron made the golden calf, he didn't call it "the calf" or "Baal" or any other name. He called it "Yahweh," rendered as "LORD" in this translation.

> When Aaron saw this, he built an *altar* in front of the *calf* and announced, "Tomorrow there will be a festival to the LORD."
>
> EXODUS 32:5

The calf wasn't a representation of *another* god, it was a *false* representation of the *true* God.

I'm using the word "idol" in the same way here. I'm not asserting that Christians have begun to worship these other things as *replacements* for God; I'm asserting that modern American evangelical Christianity has latched on to certain things as *representative* of God and his will even though they are demonstrably not. For many evangelical Christians, the things I will address are considered obvious and essential components of God's will, but I'm calling them out here as *false representations*, idols that have distracted us away from the true God. These idols are built of the wood, sticks, and straw that I and my fellow evangelical pastors are guilty of promoting in our churches. We built them up gradually. We thought they were important at the time, but over time, they have become worthless additions to our faith. They are an affront to the authority of God and the beauty of the gospel, and they must be called by name and torn down. Idolatry, wherever it is found, is unacceptable, and it's long past time for us to identify these idols by name, so we can repent of our collective sin. Since I am still in the process of learning, I imagine that I am also still blind to some of my own, but God has given me the grace to identify at least those that follow.

NAMING THE IDOLS

Individual Responsibility

One of the core doctrines of Evangelicalism is that each individual is accountable directly to God for his or her own spiritual condition. No one is saved on the basis of their community or their family. Each individual must respond as an individual to the call of God on their life to receive Jesus as their Lord and personal Savior. Consider Jesus's own words on the topic:

> Jesus replied, "Very truly I tell you, no one can see the kingdom of God unless they are born again." . . . For God so loved the world that he gave his one and only Son, that whoever believes in him shall not perish but have eternal life. For God did not send his Son into the world to condemn the world, but to save the world through him. Whoever believes in him is not condemned, but whoever does not believe stands

condemned already because they have not believed in the name of God's one and only Son.

JOHN 3:3, 16–18

Jesus taught that individual people have personal accountability before God and a personal responsibility to respond to the Son with faith, repentance, and conversion. Many other verses in the New Testament reaffirm this; however, evangelicals take it further than Jesus did.

Evangelicals have a habit of mixing biblical truths with the mythos of America. Take this biblical idea of individual accountability before God and mix it with the middle-class individualism of the American dream, and you get something not found in the Bible. You get something that fluently speaks the language of middle-class America. You get a belief in the self-made man, the idea that you can achieve success by your own efforts apart from any supportive scaffolding, the belief that in this country, effort and commitment lead to prosperity. Prosperity, the dream says, is available to all so long as they are willing to put in the work. Mix this American dream with the evangelical emphasis on personal accountability, and what you get is an idol I call **individual responsibility**. *This idol says that people are responsible for their circumstances, they get what they deserve, societal forces play a minimal role, and programs like welfare and affirmative action exist in violation of this principle.*

This idea is not biblical. In fact, the opposite is biblical:

When you have eaten and are satisfied, praise the LORD your God for the good land he has given you. Be careful that you do not forget the LORD your God. . . .

Otherwise, when you eat and are satisfied, when you build fine houses and settle down, and when your herds and flocks grow large and your silver and gold increase and all you have is multiplied, then your heart will become proud and you will forget the LORD your God, who brought you out of Egypt, out of the land of slavery. He led you through the vast and dreadful wilderness, that thirsty and waterless land, with its venomous snakes and scorpions. He brought you water out of hard rock. He gave you manna to eat in the wilderness, something your ancestors had never known, to humble and test you so that in the end it might go well with you. You may say to yourself, "My power and the strength of my hands have produced this wealth for me." But remember the LORD your God, for it is *he who gives you the ability to produce wealth*, and so confirms his covenant, which he swore to your ancestors, as it is today.

DEUTERONOMY 8:10–18

If a person has produced wealth, it is because someone else, God, in this case, has built the scaffolding to make it possible. We can never take total credit for any of our outcomes.

In their hearts humans plan their course, but the LORD establishes their steps.

PROVERBS 16:9

Individual responsibility is an idol because it sounds like it represents God when it really doesn't. *Responsibility* is not the same as *accountability*. We are accountable to God for our choices and our actions, but we are not responsible for all outcomes. Jesus proves the opposite:

As he went along, he saw a man blind from birth. His disciples asked him, "Rabbi, who sinned, this man or his parents, that he was born blind?"

"Neither this man nor his parents sinned," said Jesus, "but this happened so that the works of God might be displayed in him."

JOHN 9:1–3

According to Jesus, neither the man nor his parents were *responsible* for his blindness. Some things, even negative things, just are the way they are. Maybe it's because God has a plan in mind to bring some miraculous healing, but maybe it's just because the world is broken. Scripture affirms that people will be held *accountable* for their choices, but they are not always *responsible* for their circumstances or outcomes. We will see below how destructive this idol can be.

Sexual Ethics

Evangelical Christians are preoccupied with sin, and even though we disagree on a lot of moral issues, the one universal truth among evangelicals is that *sexual immorality is bad*. This has become so central to evangelical teaching, it is the primary concern for nearly every Christian teenager and parent. Great anguish is related to the worry that I or someone I love has violated a sexual principle found in the Bible. Here's a passage I quoted before:

> The acts of the flesh are obvious: sexual immorality, impurity and debauchery; idolatry and witchcraft; hatred, discord, jealousy, fits of rage, selfish ambition, dissensions, factions and envy; drunkenness, orgies, and the like. I warn you, as I did before, that those who live like this *will not inherit the kingdom of God*.
>
> GALATIANS 5:19–21

Although all of us are definitely prone to hatred, jealousy, rage, idolatry, and more, the teenager and his or her parent worry most about the sexual immorality. Following suit, so does the entire evangelical establishment. There's truth in our doctrine, but still, in all the ways we have talked about it, emphasized it, and applied it, we have built it into an idol. It's the idol of **sexual ethics**. This idol tells us that even secular marriage should be between a man and a woman, that health classes in public schools should teach only abstinence, that people in the LGBTQ+ community should be met with ridicule, scorn, or discrimination, and that those who find themselves unexpectedly pregnant or with an STD are getting what they deserve. There might be biblical evidence for some of these sentiments, *for Christians*, but there are at least two ways evangelicals misapply God's will on the matter of human sexuality.

First, evangelical Christians conveniently apply these ethical commitments selectively. Although evangelicals sometimes address cohabitation and divorce among church members, and although evangelicals are increasingly starting to speak out against pornography and the other exploitative practices of the sex and entertainment industries, evangelicals still broadly ignore sexual sins committed by their allies, look the other way regarding sexual abuse *within* marriage, and are more opposed to the cancel culture of the #MeToo movement than to the hidden sexual harassment that caused so many women to suffer in silence for so long even under respected church leaders. For evangelicals, sexual ethics is an idol we worship only when it doesn't impact ourselves. This is a hypocritical application of God's will regarding human sexuality.

Second, a true understanding of *biblical sexuality* begins with the recognition that the sexual commands in Scripture are only for the people of God. To be blunt, they are *laws*, not *ethics*. Laws apply only to the people who live under that law, within that kingdom. I mentioned Romans 1 before, but I'll quote it now. Here's how God handles the sexuality of the people who live outside his kingdom. In short, he lets them do what they want.

> Therefore God gave them over in the sinful desires of their hearts to sexual impurity for the degrading of their bodies with one another.
>
> ROMANS 1:24

That means God, even though he considers these behaviors sinful, impure, and degrading, is doing nothing to hinder or prevent unbelievers from indulging their desires and engaging in whatever sexual behaviors they wish. Reading further in Romans 1 informs us that sexual behaviors bear their own consequences, implying that we don't need to build any social or legal consequences for them. What's even more important for the people of God, though, is what Paul says in the first verse of the following chapter, a verse that Christians rarely quote:

> You, therefore, have no excuse, you who pass judgment on someone else, for at whatever point you judge another, you are condemning yourself, because you who pass judgment do the same things.
>
> ROMANS 2:1

Add this to something Jesus said in the Sermon on the Mount:

"But I tell you that anyone who looks at a woman lustfully has already
committed adultery with her in his heart."

MATTHEW 5:28

The point is clear. Guilt for sexual immorality is upon the head of
every single individual, and we are hypocrites if we point the finger at
others. Furthermore, it is not their law. God has made it the law only
for those who dwell within his kingdom.

But among you there must not be even a hint of sexual immorality, or
of any kind of impurity, or of greed, because these are improper for
God's holy people.

EPHESIANS 5:3

Therefore, sexual ethics is an idol because of the hypocritical ways
we hold it, the level of importance we have given to it, and the ways we
try to force it on others beyond the scope of its actual biblical context.
Furthermore, since God specifically reserves his own judgment against
the sexual behaviors of the world, for us to speak in judgment is a direct
affront to his authority. The sexual ethic embraced by evangelicals misrepresents God and is an undeniable idol.

Spiritual First

This idea might be new to you, but it's an idol core to the evangelical
experience. From my youth, I adopted a belief that what matters most
of all is the *salvation of souls* by proclaiming the message of Jesus and
teaching people they must make a personal and individual decision to
embrace it. When I would hear another church (usually one we would
label "liberal") talk about something political or mention a politician by
name, I would feel disgust over their apparent rejection of the centrality
of the gospel. They were watering down the gospel or getting distracted
from the gospel by getting involved in merely political issues. When an
African American pastor was on a news show talking about the need for
more justice in our society, I wrote it off as political and decided in my
heart that he probably wasn't a real Christian.

Evangelicalism is filled with this kind of thinking. Even as I write this, Christian news is buzzing about a prominent pastor stating that Martin Luther King "was not a Christian at all."[14] All of this is an expression of an idol I now call **spiritual first**. The spiritual-first idol tells us that because spiritual issues matter so much more than other issues, any attention paid to non-spiritual matters is likely heretical. It says we should effectively ignore all other issues until the spiritual issues are resolved. In practice, it says worshiping God, holding accurate doctrine, getting people saved, and motivating them to get other people saved are the only real concerns. Everything else is politics, liberalism, watering down the gospel, a mark of heterodoxy, or at least not worth our time.

As before, this is an idol because it misrepresents God. As important as the salvation of a soul may be, it is not the only thing on the heart of God. Throughout the gospels, Jesus talks about salvation and eternal life quite a bit, but it is not his exclusive message, nor is it ever his *first* message. He talks much more about the moral obligations his followers have to the wider world. We've already considered the Sermon on the Mount, but another important passage on this topic shows up in Matthew 25 where Jesus explicitly tells people that their lack of tangible action on behalf of the poor and oppressed is what invalidates them for eternal life.

> "They also will answer, 'Lord, when did we see you hungry or thirsty or a stranger or needing clothes or sick or in prison, and did not help you?'
>
> "He will reply, 'Truly I tell you, whatever you did not do for one of the least of these, you did not do for me.'
>
> "Then they will go away to eternal punishment, but the righteous to eternal life."
>
> MATTHEW 25:44–46

In that chapter, people are kept out of heaven not because they failed to pray the right prayer or agree to the right doctrine. They are kept out of heaven because they failed to feed and clothe the poor! The evangelical will answer, "Oh, Jesus is talking about caring for the practical needs of people who are already believers. Since they are already saved,

Jesus can now talk about caring for them." However, I'm a person who believes the text of the Scripture is more important than my self-serving interpretations of it, and I also know this one:

> "You have heard that it was said, 'Love your neighbor and hate your enemy.' But I tell you, love your enemies and pray for those who persecute you, that you may be *children of your Father* in heaven. He causes his sun to rise on the evil and the good, and *sends rain on the righteous and the unrighteous.*"
>
> MATTHEW 5:43–45

Our Father cares for people *before* they are believers, and that's the hallmark of those who are his children. A Christian or church that focuses on what is spiritual to the exclusion of what is practical is a church that has embraced a false idol.

Anointed Intellect

Evangelical training contributed to me an oddly contradictory arrogance. I call it the idol of the **anointed intellect,** but an equally accurate moniker would be **Christian supremacy.** Even though much of Evangelicalism talks about the importance of humility, all that humility goes out the window when a secular truth claim comes into conflict with a truth claim held by some evangelical. This is an idol that is ever present in evangelical thinking, even though it is never directly mentioned.

Let me explain the doctrine foundational to this idol. According to evangelical doctrine, all people are sinners by nature and separated from relationship with God. Because of that separation, the human being's spiritual condition is dead, and their fleshly condition is corrupt. The doctrinal word for this is "depravity," and most Christians call it the "flesh" or the "sinful nature." Without the spiritual renewal and mental cleansing work of the Holy Spirit, everything in that person's life (thoughts, attitudes, opinions, behaviors) is tainted by their sin. However, those who make a personal commitment to Christ have their sins washed away, are granted a spiritual awakening by the indwelling presence of the Holy Spirit, and are further given a renewed mind that they might understand God's word and the truth in it. Here are two passages that undergird the doctrine:

> As for you, you were dead in your transgressions and sins, in which you used to live when you followed the ways of this world and of the ruler of the kingdom of the air, the spirit who is now at work in those who are disobedient.
>
> EPHESIANS 2:1–2

> The person without the Spirit does not accept the things that come from the Spirit of God but considers them foolishness, and cannot understand them because they are discerned only through the Spirit. The person with the Spirit makes judgments about all things, but such a person is not subject to merely human judgments, for, "Who has known the mind of the Lord so as to instruct him?" But we have the mind of Christ.
>
> 1 CORINTHIANS 2:14–16

It's a somewhat logical conclusion that only true Christians, cleansed of sin, with a regenerated spiritual life, have the clarity of mind, heart, and spirit to actually understand truth, and therefore, evangelicals tend to believe that true Christians have an anointed intellect—that is, a superior mind.

This is arrogance, and I'll get to why in a moment, but first, I have to address the most common verse evangelicals use on this topic:

> Do not conform to the pattern of this world, but be transformed by the renewing of your mind. Then you will be able to test and approve what God's will is—his good, pleasing and perfect will.
>
> ROMANS 12:2

This verse indicates that there is the "pattern of this world" and there is "God's will." Also, this verse implies that the two are in conflict with each other. Of course, Scripture reaffirms this all the time, but Christians who believe they have an anointed intellect take this concept a step further. They define "this world" to mean everyone who isn't a believer, and since non-Christians don't have a renewed mind, all intellectual pursuits by unbelievers are untrustworthy. Unbelievers can't help but operate from the "pattern of this world" and therefore must be actively working against "God's will." No matter what kind of truth we are talking about, be it journalism, science, or art, if the source is not Christian, the result cannot be fully true. More than that, if the source is not Christian, and if the fact at hand doesn't perfectly line up with existing Christian thought, the so-called truth should be vigorously *opposed* by the Christian community. After all, if the world is opposed to the will of God, then the world must be at core demonic. What Christian would ever want to endorse something that's literally from Satan!?

Although these last points sound extreme, they are actually quite common in Evangelicalism. As one example, consider how evangelicals treated Dr. Anthony Fauci, a well-respected and highly rewarded virologist, during the coronavirus pandemic of 2020 and beyond. Early on in the pandemic, Fauci said that universal mask-wearing was not advised because there was a shortage of masks among the health-care workers in our country, and we needed to direct our available masks to them. Evangelical Christians accepted that advice and touted the wisdom of Fauci at the time. However, less than a month later, after the virus was demonstrating a rapid and deadly spread throughout various parts of the United States, and after the hospitals had become well stocked with protective equipment, Fauci began to recommend that normal people avoid crowds and wear masks in public. Soon, local municipalities began to implement lockdowns that specifically targeted poorly ventilated, potentially crowded environments, a description that fits many church buildings. From a health and safety standpoint and from a science standpoint, it made total sense. From a biblical standpoint, it also made sense. According to the New Testament, the church has never been about the building, the size of the crowd, or the meeting time, and it has always been about sacrificing our own comfort for the sake of others. But lockdowns impinged on something Christians were used to doing (going to church), and suddenly, evangelicals started doing "investigative work" to identify all the ways Fauci was not a reliable source of information. He was vilified then, and the attacks on him continue to this day. I remember a moment sitting in a room full of evangelical pastors, and when I mentioned Fauci's name, they visibly recoiled as if I had said something favorable about Satan himself! Fauci was considered evil, and many Christians saw him as emblematic of a broader evil establishment that should be opposed. They didn't care about his credentials; he was from the world and was therefore an enemy.

The common evangelical thinks Christians alone, that is, true Christians, proper Christians, other evangelical Christians, evangelical Christians who share *my* perspective, and only Christians like that, have the ability to discern truth. If a truth claim doesn't come from an evangelical Christian like me, then it can't be trusted. Science loses. History loses. Cultural analysis loses. Journalism loses. Academic rigor loses. In that environment, conspiracy theories, pseudoscience, anecdotes, gut feelings, and "prophecies" win because the only thing that matters is whether the idea in question is coming from another Christian or confirms an idea that came from another Christian or confirms the way I, a Christian, already think. This is the *genetic fallacy*; it's *confirmation bias*; it's arrogant and wrong.

The anointed intellect is an idol as much as any other because it misrepresents God, and it misrepresents the image of God he placed in every single human being. Scripture claims that the mind of a believer is better equipped to understand *spiritual* matters or the *will of God*, but nowhere does it claim that Christians understand *math, medicine,* or *literature* better than unbelievers! God, who wired all humans with the ability to represent him in stewardship of this world and in relationship with each other, infused basic rationality into every single one of us (in varying degrees). Regardless of doctrinal belief, each individual person bears the image of God as a fundamental component of his or her being.

On top of that, the idea of an anointed intellect misrepresents the way God works in this world. God has never given his gifts only to his followers. God gives to every single individual what theological scholars call "common grace." It is the idea that God gives a measure of grace to each person regardless of their spiritual condition. As I quoted before,

"[God] causes his sun to rise on the evil and the good, and sends rain on the righteous and the unrighteous."

MATTHEW 5:45

God does not reserve his gifts for the believer alone, and the image of God has not been utterly destroyed in the natural man. A person's intellectual condition is not entirely linked to their spiritual condition, and Christians do not have a monopoly on truth, even if the modern evangelical church is inclined to believe otherwise.

Color Blindness

Riding the coattails of individual responsibility and spiritual-first sentiments, fundamental evangelical doctrine holds that every single person is *equally spiritually* accountable to an *objective* God. Since each of us has choices to make, and since each of us will be accountable for those choices, evangelicals presuppose that *circumstances* do not change our moral or spiritual obligations. Therefore, since all people have *equal* standing before God, and since circumstances do not modify our moral obligations, the natural conclusion is that earthly attributes like hair color, skin color, economic standing, family of origin, and more are irrelevant to your spiritual condition. Further, since evangelicals emphasize a person's spiritual condition over all other concerns, they believe that what's irrelevant spiritually should be considered irrelevant generally. If it doesn't affect your spiritual condition, it should be effectively ignored by *you* and by the people around you.

This is why evangelicals embrace an attitude of **color blindness**. We even consider ourselves racially enlightened by this attitude. After all, we can appeal to Dr. Martin Luther King Jr:

> I have a dream that my four little children will one day live in a nation where they will not be judged by the color of their skin, but by the content of their character.[15]

We think we are being noble and anti-racist by embracing this one line, but we have fully ignored other lines from that same speech:

The Negro still is not free. One hundred years later, the life of the Negro is still sadly crippled by the manacles of segregation and the chains of discrimination. One hundred years later, the Negro lives on a lonely island of poverty in the midst of a vast ocean of material prosperity. One hundred years later the Negro is still languished in the corners of American society and finds himself in exile in his own land. And so we've come here today to dramatize a shameful condition. In a sense we've come to our nation's capital to cash a check.[16]

King never advocated an ignorance of race or a denial of race. He was lamenting the tangible reality of racism's results. His dream of equal brotherhood could come only *after* the difficult work of affirmative, racial justice. Evangelicals lie to ourselves, pretending color blindness is a principle to embrace now and not a future dream to pursue. We ignore the fact that Jesus intentionally went out of his way to elevate the outcasts of his society—lepers, sinners, Samaritans, and more.

I used to strongly promote color blindness, and even though I now see it as self-righteous and ignorant, I also know that most evangelicals are holding to it in good faith. They simply haven't experienced the realities of racism in the world, they haven't listened to the pleas of Black people, and they have found biblical reasons for color blindness. To support it, they quote verses like the following:

> For all of you who were baptized into Christ have clothed yourselves with Christ. There is neither Jew nor Gentile, neither slave nor free, nor is there male and female, for you are all one in Christ Jesus.
>
> GALATIANS 3:27–28

The pious evangelical response to this verse is that color blindness is not a goal or a principle; it's just the Christian reality, and it's the *noble* worldview. Race, gender, and all other external attributes of a person are *spiritually* insignificant and should be ignored and dismissed as *socially* insignificant. By dismissing these attributes of people, American evangelicals build for themselves a self-righteous monoculture that looks indistinguishable from the majority culture, and they give themselves an excuse to downplay or disregard anyone who claims they have experienced the world differently.

Let me illustrate how this worked in my life. From my overly white experience, I developed a belief that racism was a problem only when Black people made it a problem. In my church context, if a Black person showed up, they were welcomed into the church family and treated warmly just like we treated everyone else. Therefore, I took it as proof that my church context wasn't racist. If a Black family chose to join us (it was rare, but it happened), that meant they didn't have a problem with us, and of course, we didn't have a problem with a new family joining our church. We loved it when people chose to join our church, but we were also clear in many ways that by choosing us, any family was affirming us, desiring to assimilate with us. As long as a family was willing to become like us, we were eager to receive them! In joining us, they were expressing approval of us. In welcoming them, we were proving we weren't racists, and silently, I convinced myself that Black people were the real racists. They had their all Black churches, their all Black TV shows, their all Black magazines, and their all Black beauty pageants. We were the noble ones; we were the color-blind. We were welcoming to all! Together with many other evangelicals, I believed that if people in our society could just get past race, we would all find harmony! I believed if Black people could just get over the past and choose to assimilate into the wider (white) culture and take on some individual responsibility, they would come to see that racism doesn't exist here.

However, I have come to learn that color blindness is its own kind of racism. Color blindness expects the minority to assimilate and accommodate itself to the majority. Color blindness disregards the experience of the minority and is dehumanizing to them by ignoring a core component of how they have experienced the world. Color blindness then judges the minority for failing to assimilate or for celebrating their uniqueness, and therefore color blindness *empowers* prejudice by giving the majority a "moral" reason for discriminating against the minority. Color blindness is certainly better than the horrifically racist practices of slavery and lynching, but it's still racism in its own way.

But more than all that, for a Christian, color blindness is an idol because it misrepresents God's love for the people he has made. People who aren't like me have experiences that are unlike mine, and I will never understand them until I recognize that my perspective is limited. Any attempt at color blindness will always result in me viewing *their* experience through *my* perspective, and that is intrinsically dehumanizing and delegitimizing to them. By nature, this attitude rejects the image of God *in them*, and it prevents me from loving them *as myself*. Furthermore, color blindness does not represent the character of God or his will for humanity. God created the diversity of human *biology* and sympathizes with us in the diversity of human *experience*. The incarnation of Christ proves that God accommodates himself to us and enters into our experience. Therefore, rather than ignoring or disregarding a person's racial experience, love calls me to *enter* it as much as I can so that I can develop sympathy, compassion, and a Christlike incarnational relationship with them.

Cultural Conservatism

And finally, ever present in evangelical Christianity is the idea of "keeping the word," that is, obeying the Bible. To explain what that means, I need to discuss how evangelicals view the Bible, and I need to revisit the strange relationship evangelicals have with the concept of obedience.

First, evangelicals view the Bible as the authoritative word of God, and most evangelicals also believe that the text of Scripture was fully without error when it was originally written—it is *inerrant* in the *original manuscripts*. Evangelicals believe the text of the Bible is the literal breath of God.

> All Scripture is God-breathed and is useful for teaching, rebuking,
> correcting and training in righteousness, so that the servant of God
> may be thoroughly equipped for every good work.
>
> 2 TIMOTHY 3:16–17

This perspective requires evangelical pastors to focus on *author intent* when trying to teach the text, and we encourage people to do the same when they are studying it themselves. This also implies that the oldest understanding of the text is best. Evangelicals take a conservative perspective and are generally skeptical of progressive or liberal interpretations. This is how evangelicals view the Bible, but this perspective also tempts evangelicals to view all old documents through that same interpretive lens. For many, even the US Constitution should be seen through the lens of original intent. Additionally, our preference for older interpretations leads us to prefer older behaviors, older perspectives, and older rules. Biblical conservatism easily morphs into social conservatism.

Second, let's revisit the evangelical relationship to obedience. Remember, the narrow evangelical version of the gospel says that faith (commitment to correct doctrine) can get you a place in heaven, but works (good behavior) cannot. There is biblical support for this, of course, and I've discussed it earlier, but now, I need to expose where this thinking leads. When you say faith matters more than works, you imply that doctrine matters more than behavior, but, since no evangelical believes behavior is pointless, you have to decide which behaviors actually matter and how to prioritize them. There are religious behaviors like going to church, getting baptized, praying a salvation prayer, or speaking in tongues, but there are also social behaviors like abstaining from alcohol, reading a specific translation of the Bible, or voting conservatively. We have to prioritize them, but we don't agree. We each have our own moral code, and we point fingers at others for the styles of music they embrace, the quantity of alcohol they allow, the translations of the Bible they use, the standards of modesty they promote, and more. Nevertheless, we know we are called to be a unified body of Christ engaged with the world, and therefore, if we are to have any unity, we need to find some lowest common denominator of morality, and we found it by focusing on a few *big sins*, such as sexual immorality and substance abuse.

Therefore, when evangelicals started working together as a cultural movement, we tossed our conservative approach to things of importance and all our different moralities into the same fire, and a shiny gold idol emerged. It's called **cultural conservatism**, a doctrine that something in the past is better than today, that progress is suspect, and that a universal moral code compatible with Christianity can apply to all people at all times.

We don't always use the words "cultural conservatism." In fact, most evangelical preachers prefer to use two other words, "salt" and "light," but when those words are on their tongue, social conservatism is often in their heart. Evangelicals tell themselves that "salt" means we should *preserve the world from the forces of corruption*, and "light" means we should *shine a revealing light into the places of darkness* (evil) in the world. Practically speaking, evangelicals think the goal of being salt and light is to enforce Christian morals on the world around us, using whatever means we can. Christian culture and Christian morality would slow down the societal rot just like salt preserves food. Shining a Christian spotlight on social sins would bring them to everyone's attention, shame those who would commit such sin, and hopefully bring about their repentance.

Moreover, in the hands of evangelical Christian pastors like myself, the salt and light metaphors get mixed with a bit of American mythology. Many evangelicals believe a myth that this nation was founded in some way as a Christian nation and that Christian culture is this nation's original culture. Therefore, being salt and light means evangelicals view themselves as conservers of a Christian national heritage and culture. In practice, though, this work of conservation is little different from simply pushing our moral hypocrisies on the broader society around us.

This is idolatry. Cultural conservatism misrepresents God's will for his people in the world. Remember how Jesus ended his statement about salt and light:

> "In the same way, let your light shine before others, that they may see your good deeds and glorify your Father in heaven."
>
> MATTHEW 5:16

Turning salt into a preservative and light into a spotlight might accurately represent the physics of salt and light, but it misrepresents Jesus's intent by the metaphor. Worse, it leads directly to the misunderstanding that Christians are supposed to shame the culture and restrain the culture. Getting the metaphor wrong is at the heart of cultural conservatism. No Scripture ever instructs Christians to create or promote Christian behaviors in the broader society or to leverage political power to do so. Of course, as I have previously shown, there are a few values that Christians *should* promote in the broader society, but those values do not include specific Christian *behaviors*. Furthermore, there are behaviors that should be part of a *Christian's* life, but Scripture never tells us to enforce or even promote those behaviors outside the context of the Christian community.

TEMPLES

While the aforementioned idols are ones that grow directly out of evangelical doctrines, they are not the only structures of wood, hay, and straw we evangelical pastors have been building. The human tendency is not to simply build an idol but to build temples to house the idol and systems to support its worship. Then, once the temple is built, we give it the same level of importance as the idol it contains, sometimes worshiping the temple itself. The previous items are idols in the sense that Christians actually believe they represent God and his will for us somehow, but the following items are temples in the sense that they insulate and protect the idols. The previous items are treated with special care and are mentioned quietly, but the following items have ornate outsides; they are the things Christians say more loudly; they make up the content of our public policies. We would never make a law that everyone should be individually responsible, but we *can* make a law that a young, single, pregnant mom must bring her baby to term and pay all the consequences of her indiscretions. Nonetheless, the temples are misrepresentations of God just the same and deserve tearing down.

Pro-life

To support individual responsibility, our sexual ethics, and cultural conservatism, we built a temple called **pro-life**. As I said before, a more accurate name for this position would be antiabortion, because many things that favor life are missing from the pro-life platform. Quoting myself in the earlier chapter, I said,

> *For some reason*, evangelicals are comfortable with activism that opposes abortion. For some reason, that activism has been sanctified,

but any activism related to racial equity, the elimination of the death penalty, the expansion of health care, adoption, or financial assistance to moms is disallowed.

In that chapter, I didn't say what the reason was, but I will now. It's the worship of our idols.

Pro-life sounds like it would be against the death penalty, but the other idols say criminals should pay for their actions even with their lives. Pro-life sounds like it might be in favor of universal medical care, but individual responsibility says people should be responsible for their own medical needs and that parents alone should bear the responsibility for the expenses of their children. Pro-life sounds like it might be in favor of stronger restrictions on deadly weapons, but individual responsibility says people are responsible to protect themselves and the people around them, and cultural conservatism reminds us that ages ago, people needed guns. Pro-life sounds like it might be in favor of medical and financial support for the pregnant woman, but sexual ethics calls her reprobate and the other idols want her to pay for her indiscretions. Pro-life sounds like it might want to provide material support for the young family, but cultural conservatism and individual responsibility want to blame the parents for their poor planning.

There are many things that promote life and elevate human dignity, but most of those things don't adequately serve our idols. Opposing abortion does. Many other life-affirming actions a government might take infringe on some principle of individual responsibility, sexual ethics, or cultural conservatism and therefore are removed from this temple. Please don't misunderstand me. I still see it as the responsibility of parents to take care of their children whether born or unborn, and I see it as the responsibility of the government to dignify the life of every person, born and unborn. However, we have to admit that so long as pro-life is only committed to being against abortion, it's a deceptive temple constructed to protect false idols.

This is an especially attractive temple for evangelical Christians because it seems to have strong biblical support. The Bible affirms infants are designed by and known by God even in the womb (Ps. 139); it affirms that the death of an unborn infant is equivalent to murder in the same passage where the principle "life for life" is mentioned (Exod. 21:22–25); also, the Bible frequently supports the death penalty as a universal principle that extends beyond ancient Israel (Gen. 9:6, Lev. 24:17–23); and as mentioned above, there is ample evidence that people bear responsibility to take care of their family and their own financial needs. In other words, being against abortion sounds more biblical than other life-affirming policies.

However, pro-life as an agenda that focuses only on abortion policy is still idolatrous because it misrepresents the God who loves humans from the cradle to the grave. There is ample evidence in Scripture that God opposes the practice of abortion, but there is ample evidence that a God-honoring approach would embrace many more life-affirming policies than are allowed in the pro-life temple. Consider the words of Jesus in the Sermon on the Mount where he undoes the "eye for eye" principle while also raising serious questions about self-defense:

> "You have heard that it was said, 'Eye for eye, and tooth for tooth.' But I tell you, do not resist an evil person. If anyone slaps you on the right cheek, turn to them the other cheek also."
>
> MATTHEW 5:38–39

Consider the account in John 8 where Jesus unravels the death penalty while also taking up the cause of the adulterous woman:

> When they kept on questioning him, he straightened up and said to them, "Let any one of you who is without sin be the first to throw a stone at her." Again he stooped down and wrote on the ground.
>
> At this, those who heard began to go away one at a time, the older ones first, until only Jesus was left, with the woman still standing there. Jesus straightened up and asked her, "Woman, where are they? Has no one condemned you?"
>
> "No one, sir," she said.
>
> "Then neither do I condemn you," Jesus declared. "Go now and leave your life of sin."
>
> JOHN 8:7–11

God calls his people to be advocates for human dignity and justice, and those efforts should include all the ways we can care about and support the lives of others. Certainly our efforts to aid the weak and vulnerable should include the cause of the unborn, but advocacy for the unborn without equal advocacy for the pregnant mom is not being an advocate for the weak and vulnerable. Rather, it is a prejudicial advocacy prioritizing one specific life over all the concerns of other lives. I'm not saying it's easy to compare the life of the mother with the life of the unborn child. I'm saying Christians should be equal advocates for both! God in heaven loves both the mother and the child, and therefore a false priority of one over the other misrepresents the heart of the one who made them both.

The pro-life temple is idolatrous also because it misrepresents the will of God for the activism of his followers. Ages ago, Christians made a name for themselves in the empire of Rome by rescuing babies who had been left at the outskirts of towns to die of exposure. Likewise today, a group of Christians who are opposed to abortion could stand in front of an abortion clinic and offer to pay each mother's medical bills, cover her day-care costs, or even adopt her baby. That would be newsworthy! *Good news* even. That would be flavorsome and illuminating, salt and light, in a world that needs both. But we have instead taken the approach of aggressive picket lines and legislation. By promoting the pro-life agenda the way we have, we have embraced an activism that can't be supported by Scripture and have begun to worship in an unbiblical temple.

Personal or Religious Freedom

To further promote our idols, especially individual responsibility, we built the temple of **personal freedom**. It promotes a doctrine that each individual should be unhindered by external forces, taxes should be low, and government should be small. Anything that limits a person's ability to express his or her autonomy is not allowed entrance in this temple. However, like the other idols we have seen, evangelical Christians are hypocritical when it comes to applying this principle.

Sometimes, evangelicals apply it to Christians and unbelievers equally. Here are just a few examples. We say that none of us should be forced by the government to provide for the poor because we think *all* people should freely choose to give money to churches and Christian nonprofits so Christians can willingly care for the poor and so the government can stay out of it. When it comes to parental freedom, we say *all* parents should be able to choose their schools, choose their vaccination schedules, and make their own decisions regarding public health measures. When it comes to firearms, we are again in favor of freedom for all people. We say *all* people should be able to arm themselves to defend their freedoms.

However, we evangelicals are just as likely to apply the idea of personal freedom differently to ourselves when it benefits us. After all, we also need to house the idol of anointed intellect. In this case, the temple gets renamed to **religious freedom**. But it should more accurately be called **Christian preference**. Everyone should be free, but we are special and should be treated so. We go to court to defend the rights of Christians (and only Christians) to discriminate against others for their beliefs. We think Christian businesspeople should be exempt from federal requirements concerning health care for employees. We think Christians should be able to worship when and how they want. We think Christians should be able to say whatever they want in whatever forum they choose without fear of being canceled. We think the world should make an exception for us because Christians are the ones "speaking the truth."

These principles are illogical in their fundamental inconsistency, and they represent a level of individual arrogance that should be anathema for the people of God, but worse, they misrepresent God and his will for his people. Neither personal freedom nor religious freedom is ever described as a value in Scripture. Dignity and justice are biblical values, but freedom and independence are not. Moreover, both Testaments promote the idea of people using their own power and authority to *defend the dignity of other people* even when upholding the dignity of another results in injustice or indignity *to themselves.* The whole idea of defending one's own personal or religious freedom is antithetical to the teaching of Jesus. We've seen this instruction before, but it bears repeating. In Matthew 5, he commands his followers to lay down their own freedoms even to the point of letting others exploit them!

> "But I tell you, do not resist an evil person. If anyone slaps you on the right cheek, turn to them the other cheek also. And if anyone wants to

sue you and take your shirt, hand over your coat as well. If anyone forces
you to go one mile, go with them two miles. Give to the one who asks
you, and do not turn away from the one who wants to borrow from you."

MATTHEW 5:39–42

An important Christian value is *human dignity*, and the related
Christian behavior is to promote the dignity of *others*. **Personal freedom** sounds similar, and **religious freedom** sounds noble, but they are
false representations of true Christian values.

Blessing (Capitalism)

To promote and protect *all* our other idols, we built an ornate temple
that I call the temple of **blessing**. The nuances of this temple are terribly important to understand, and they are deeply enmeshed in the
American subconscious, because they blend so well with the material
concepts of capitalism.

The doctrine of this temple says that *if people do the right thing,
God will bless them, and if they don't do the right thing, they will get what
they deserve.*

This sounds exactly like the popular idol of individual responsibility,
but actually it's much worse. In the temple of blessing, we apply the doctrine in reverse, and we use it to justify even terrible behaviors. Here's
how it works. If a person is "blessed" (usually identified by some American metric of success like financial wealth, or in the case of a church,
offerings and attendance), that success is taken as evidence they did
the right thing or are doing the right thing. After all, God wouldn't bless
something wrong, right? Their blessing proves they have God's approval,
doesn't it? Because of this, evangelical Christians often value rich people
more than poor people and can even feel disdain for poor people because their poverty proves they are under God's judgment. Why should
we help them? After all, who are we to intervene in God's judgment?

Very few evangelical Christians will admit to this line of thinking,
but it shows up often and repeatedly in the context of churches, individual relationships, and even politics too. Christians will talk about how
God is blessing a church when the attendance is on the rise even if the

church is doing something otherwise outside of God's will. Perhaps the pastor is an abusive person, perhaps the sermons are likewise aggressive and abusive, and perhaps people in the church are being wounded or wounding others, but if the church is growing, people will say, "Look at the fruit." On the other hand, perhaps the pastor is loving and caring, and the sermons are biblical but boring. The church might decline in attendance or funding, and more people will leave the church assuming it is no longer under God's blessing because, they say, "There is no fruit." Regardless of any other metric, decreasing attendance then becomes the reason for people to leave, which of course decreases attendance even more. The burden of being a pastor in that climate is heavy, and the pressure to do what must be done to regain the favor of the people is enough to make a diamond.

It's true outside the church too. Perhaps a politician is evil in nearly every sense of the word, but if he is wealthy (and convincingly conservative, of course), evangelical Christians will point to the wealth as an example of God's blessing *in spite of* the moral failings. A man might have obtained billions through deceit and the exploitation of others, but if he's conservative in some important policy or tied to the Republican party, evangelicals will conclude he has God's blessing and will vote for him. Strangely, though, if the politician is a liberal, evangelicals will point to the wealth as an example of worldly corruption.

This blessing rhetoric is not applied equally in all circumstances.

Worst of all, this rhetoric is often used to justify the inequities and atrocities of the United States itself. Evangelical Christians embrace a strange kind of nationalism that is based upon viewing our national prosperity as God's blessing on this nation. Because we are the richest nation, the conclusion is that we are incredibly blessed by God, ergo God must be incredibly pleased with us. This has incredibly dangerous implications.

For many evangelical Christians, the state of the economy determines God's pleasure with our nation. Therefore, for many evangelical Christians, all you have to do is to point to a time in our national history when the economy was good, and you'll have a time when God was pleased with us. If the economy is strong now, it's because our *current* state is the state God is blessing and we need to conserve it. Any progressive moves might break what God is obviously pleased with today. Also, if we can find any times of great financial success in the past, maybe we should actually try to move backward to rediscover those days. Maybe America's greatness is in the past. Maybe we should try to make America great again!

Very few evangelicals would admit to worshiping in the temple of blessing as I have described it, but ask any evangelical on the National Day of Prayer what they are praying for, and you'll hear the not-so-coded answer as they quote from 2 Chronicles:

> "If my people, who are called by my name, will humble themselves and pray and seek my face and *turn* from their wicked ways, then I will hear from heaven, and I will forgive their sin and will *heal their land*."
>
> 2 CHRONICLES 7:14

The unspoken (and sometimes spoken) belief of nearly every evangelical who reads that verse is that our nation needs to repent and turn (back) to God so he will return his blessings to us. I can hardly contain myself when I hear people misuse Scripture that way. They think this is a passage about making Christianity the national morality when really it's a passage about the people of God needing to leave their idolatry.

Read the verse in context, and you see God promising restoration *after judgment*. If they fail him, he will send them into exile, but if they later turn back to him, he will bring them back. Do you know your Old Testament history? Do you know that the people of Israel eventually *did* fail God? Do you know *how* the people failed God? Isaiah tells us.

> "Declare to my people their rebellion and to the descendants of Jacob their sins. For day after day they seek me out; they seem eager to know my ways, as if they were a nation that does what is right and has not forsaken the commands of its God. They ask me for just decisions and seem eager for God to come near them. 'Why have we fasted,' they say, 'and you have not seen it? Why have we humbled ourselves, and you have not noticed?' Yet on the day of your fasting, you do as you please and exploit all your workers. . . .

"Is not this the kind of fasting I have chosen: to loose the chains of injustice and untie the cords of the yoke, to set the oppressed free and break every yoke? Is it not to share your food with the hungry and to provide the poor wanderer with shelter—when you see the naked, to clothe them, and not to turn away from your own flesh and blood? Then your light will break forth like the dawn, and your healing will quickly appear; then your righteousness will go before you, and the glory of the LORD will be your rear guard. Then you will call, and the LORD will answer; you will cry for help, and he will say: Here am I."

ISAIAH 58:1–9

Despite their religious activity, they failed to care for the poor in their midst! The National Day of Prayer movement drips with Isaiah's irony as they call Christians to fast and pray but say little to nothing about the injustice and economic exploitation pervasive in *our* land! We can't see the irony because we are standing too deeply in the idolatrous temple of blessing.

This temple is explicitly antibiblical. God never said that prosperity is proof of his favor even if he sometimes promised it as a reward. Before the people of Israel entered the promised land, the land was already quite prosperous. Did that mean God was happy with the Canaanites? According to the book of Joshua he wasn't. What about David? From an earthly perspective, David was the least blessed of all his brothers, but he was the one God chose as king.

More than that, this idea of wealth being an indication of God's favor is directly countermanded in the book of James. See how James separates the idea of blessing from human wealth and castigates both the rich and those who show favor to the rich:

But the rich should take pride in their humiliation—since they will pass away like a wild flower. For the sun rises with scorching heat and withers the plant; its blossom falls and its beauty is destroyed. In the same way, the rich will fade away even while they go about their business. . . .

If you show special attention to the man wearing fine clothes and say, "Here's a good seat for you," but say to the poor man, "You stand there" or "Sit on the floor by my feet," have you not discriminated among yourselves and become judges with evil thoughts?

JAMES 1:10–11; 2:3–4

The focus on earthly blessings, prosperity, success, and wealth is unimaginably dangerous. Not only is success a false method of seeing God's favor on a person, but it also allows us to excuse immoral behaviors whether by a leader, a group, or an entire society. If the economy is going up, we view it as *God's blessing* even if we are actually on a path toward God's judgment. This temple must be brought down.

Political Conservatism

And finally, to promote all these other idols, we built the idol of **political conservatism** or to just be frank, **Republicanism**. This is different from cultural conservatism, because it is bound not to a set of doctrines but to a political party that has for decades promised Christians it would serve their other idols and fund their other temples. Cultural conservatism is the idea that our whole culture needs to move back to a previous morality centered on Christian ethics, one that favors the Christian worldview. However, political conservatism is the temple that says we can accomplish our Christian goals by aligning ourselves with powerful non-Christians who also want to restrict social progress or even move it backward. *Political* conservatism is the temple where we embrace the politicians and the political party that promises to support our favorite idols too.

Over the past forty or fifty years especially, white evangelicals in the United States have banded together to leverage political power to promote these idols and temples in their various forms, and though there isn't anything wrong with using our voice collectively as the church to promote things that are truly on God's heart, there is something terribly wrong with forming an uncritical alliance with a platform that supports only the idols and temples of Evangelicalism without embracing the authentic values of Jesus. The evangelical allegiance to the Republican party and to the political conservative platform is itself idolatrous. We have embraced an allegiance to whichever party promises to promote the worship of personal freedom, individual responsibility, pro-life, and cultural conservatism, the party that pats us on the back for our anointed intellect, the party that promises more blessing for us. That party is currently the Republican party, and our allegiance has made us complicit in all the policies of the Republican party that disadvantage the poor, perpetuate gun violence, encourage police violence, dehumanize immigrants, and reject refugees. We put up with fiscal irresponsibility, out of control governmental debt, expensive wars, and unethical leaders simply because *we have decided that we need the particular political power that the Republican party promises us.* In my evangelical circles, even voting for a Democrat once is seen as turning from the faith and is likely to initiate a spiritual intervention from friends.

Political conservatism is a false temple. The entire notion of political power might be an idol in itself, but the alliance with political conservatism and specifically the Republican party is most certainly an idolatrous one. No earthly allegiance to any earthly group other than the body of Christ itself is proper for a Christian. We might choose to cooperate at times with earthly groups, but *allegiances* to those groups are idolatrous, because at best they can represent only a small portion of God's will for his people.

NOW LIBERATED!

All of this false worship I have mentioned used to be my own. These things used to be obvious Christian ideals to me, and I can still see why other evangelicals view them as obvious Christian values, but every idol that has ever been erected made sense to the people who built it. Every temple ever built made sense to the builders. Still, the time is long overdue for Christians to step out of these false temples and turn their backs on these false idols. None of these false doctrines is endorsed by Scripture, and none of them represents the heart of God. It's time for us to grind these idols to bits, set the temples on fire, and get back to what Jesus has actually called us to be and to do in this world.

For modern evangelicals, a life without these idols and temples seems scary. What will we do if the world goes to hell in a handbasket? What will we do if the persecution of the church gets stronger? What will we do if socialism erases individual prosperity in this country? What will we do if open immigration or affirmative action means my son can't get a good job? (The list of fears is long, I think, because the lack of faith is real.) However, if you and I rid ourselves of these idols, we will be liberated to be fully engaged Christian citizens in a world that needs our salt and light, a world that is desperate for a uniquely Christian form of social engagement, an activism that represents our Creator and looks like Jesus himself!

Once we manage to tear down our high places, temples, and the idols therein, we will be able to see clearly what an authentic Christian response to our current world might be! Consider these potential benefits:

- If a politician claims to be a follower of Christ but fails to display Christlikeness in their actions or decision making, we are liberated to vote against them regardless of their political associations.
- If a politician supports policies we don't like but nevertheless has an overall position of elevating the dignity of individuals and is committed to working for justice for all, we are liberated to vote for that person regardless of their few disagreeable policies.
- If a politician we voted for is embracing a policy or position that is outside the parameters of our key values, we are liberated to speak out against that policy or position even if we still intend to vote for them in the next election for other reasons.
- If a new study (climate science, evolution, critical race theory) arises and challenges our previous understanding of the world, we are liberated to learn about it, accept its truths, and to grow from it.
- If it's Black History Month, we are liberated to attend events and learn Black history without feeling that we are violating principles of color blindness.
- If the government puts forth a particular public health measure or antidiscrimination law, we are liberated to go along with it, because protecting personal freedom and the enforcement of cultural conservatism are no longer our guiding principles.
- If the world around us falls into rampant sexual promiscuity, we are liberated to let it happen. We can and will focus on our own sexual

integrity, we can and will speak with our brothers and sisters in Christ about theirs, and we can and will speak out against the exploitation that so often accompanies sexual promiscuity in the society, even coming to the aid of the exploited, but we are free of the burden to police the sexual ethics of our society.

- If the world around us begins to act in ways that appear detrimental to the mission of the church, we are liberated to not worry about it! We don't need to worry about cancel culture or antidiscrimination laws because we are too focused on promoting human dignity and equity wherever we can, too focused on living like Jesus! And if our authentic Christian behavior ever incites the ire of the world, we are free to embrace persecution without feeling the need to fight for religious freedom. We are free to keep shining our winsome light and sprinkling our life-enhancing salt while hoping that the world around us will eventually see our good deeds and glorify our Father in heaven!

The recognition and rejection of the idols associated with evangelical Christianity is the key step in liberating evangelicals like me to be authentically Christian and properly engaged in this current world.

If you are with me, if you too agree that the time is ripe for Christians to discard our false idols and move into a brand-new world of biblical truth, moral accuracy, and social engagement that brings glory to our Father in heaven, then let's press on. We have only one thing left to do, and it is to consider what living this way means for us and our churches. In the next chapter, I'll address the practical matters of what we need to be doing about it, calling us to embrace a new kind of mission.

CHAPTER 12

Mission and Strategy

THE WORK TO GET HERE has been difficult. We have wrestled with defining the foundation of the Christian faith, revealed how our divisions
damage our ability to even understand that foundation, let alone build
on it, confessed ways that we have built poorly on top of that foundation, and have set ourselves a vision for what could and should be.
Nevertheless, along the way, I have most certainly offended many of
my evangelical brothers and sisters by calling their deep convictions
idolatry. Additionally, even for those who agree with me, we will still
disagree about what we should do about it. The words I have shared
seem innately divisive regardless of my intent.

Am I contributing to disunity?

Sitting in that room years ago as the elders of the church accused me
of being too political, one of their main points was that I was bringing
division to the church. The idea of church division pains me deeply.
After all, the New Testament is powerfully clear on the point that the
body of Christ is to be unified. It was the central thing on Jesus's heart
the night before he went to the cross.

> "My prayer is not for them alone. I pray also for those who will believe
> in me through their message, that all of them may be one, Father, just
> as you are in me and I am in you. May they also be in us so that the
> world may believe that you have sent me. I have given them the glory
> that you gave me, that they may be one as we are one—I in them and
> you in me—so that they may be brought to complete unity. Then the

world will know that you sent me and have loved them even as you have loved me."

JOHN 17:20–23

It was top of mind for the apostle Paul.

Therefore if you have any encouragement from being united with Christ, if any comfort from his love, if any common sharing in the Spirit, if any tenderness and compassion, then make my joy complete by being like-minded, having the same love, being one in spirit and of one mind. Do nothing out of selfish ambition or vain conceit. Rather, in humility value others above yourselves, not looking to your own interests but each of you to the interests of the others.

PHILIPPIANS 2:1–4

Christian unity was also a primary reason I got into pastoral ministry to begin with.

So, if Christians are supposed to be united as the one body of Christ, isn't it better to just let everyone have their own opinion? Why would we speak up and draw attention to issues that divide us? Isn't the mission of the church to get people saved and not deal with all these politics and matters of opinion?

Well, that's a loaded set of questions, isn't it?

It's too convenient for us to divide ourselves from others who don't share our exact formulation of the gospel, or to divide ourselves from Christians who do or don't agree with us on some pressing cultural issue. It's too easy for me to separate from you and blame you for holding such a divisive opinion. (I always find it hypocritical when a person leaves a church with the accusation that someone *else* is being divisive.) Perhaps divisiveness is a bad metric. Perhaps a better metric is to figure out where the boundaries of the Christian family and mission really are.

When it comes to living out the gospel in the current world, we've addressed some important questions, but one remains:

Where is there room for disagreement?

I think it will help us to understand the difference between the overall *mission* of the body of Christ and an individual church's *strategy*. In my view, there is no room for disagreement over the mission of the universal church, but there is a great deal of room for differences over any specific church's strategy.

MISSION

Every church will use different words to describe its mission, but the overall mission of the church is given to us by Jesus in the two passages we call the Great Commandment and the Great Commission.

In Matthew's account, these two concepts are recorded like this:

THE GREAT COMMANDMENT

Jesus replied: "'Love the Lord your God with all your heart and with all your soul and with all your mind.' This is the first and greatest commandment. And the second is like it: 'Love your neighbor as yourself.' All the Law and the Prophets hang on these two commandments."

MATTHEW 22:37–40

THE GREAT COMMISSION

"Therefore go and make disciples of all nations, baptizing them in the name of the Father and of the Son and of the Holy Spirit, and teaching them to obey everything I have commanded you. And surely I am with you always, to the very end of the age."

MATTHEW 28:19–20

Even though I've spent a good amount of time promoting proper Christian activism, the essential values of that activism—speaking for human dignity and justice, embracing what is good and true, and caring for the Earth and its inhabitants—are all merely the non-religious outgrowth of these two fundamental commands Jesus gave his followers. Living like Jesus dovetails with living as image-bearers caring for the Earth and other image-bearers, with valuing truth and goodness, and with loving our neighbors as ourselves. Nevertheless, we can't forget the overtly spiritual components of our mandate. We can't forget our *mission*.

The mission of the church requires at minimum these things: loving God, loving people, sharing the message of Jesus, and training others to follow him and do the same. All the other instructions Jesus gave—to live in purity, to be salt and light in the world, to care for the weak, to speak out against hypocrisy, and more—fall under the umbrella of these two passages. However, it would be wrong of any church or any Christian to accept these basic statements only in principle without ever letting them form the core of their actual behavior. "Love your neighbor as yourself" is not a statement for a banner. It's an action we must do. Therefore, even though these two passages form the foundation of any Christian's and any church's understanding of the mission, the mission is not completed by a doctrinal definition. Each church must adopt a *strategy* regarding these statements of mission, and that strategy must encompass all that I have covered so far—a gospel that is both accurate and transformative, an activism that properly represents Christ to the world, and a discipleship that tears down the wood, hay, and straw of earthly idols and all allegiances that fight against our allegiance to Christ. Because strategy is intrinsically contextual, it will be different for different churches and different individual Christians, but it must still be made of good materials on the right foundation. What does it take to build a good strategy, unique to a specific church, built on the firm foundation of our Christ-given mission?

STRATEGY

Early on in the book of Acts, it becomes clear that certain aspects of the life of the church were open to the judgment of the early leaders. They developed practical strategies regarding the selection of new leaders, caring for the poor in their fellowship, responding to persecution, welcoming gentiles, and more.

Consider the problem of selecting a replacement for Judas. Peter took the lead, saying,

> "Therefore it is necessary to choose one of the men who have been with us the whole time the Lord Jesus was living among us, beginning from John's baptism to the time when Jesus was taken up from us. For one of these must become a witness with us of his resurrection."
>
> ACTS 1:21–22

Nothing in Jesus's teaching gave any guidelines regarding how to replace Judas. Peter and the others simply came up with their own strategy and acted on it.

We see it again in Acts 6:

> In those days when the number of disciples was increasing, the Hellenistic Jews among them complained against the Hebraic Jews because their widows were being overlooked in the daily distribution of food. So the Twelve gathered all the disciples together and said, "It would not be right for us to neglect the ministry of the word of God in order to wait on tables. Brothers and sisters, choose seven men from among you who are known to be full of the Spirit and wisdom. We will turn this responsibility over to them and will give our attention to prayer and the ministry of the word."
>
> ACTS 6:1–4

Again, there was no guidance given by Jesus regarding how to make sure Hebraic widows and Hellenistic widows were treated equitably. They knew equity was important. Jesus taught that. But they had to develop an implementation strategy to make equity happen.

Then, as we have seen in Acts 15, the leaders of the church collectively developed a strategy for how to welcome gentiles into the faith even though doing so was violating the existing value system (circumcision) of many Christians. Their strategy for the gentiles discarded circumcision but included other recommendations. It was a sensible strategy for the time, but it wasn't universal or forever.

Furthermore, at the end of Acts 15, Paul and Barnabas had a disagreement not about the need to disciple people or to spread the gospel but about which of those two things they would do *next*—which *strategy* they would employ. Paul wanted to get back on the road, spreading the gospel far and wide, but Barnabas wanted to rehabilitate his cousin. They both had the same mission to make disciples who looked like Jesus, but their strategies were incompatible. As a result, they went in different directions, and we now praise God for that separation. Barnabas's work transformed John Mark (who wrote the Gospel of Mark), and God did great things through Paul's next journey (including the discipleship of Luke, who ended up writing two books himself). Think of all we might have lost if Paul and Barnabas hadn't embraced incompatible strategies!

The early church is filled with examples like this where different contexts and different needs result in different strategies, and that's a good thing. Our modern strategies should follow their example. We need to take what it means to follow Jesus and contextualize it to the moment we're in. Here are some guidelines and suggestions for doing that.

Strategy Guidelines

First, and most obviously, Christians and churches should employ strategies that recognize and live out our core Christian values. A strategy that attempts to advocate for environmental concerns while not addressing human dignity is not a good strategy. Likewise, a strategy that encourages Christians to pursue some activism goal while avoiding personal holiness is not a good strategy.

Second, Christians and churches should be clear about which values are internal and which values should be promoted in the wider world. Any strategy that knowingly or unknowingly attempts to press an internal value upon the broader society is a bad strategy. On the flip side, any strategy that prevents an individual Christian or any church from embracing proper Christian activism is a bad strategy.

Third, regardless of all other strategic choices, Christians and churches should categorically reject false idols and their doctrines and never allow them to influence their strategy or infect their mission. It's desperately important that Christians remove the idols and temples from their lives, and therefore, it's additionally important that we remove them from our strategies. Any infiltration of an idolatrous perspective into our strategy will reinforce that idol to ourselves and our fellow believers, and it will also misrepresent our God to the watching world. Not only do the idols lead us astray from our Father but they also dilute or dissolve our witness of the one true God.

That still leaves a broad swath of room for disagreement over strategic decisions like how to do children's ministry, how to do music, how to handle staff payments, how to handle building issues, and more. Additionally, if following Jesus involves a uniquely Christian activism, then we must develop strategies around that too, and praise God, he gives us room for different strategies there as well.

These strategies will be different for each and every Christian and each and every church. And that's okay! So long as a church or Christian is striving to live out the mission, honor the key values of Scripture, keep lines of demarcation between what is internal to the church and what is external, and reject the temptation toward idolatry, that church has employed an *acceptable* strategy. It might not be the most effective or the most desirable, but that doesn't invalidate it as a God-honoring strategy!

Another important realization about strategy is that strategies are not only contextual to the church, but they are also contextual to the moment. In other words, the strategy for *today* doesn't need to match the strategy for *yesterday*. Specifically, it can be helpful to indicate that in the formation of the strategy itself. For example, rather than asking the big, bold, and probably impossible to answer question, "What is the best way for our society to elevate human dignity and justice?" consider asking this question: "What is the *next* way for our society to elevate human dignity and justice?" or even "What is the next way for our church to get involved in the advocacy for human dignity and justice?" In other words, rather than asking a question about what is best, simply ask the question of what could be *next for you now*.

This gives individual Christians and the larger church community incredible freedom to intersect with society over politically charged issues.

- What is the next way for our society to address the inequalities of racism as they are displayed in police-inflicted injury, and what role can we play?
- What is the next way for us to advocate for the cause of the unborn and the life of the living?
- What is the next way for us to elevate truth and beauty and work against the tide of misinformation and vitriol?
- What is the next way for us to address global environmental and humanitarian concerns?
- Who is the next person we should support in leadership regarding these and other issues?

These questions are not uniquely Christian. They might be asked by anyone, and they might be answered by anyone. Nevertheless, *we* ask them because these are the questions that Christians are uniquely *moti-*

vated to ask and uniquely equipped to answer. The world of economic and political power has no real reason to ask questions about human dignity, moral integrity, or environmental concern, but as we have seen, these issues have always been fundamentally Christian concerns, and therefore, *even if no one else in the society asks these questions, Christians still must.*

Additionally, these questions illustrate by their very wording that the answers are impermanent. A Christian might answer the question one way this year and a different way next year, and that's perfectly fine. Two churches or two Christians might disagree over their answers to these questions this year, but next year, they might find alignment. Strategy is fluid and time-bound, and therefore, when it comes to answering these questions, different strategies need not create animosity between Christians. We can be united over the cause of human dignity and justice in our world even if we disagree over the next course of action to be taken.

Sometimes, Christians will find large consensus over one of these questions, and when we are so united, we will have significant political power. But we need to remember that political power is not our goal. Our goal should be to answer questions such as these in a way that honors our Savior and then to live out our answers to the best of our ability. And living them out in a society that promotes freedom of expression and the democratic process just might involve Christians and churches exercising those freedoms. Running for office or embracing activism just might be the correct strategic decision for a Christian to make even if other Christians would employ different strategies. Each individual Christian and each individual church must ask the question about strategy and come to a decision about it, but we also need to give each other the space to come up with different answers.

Acceptable Strategies

We might *say* there is space for different strategies, but we still *feel* like ours is the only way or the best way, so let's be specific and recognize at least three general strategies a Christian or church might take.

The Encouragement Strategy

Taking their cue from passages like this:

> Do not let any unwholesome talk come out of your mouths, but only
> what is helpful for building others up according to their needs, that
> it may benefit those who listen. And do not grieve the Holy Spirit of
> God, with whom you were sealed for the day of redemption. Get rid of
> all bitterness, rage and anger, brawling and slander, along with every
> form of malice. Be kind and compassionate to one another, forgiving
> each other, just as in Christ God forgave you.
>
> EPHESIANS 4:29–32

> Be wise in the way you act toward outsiders; make the most of every
> opportunity. Let your conversation be always full of grace, seasoned
> with salt, so that you may know how to answer everyone.
>
> COLOSSIANS 4:5–6

*Some churches and some Christians will decide to stay fully silent on
divisive issues nearly all of the time in order to focus on encouragement.*
Because certain issues are so fraught and so loaded with prejudices
and connotations, these churches will avoid such issues almost always
unless the context for addressing them is maximally conducive to building people up. In general, they will ignore contentious issues and use
their limited resources to proclaim the most encouraging and winsome
aspects of Christianity. They might not directly talk about the Christian
idols from public platforms, but they will still root them out internally,
and intentionally avoid any expression of those idols. They might not
talk about the problems with *specific* political allegiances, but they will
still warn people against *having* political allegiances. They might not
discuss the societal ills of the day, but they will still do work that *ad-
dresses* them. Nevertheless, when the time is right, when the context is
one of edification, and when the opportunity is at hand, they will make
the most of that moment to add their voice to the global work of proper
Christian activism.

The Education Strategy

Recognizing that sometimes the truth is hard to hear, and taking their
cue from passages like this:

Better is open rebuke than hidden love. Wounds from a friend can be trusted, but an enemy multiplies kisses. . . .

Perfume and incense bring joy to the heart, and the pleasantness of a friend springs from their heartfelt advice. . . .

The prudent see danger and take refuge, but the simple keep going and pay the penalty.

PROVERBS 27:5–6, 9, 12

Or this:

Then we will no longer be infants, tossed back and forth by the waves, and blown here and there by every wind of teaching and by the cunning and craftiness of people in their deceitful scheming. Instead, speaking the truth in love, we will grow to become in every respect the mature body of him who is the head, that is, Christ. From him the whole body, joined and held together by every supporting ligament, grows and builds itself up in love, as each part does its work. . . . Therefore each of you must put off falsehood and speak truthfully to your neighbor, for we are all members of one body.

EPHESIANS 4:14–16, 25

Some churches and some Christians will decide to take the approach of honest and open internal discipleship coupled with public nonactivism. They will recognize that sometimes truth hurts, but it is always good. They will openly discuss controversial matters, sharing their honest answers and welcoming contrary opinions. However, they will not go silent when truth is under attack. They will be unafraid to call sin sin even when that sin is coming from within their own ranks or from their brothers and sisters in the larger body of Christ. They will not shy away from opportunities to speak about the moral issues God desires for all people of all time even in the public sphere and even when it is unpopular. They will in fact encourage people to pursue the truth wherever it may be found, but recognizing their own propensity to error, they will only rarely and cautiously ever advocate any specific action in the public sphere. They will talk about Christian values, both those for the church and those for the world, but they will focus on individual transformation, not any specific public activism. Nevertheless, when the time calls for it, they will not be afraid to use their voice to advocate for human dignity, what's true and good, and the care of the Earth.

The Prophetic Strategy

The goal of the prophets of old was never to give information but to provide a voice of warning and a call for social transformation. Taking their cue from passages like these:

> "Then you will call, and the LORD will answer; you will cry for help, and he will say: Here am I. If you do away with the yoke of oppression, with the pointing finger and malicious talk, and if you spend yourselves in be-half of the hungry and satisfy the needs of the oppressed, then your light will rise in the darkness, and your night will become like the noonday."
>
> ISAIAH 58:9–10

> But when he saw many of the Pharisees and Sadducees coming to where he was baptizing, he said to them: "You brood of vipers! Who warned you to flee from the coming wrath? Produce fruit in keeping with repen-tance. And do not think you can say to yourselves, 'We have Abraham as our father.' I tell you that out of these stones God can raise up children for Abraham. The ax is already at the root of the trees, and every tree that does not produce good fruit will be cut down and thrown into the fire."
>
> MATTHEW 3:7–10

> "The King will reply, 'Truly I tell you, whatever you did for one of the least of these brothers and sisters of mine, you did for me.'"
>
> MATTHEW 25:40

Some churches and some Christians will decide to take the approach of humble, intentional public activism. Internally, they will do all that the previous strategy does, but they will also embrace *visible vulnerability.* Toward themselves and other Christians, they will expose their failings to the light of Scripture and call each other to repentance. In view of the world, they will intentionally root out their own sin and will rigorously refrain from pronouncing judgment on others. However, they will also personally and corporately embrace a stance of activism in this world that represents the heart of God for his people *and* for the wider world. They will answer the preceding questions definitively and promote specific and concrete action for themselves and others. They will promote certain actions for fellow believers and other actions for the wider world, but maintaining humility, they will continually reevaluate their approach in light of the values of Scripture and never lock themselves into a specific political platform or framework.

CONCLUSION

Any of these strategies or even others might be God's desire for a particular Christian or particular church, and we should all extend the freedom to each other to adopt the strategy that makes the most sense to them in the context where God has placed them. There is a lot of room for disagreement regarding how we answer the various political questions and how we act in response to those answers, but the answers need not divide Christians or make us antagonistic toward each other.

However, as I bring this to a close, I want to point out that two strategic extremes are inappropriate for any Christian or church that desires to follow Jesus.

- Churches and Christians that never address difficult questions in any public way are hiding their light under a bowl and failing to fulfill their mission in the modern world.
- Churches and Christians that align themselves fully with a specific political framework and adopt an activist mentality from that perspective are extinguishing the unique light of Christ within themselves in favor of the whims of earthly groups and current societal fads.

Our calling in this world is to integrate the whole gospel deeply into our own personal lives and in the Christian community where we worship, to pursue the Great Commission and the Great Commandment in full view of the world, to live out our Christian values with integrity and authenticity, and to invite the world higher toward the fundamental principles of God's kingdom that always and forever transcend our human differences and shine a light not our own.

Sixty years ago, Dr. Martin Luther King Jr., sitting in a jail cell, wrote these words to some pastors in Birmingham:

> There was a time when the church was very powerful—in the time when the early Christians rejoiced at being deemed worthy to suffer for what they believed. In those days the church was not merely a thermometer that recorded the ideas and principles of popular opinion; it was a thermostat that transformed the mores of society. . . . By their effort and example they brought an end to such ancient evils as infanticide and gladiatorial contests. Things are different now. So often the contemporary church is a weak, ineffectual voice with an uncertain sound. So often it is an archdefender of the status quo. Far from being disturbed by the presence of the church, the power structure of the average community is consoled by the church's silent—and often even vocal—sanction of things as they are. . . .
>
> But the judgment of God is upon the church as never before. If today's church does not recapture the sacrificial spirit of the early church, it will lose its authenticity, forfeit the loyalty of millions, and be dismissed as an irrelevant social club with no meaning for the twentieth century. Every day I meet young people whose disappointment with the church has turned into outright disgust.[17]

The world is tossing out the church because the church has lost its saltiness. The world is turning off to the church because the church has turned off its light. But it need not stay that way. We have a winsome light. Our light is the light of Christ, the one who sacrificed himself so others might be blessed, and if he be lifted up, he will draw people to himself. May the light we shine look like him.

> *May we, as followers of Jesus, the only true Savior of the world, leave the temples, discard our idols, burn the scaffolds, embrace our mission, and be creatively strategic, using whatever means we can to display the glorious light of our heavenly Father before a desperately dark world!*

The Way of Christ

Who has believed our message
   and to whom has the arm of the LORD been revealed?
He grew up before him like a tender shoot,
   and like a root out of dry ground.
He had no beauty or majesty to attract us to him,
   nothing in his appearance that we should desire him.
He was despised and rejected by mankind,
   a man of suffering, and familiar with pain.
Like one from whom people hide their faces
   he was despised, and we held him in low esteem.
Surely he took up our pain
   and bore our suffering,
yet we considered him punished by God,
   stricken by him, and afflicted.
But he was pierced for our transgressions,
   he was crushed for our iniquities;
the punishment that brought us peace was on him,
   and by his wounds we are healed.
We all, like sheep, have gone astray,
   each of us has turned to our own way;
and the LORD has laid on him
   the iniquity of us all.
He was oppressed and afflicted,
   yet he did not open his mouth;

he was led like a lamb to the slaughter,
and as a sheep before its shearers is silent,
so he did not open his mouth.
By oppression and judgment he was taken away.
Yet who of his generation protested?
For he was cut off from the land of the living;
for the transgression of my people he was punished.
He was assigned a grave with the wicked,
and with the rich in his death,
though he had done no violence,
nor was any deceit in his mouth.
Yet it was the LORD's will to crush him and cause him
to suffer,
and though the LORD makes his life an offering for sin,
he will see his offspring and prolong his days,
and the will of the LORD will prosper in his hand.
After he has suffered,
he will see the light of life and be satisfied;
by his knowledge my righteous servant will justify many,
and he will bear their iniquities.
Therefore I will give him a portion among the great,
and he will divide the spoils with the strong,
because he poured out his life unto death,
and was numbered with the transgressors.
For he bore the sin of many,
and made intercession for the transgressors.

ISAIAH 53

The eunuch asked Philip, "Tell me, please, who is the prophet talking about, himself or someone else?"

ACTS 8:34

"What things?" he asked.

"About Jesus of Nazareth," they replied. "He was a prophet, powerful in word and deed before God and all the people. The chief priests and our rulers handed him over to be sentenced to death, and they crucified him; but we had hoped that he was the one who was going to redeem Israel. And what is more, it is the third day since all this took place. In addition, some of our women amazed us. They went to the tomb early this morning but didn't find his body. They came and told us that they had seen a vision of angels, who said he was alive. Then some of our companions went to the tomb and found it just as the women had said, but they did not see Jesus."

He said to them, "How foolish you are, and how slow to believe all that the prophets have spoken! Did not the Messiah have to suffer these things and then enter his glory?" And beginning with Moses and all the Prophets, he explained to them what was said in all the Scriptures concerning himself.

LUKE 24:19–27

NO ONE EXPECTED A CROSS when they thought of the Messiah.

For hundreds of years before Jesus, the text of Isaiah was just sitting there. People read it, but no one understood the real meaning of chapter 53. Consider the eunuch. He was the servant of the queen of Ethiopia. He was surrounded by scholars. Surely this wasn't the first time he had been exposed to the prophet Isaiah. If so, how was he already in chapter 53, and how did he even acquire a personal copy of the scroll of Isaiah in those days? Clearly, he viewed the prophecy as extremely important, and yet he didn't understand it. For centuries, none of the scholars realized what it meant.

Consider the men on the way to Emmaus. They were defeated and despondent. They had put their hopes in something that hadn't panned out. They were disappointed and even incredulous regarding the reports of the empty tomb. But they shouldn't have been. Just three days prior, Jesus quoted directly from Isaiah 53. Luke records it:

"It is written: 'And he was numbered with the transgressors'; and I tell you that this must be fulfilled in me. Yes, what is written about me is reaching its fulfillment."

LUKE 22:37

Jesus was the suffering servant, and he knew it. He quoted directly from the final words of Isaiah 53; he spoke the literal words after Isaiah's line "he poured out his life unto death." And yet, after his literal death literally fulfilling Isaiah's prophecy, fulfilling *his own* prophecy, these two lost hope, gave up, and were just wandering off to Emmaus, *even after hearing of an empty tomb*!

Literally no one understood Isaiah 53 until they had the blessing of hindsight and the help of someone who saw the bigger picture.

How were they all so blind?

Well, for the same reason we are blind. Idolatry.

Before the resurrection, the concept of Messiah among the Jewish people was an idol. They thought they were waiting for something God had promised, but the picture they constructed of their Savior was as malformed as the golden calf, and it's obvious throughout the Gospels:

> After the people saw the sign Jesus performed, they began to say, "Surely this is the Prophet who is to come into the world." Jesus, knowing that they intended to come and make him king by force, withdrew again to a mountain by himself.
>
> JOHN 6:14–15

Their messiah idol was going to be a prophet, but he was also supposed to be the king. More than that, he was supposed to be the kind of king who would claim his kingdom through violence. Their idol messiah was going to use force and violence to destroy their oppressors like the judges of old, like David against Goliath, but Isaiah 53:12 described how the real Messiah would gain his power: "I will give him a portion among the great . . . because he poured out his life unto death."

They couldn't see the real Messiah right in front of them because their idol was too prominent. They were effectively worshiping a bronze snake while the true Savior was in their midst. They were waiting for a hero to defeat their enemies while the Lord of Hosts was *right there*. They were blinded by their expectations, and the more Jesus spoke, the less he sounded like what they wanted.

He then began to teach them that the Son of Man must suffer many things and be rejected by the elders, the chief priests and the teachers of the law, and that he must be killed and after three days rise again. He spoke plainly about this, and Peter took him aside and began to rebuke him.

MARK 8:31–32

Oh, the arrogance! Peter was standing before the man who calmed the storm, healed the lepers, gave sight to the blind, raised the dead, and taught with supernatural authority. Peter, standing before that man, opened his mouth in rebuke. Utterly insane! Or more accurately, blind. Peter was entirely blinded to Isaiah 53 because he had a messianic idol in his heart.

If you're blinded by the glimmering gold of a metallic baby cow, or if you are taken captive by the stories of a magical bronze snake, you'll never be able to evaluate the true worth of the real healer in your midst.

They had established an idol of the Messiah in their hearts.

They had taught it to each other.

They had built scaffolding of religious systems around it.

They added to the temple a system of synagogues, rabbis, Pharisees, Sadducees, scribes, and others. They had an unending list of rules, regulations, and traditions added to God's law.

It was wood and hay and straw constructed around more wood and hay and straw, protecting their idols, and they were all blind to it. They couldn't see their own idolatry, and they were willing to fight to protect it too.

So Peter rebuked Jesus.

Jesus rebuked Peter right back:

But when Jesus turned and looked at his disciples, he rebuked Peter. "Get behind me, Satan!" he said. "You do not have in mind the concerns of God, but merely human concerns."

MARK 8:33

Peter thought he knew what God was like, but he was speaking the words of Satan.

The greatest problem the people of God ever have is idolatry. Not the overt kind where you abandon God and adopt some rival god. Not the obvious kind where you add an extra god to your personal list and share your religious time between shrines. Not even the visible kind where you construct a physical object and bow down to it. Those idolatries exist, but they have never been the most troublesome. The real idolatry has always been this: *Thinking this or that is the true representation of God.* Worded more personally, it goes like this: *I know what God is like.*

Do you have words to describe God? Fine, you probably should, but you should probably realize that your definition for each of those words is inadequate. Remember what the angels sing about God:

> Each of the four living creatures had six wings and was covered with eyes all around, even under its wings. Day and night they never stop saying: "'Holy, holy, holy is the Lord God Almighty,' who was, and is, and is to come."
>
> REVELATION 4:8

What's the key word used to define God?

Holy—a word that literally means "set apart."

The number one attribute of God is that he's different, not like anything else.

The Bible tells us God is love, but he's not like anything else. Our definition of love is too small.

The Bible tells us God is righteous, but he's not like anything else. Our understanding of righteousness is too limited.

The Bible tells us God is just, merciful, full of wrath and patience and jealousy, but he's not like anything else. All those words are inadequate for God if we bring our own definitions to them.

There are only two things we know for certain about God:

He's not *really* like anything you can imagine. All idols and all images are inadequate.

He's been fully revealed to us through Jesus, the ultimate image of God.

The Son is the image of the invisible God, the firstborn over all creation. For in him all things were created: things in heaven and on earth, visible and invisible, whether thrones or powers or rulers or authorities; all things have been created through him and for him. He is before all things, and in him all things hold together. And he is the head of the body, the church; he is the beginning and the firstborn from among the dead, so that in everything he might have the supremacy. For God was pleased to have all his fullness dwell in him, and through him to reconcile to himself all things, whether things on earth or things in heaven, by making peace through his blood, shed on the cross.

COLOSSIANS 1:15–20

You want to get rid of your idols? You want to really get a glimpse of what God is like?

Look to Jesus.

> He came to the earth he created
> Wrapped himself in flesh he formed
> Inhaled the breath that he breathed out
> Touched the lepers
> Washed the feet
> Received the wounds
> Died on a hill he lifted up
> Hung on a tree he planted
> Was buried in a tomb he borrowed
> Rose again in victory
> Is now reconciling the world to the Father
> Is coming soon in power and great glory.

That's what God is like.

Everything else is idolatry.

Everything else is wood, hay, straw.

Everything built on the foundation of him that doesn't look like him is doomed to burn.

WE ARE TERRIBLY BEHOLDEN to our idols. We love them, we worship them, and seeing them for what they are is painful at best. We might disagree on many things. But I pray you agree with me that this one thing is true:

The life of a Christian should look like Christ.

Loving, serving, sacrificial, faithful, forgiving, gracious, just, and honest. Jesus.

At minimum, let's do that.

Humbly.

For his glory, not ours.

Notes

1. Nambi Ndugga, Latoya Hill, and Samantha Artiga, "COVID-19 Cases and Deaths, Vaccinations, and Treatments by Race/Ethnicity as of Fall 2022," *KFF*, November 17, 2022, http://tinyurl.com/3vbb7xv7.

2. Paul Doellinger, "Luther's Breakthrough in Romans," *Lutheran Reformation*, October 27, 2017, http://tinyurl.com/yja7rt.

3. Ronald Numbers, *The Creationists: From Scientific Creationism to Intelligent Design* (Cambridge: Harvard University Press, 2006), 7.

4. Henry Morris, *The Beginning of the World*, 2nd ed. (Green Forest: Master Books, 1991), 147-48. Quoted by Richard Trott and Jim Lippard, "Creationism Implies Racism?," *TalkOrigins*, last updated July 17, 2003, http://tinyurl.com/huk39uen.

5. Jemar Tisby, *The Color of Compromise: The Truth about the American Church's Complicity in Racism* (Grand Rapids: Zondervan, 2019), 135.

6. Resolution on abortion, adopted by the Southern Baptist Convention, June 1971.

7. Randall Balmer, *Bad Faith: Race and the Rise of the Religious Right* (Grand Rapids: Eerdmans, 2021), 48-49.

8. Russell Moore, *Losing Our Religion: An Altar Call for Evangelical America* (New York: Sentinel, 2023), 86.

9. See Cynthia Long Westfall, *Paul and Gender: Reclaiming the Apostle's Vision for Men and Women in Christ* (Grand Rapids: Baker Academic, 2016).

10. David W. Bebbington, *Evangelicalism in Modern Britain: A History from the 1730s to the 1980s* (London: Unwin Hyman, 2003), 2-17.

11. Isaac Newton, "General Scholium," in book 3 of *The Mathematical Principles of Natural Philosophy*, trans. Andrew Motte.

12. "How Great Thou Art," Carl Boberg, 1886.

13. *The Consensus Project*, September 24, 2021, theconsensusproject.com.

14. Mark Wingfield, "John MacArthur Says MLK Was Not a Christian and The Gospel Coalition Is 'Woke,'" *Baptist News Global*, March 3, 2024, https://tinyurl.com/332mrzpd.

15. Martin Luther King Jr., "I Have a Dream" (delivered August 28, 1963), African Studies Center, University of Pennsylvania, http://tinyurl.com/2b6mycmy.

16. King, "I Have a Dream."

17. Martin Luther King Jr., "Letter from a Birmingham Jail" (letter dated April 16, 1963), African Studies Center, University of Pennsylvania, http://tinyurl.com/27nycjps.

For Further Reading

biologos.org

>   If you are interested in thoughtful theology that isn't afraid of science, you can do no better than biologos.org. I can't endorse everything they write, of course, but their articles regularly inspire me as they express thoughtful, devoted, Christ-focused Christianity.

Balmer, Randall. *Bad Faith: Race and the Rise of the Religious Right*. Grand Rapids: Eerdmans, 2021.

>   Were you told that the pro-life agenda was the unifying force bringing Fundamentalists and other conservative Christian groups together? I was. Nevertheless, Randall Balmer expertly proves the case that the root of modern Evangelicalism was racism and money. The first truly unified act of conservative Christians was to rise up in support of segregationist schools that were losing tax-exempt status. The antiabortion agenda came later and served as an effective smoke screen for the cause.

Du Mez, Kristin Kobes. *Jesus and John Wayne: How White Evangelicals Corrupted a Faith and Fractured a Nation*. New York: Liveright, 2020.

>   As I began my journey of disillusionment with the evangelical church, I knew I needed help to figure out how I had misunderstood my own tradition. This was a book I needed to read, and it has been perhaps the most important book in my journey because it gave me new lenses to see the difference between true Christian doctrine and evangelical culture.

King, Martin Luther, Jr. "Letter from a Birmingham Jail." African Studies Center, University of Pennsylvania. http://tinyurl.com/27nycjps.

If you have never read Dr. King's remarkable letter, you must. The principles discussed are still as relevant to the modern American church as ever. His concept of proper Christian activism is brilliant and biblical. His assessment of racial injustice, the complicity of the church, and the possibility of solutions is both eloquent and tragic. I found it convicting when I first read it, and additionally touching every time since.

Numbers, Ronald L. *The Creationists: From Scientific Creationism to Intelligent Design.* Cambridge: Harvard University Press, 2006.
The widespread adoption of Young Earth Creationism among Christians is a recent phenomenon. To get a pretty thorough history of the development of the idea, you might want to check out this book. It's out of print, but it can be borrowed for free online at the Internet Archive: http://tinyurl.com/3mbv6yvf.

Tisby, Jemar. *The Color of Compromise: The Truth about the American Church's Complicity in Racism.* Grand Rapids: Zondervan, 2019.
In those early days, I also turned to Tisby's book specifically because I needed to learn more about racism in America. I also had a suspicion that my evangelical church tradition wasn't just in denial about racism but that there were deeper prejudices at work too. Like *Jesus and John Wayne*, this book is an uncomfortable read if you haven't already given yourself some time with these ideas.

Westfall, Cynthia Long. *Paul and Gender: Reclaiming the Apostle's Vision for Men and Women in Christ.* Grand Rapids: Baker Academic, 2016.
This is an academic work, and I don't agree with everything she says in it. I find it deeply challenging to my conservative, complementarian reading of the Bible. I mention it here because I value the dialogue and want to honor the work she's doing even though I disagree. Her deep commitment to the Scriptures blesses me.

Index

Aaron, 183

abortion activism, 90-94, 149-50, 201-4. *See also* pro-life platform, "temple" of

accountability *vs.* responsibility, 186

activism, 147-81; Christian influence in, 109, 148-50; of early church, 108-9, 204; for environmental stewardship, 157, 178-80; for equity, 152, 154, 156, 161-66; gospel incongruity and, 107-8; for human dignity, 152, 154, 156, 161-66, 204, 205-6; internal values in tension with, 126-27, 155, 163-65; of John the Baptist, 107, 108; for justice, 131-32, 148, 154, 156, 161-66; love for neighbors in, 155, 158-60; mission and, 216-17; of prophets, 131-32; repentance and, 212-13; strategies for, 219, 222, 223-25; theology of, 99-105, 107-8; translatable values guiding, 152, 154, 155, 156-57, 163-64; for truth, goodness, and beauty, 157, 166-67, 176-78, 216

activism, priorities in: Christian preference/favoritism, 88-89, 90, 205; cultural norms, 142-45, 181; evangelism and, 158-60; in history of Christianity, 156; hypocrisy and, 88-89, 93-94, 148, 150, 151, 162; idolatry and, 202-4; individual responsibility, 149, 202; political commitments, 92-93, 150-55, 200-201; pro-life platform and, 201-4; promotion of internal values, 143, 146, 150, 153, 155, 200-201; racism and, 86-87, 91-94, 148; sexual ethics, 202

Acts 15 path, 51-55

anointed intellect, as idol, 76, 191-95, 205

art, 169-70, 175-76

Bad Faith (Balmer), 92

Balmer, Randall, 92

Barnabas, 51, 218

beauty, 123-24, 175-76. *See also* truth, goodness, and beauty

Bebbington, David, 147

neo-evangelicals, 91–92

New Testament: breadth of gospel in, 41–42, 44; social context for, 135–36; unpleasant truths in, 167–68. *See also* church, early; Paul

Newton, Isaac, 168–69

obedience, 198–99

Old Testament: Christian moral values guided by, 118–19, 128–32, 137; idolatry in, 15–17; Jesus's references to, 22, 100–103, 138, 230; social context of, 134–35. *See also* Genesis 1–2

O'Neal, James, 87

On the Origin of Species (Darwin), 82–83

opinions, political, 152–55

Paul: approach to conflict, 52–53, 54–55, 218; on Christian unity, 215; on cultural accommodation, 143–45; cultural context of, 144–45; doctrine of, 38–41; evangelical reading of, 36–37, 62–64, 69–72; gospel according to, 21, 25–26, 28–29, 36–41; idolatry metaphor, 11–12; liberated from prison, 105; mission and strategy of, 218

Paul, moral teaching of: individual and social implications of, 69–70, 71, 165–66; internal values and, 119–28, 133, 165; on judgment of unbelievers, 126–27, 142–43, 155, 188; selective application of, 65, 69–72, 120

personal or religious freedom, "temple" of, 150, 204–6. *See also* religious and personal freedom

Peter, 48, 105, 167, 217–18, 231–32

Philip, 226

policies, public and political, 154–55, 201

"political," use of term, 94, 150–51, 154–55, 189

political conservatism, "temple" of, 148, 149, 210–11

political opinions, 152–55

political parties, 148, 149–50, 153–54, 181, 211

political policies, 154–55

poor and oppressed people, care for: activism and, 108–9, 130–32, 137, 156, 157, 204; salvation and, 190–91; as translatable value, 137–38, 157. *See also* dignity, human

prayer in schools, 88–89

"progressive," use of term, 61, 65

progressive Christianity, 27

Prohibition, 148

pro-life platform, "temple" of, 92–94, 201–4

prophetic strategy, 224–25

Protestantism, 26–27, 28

psychology, 169

public policies, 154, 201

racism: in Christian activism, 86–87, 91–94, 148; color blindness as, 85–87, 195–97; evangelical silence about, 85–88, 93, 94, 226; George Floyd murder and, 7–8, 71;